Of Presidents,
Prime Ministers
and Princes

BOOKS BY ANTHONY HOLDEN

Of Presidents, Prime Ministers and Princes

A Decade in Fleet Street

Anthony Holden

With a Preface by Harold Evans

Atheneum   New York   1984

In memoriam IVAN SHARPE (*1889-1968*)

Library of Congress Cataloging in Publication Data

Holden, Anthony, ———
    Of presidents, prime ministers, and princes.

    1. Great Britain—Politics and government—1964-1979—
Addresses, essays, lectures. 2. Great Britain—Politics
and government—1979-   —Addresses, essays, lectures.
3. United States—Politics and government—1977-1981—
Addresses, essays, lectures. 4. United States—Politics
and government—1981-   —Addresses, essays, lectures.
I. Title.
DA589.7.H65 1984   973.9   83-45074
ISBN 0-689-11400-1

The articles in this book originally appeared in
the *Sunday Times*, the *Observer*, *Punch*, the
Spectator, the *New Statesman*, the *Times Literary
Supplement*, the *Tatler*, the *New Republic*, and
the *Sunday Express*. The author and publisher
are grateful to their editors for permission to
reproduce them now.

Contents

Preface

Anthony Holden plays poker every Tuesday when he is in London. The competition is provided by a sly poet and a ferocious professor. His annual birthday treat is to take himself off to the professional world series in Las Vegas where he monitors the play of the likes of Amarillo 'Slim' Preston, Stuart 'The Kid' Ungar, Doyle 'Texas Dolly' Brunson and Johnny 'The Man' Moss, and joins in a tense five-and-ten dollar stud sidegame at The Golden Nugget. He got beaten by Silent Harry, and it is bravely acknowledged in this book, but in the British championships he suckered Bullethead in the consolation finals.

It is necessary for the reader to know these things before dipping into this collection of Holden's varied journalism. Here is a deceptive fellow. He is the biographer of Prince Charles, the *Observer*'s chronicler of Carter's Washington, a front-line foreign reporter for the *Sunday Times* as well as the successor as Atticus to Ian Fleming and Nick Tomalin. But he makes no large claims for himself. He produces no elegant theories, from his many encounters, on the nature of political leadership, no analysis, from his wide travels, of national character. It is just like his poker. He looks a pushover but he is holding two pairs, aces up. The articles he wrote for the moment survive as a collection because they represent good reporting by someone you feel you can like. They are refreshingly free from stereotype or the bogus immediacy of 'news' and altogether unencumbered by punditry. This is the way it was with Jimmy Carter steaming down the Mississippi, a grinning rain-soaked figure in T-shirt, blue jeans and sneakers shrilling through the gathering darkness 'Hello, Fort Madison, I love ya'. This is the way it was with the candidate for the Republican nomination in the grassroots of Alabama: 'Ask him if he dyed his hair and his head would sink between his knees with an invitation to run your fingers through it, looking for clues in the roots. Ask him if he had a facelift and down it went again, "Look behind the ears for those tell-tale scars".' It adds to the fun, of course, that Ronald Reagan is still around, and that Holden perfectly caught the nature of his appeal to the voters as he did their disillusion with Carter.

Holden glides into the proximity of the great and the powerful, unnoticed and undemanding, and he misses nothing: the signs of strain on Prince Charles on tour in Canada, Mrs Thatcher's scrutable way with the Chinese leaders in Peking, Carter's White House symbolized by the announcement of the dismissal of the entire Cabinet being made by the press secretary with his feet propped nonchalantly on his desk. (This collection, like others, may be read at random with pleasure, but 'Reporting America' has an extra excitement if it is taken in its sequence.)

Holden was initiated into journalism by his grandfather, Ivan Sharpe, to whom he has dedicated this book. Ivan wrote football reports from Manchester for the *Sunday Chronicle* (and later the *Sunday Times*) and young Holden was allowed into the press box to keep count of the number of corners, fouls and shots at goal, a commonplace today but a statistical touch which Sharpe introduced to football then and which gave Holden a valuable appreciation of professionalism. It served him well. He came to my attention as an editor when he came top of the proficiency examinations run by the National Council for the Training of Journalists. Many aspiring young journalists fresh from Oxbridge, as he was, look with disdain on the scuffed rungs of the ladder from provincial newspapers, shorthand and local government lessons, to Fleet Street. Holden was more modest and more canny. Having come top, he spent his prize money on a trip to the United States where he wrote an article good enough for the *Sunday Times Review* front on the American Health Service. He crowned his training on the *Evening Echo* at Hemel Hempstead by writing a book on the Hertfordshire poisoner Graham Young: there is a fascinating extract in this collection. When he joined the *Sunday Times* reporters' room he unassumingly immersed himself in the arts of hard reporting with a grim spell in Ulster. It is no surprise to me that when he was admitted to the Oval Office in the White House for a short ceremonial he made a note of the President's private telephone number. Just in case.

I have properly warned the reader that there is more to Holden than meets the eye. I have, it should be noted, cause to be grateful for that. When in 1982 I was under pressure from Rupert Murdoch to resign the editorship of *The Times*, and saying nothing either privately or publicly, it was Holden, un-prompted by me or anyone else, who spoke out about some of the issues with which he was familiar as features editor, and who, in the end, gave up without compensation a job he loved without thought for the effect on his own career. He took me and others by surprise; and though he felt passionately about the issues, he did it with coolness and good temper. 'Smile when you call me that,' said Owen Wister's Virginian when faced with a lethal insult at the poker table. It is very much the Holden ethic. Certainly his good nature informs this collection and makes it pleasant as well as rewarding reading.

Harold Evans
November 1983

Introduction

On the Ides of March 1973, towards the end of my apprenticeship on a provincial daily paper, I spent the afternoon sitting in the outer office of Harold Evans, then editor of the *Sunday Times*, refusing to budge until he saw me. As the hours crept blankly by, I became ever more convinced that Shakespeare's soothsayer had got it right. Evans had a rather frightening secretary in those days, and this was one of the less comfortable 'doorstepping' jobs I had yet attempted. But the long wait was worth it: around dusk I made it past Cerberus, and was hired as a junior reporter.

On the Ides of March 1982, just nine years later, the soothsayer got his revenge. I resigned my position as features editor of *The Times*, in protest at the manner in which Rupert Murdoch had abruptly terminated the editorship of that same Harold Evans. Our ways had parted in between; I had left the *Sunday Times* for a year to write a book, and then 'defected' to the *Observer* as Washington correspondent. But Harry, on moving to *The Times*, had rehired me; and when that extraordinary twelve-month adventure ended so abruptly, some kind of bumpy wheel had turned full circle.

This collection amounts, in digest form, to what happened in between. There is a little blurring at the edges: I have included, for instance, one article I wrote for Anthony Howard's *New Statesman* in 1972, among the first pieces of mine to appear in a national publication. I have also added a few of the pieces written in the unwonted self-employment which has recently been my lot. But the selection really represents those hugely enjoyable ten years, 1973-83, my first decade in Fleet Street. For newspapers alone, by a rough calculation, I wrote well over a million words in that time, so this sample amounts to rather less than ten per cent of what went on.

My initial role at the *Sunday Times* was Education Correspondent. The then news editor, Derrik Mercer, had been a zealous holder of the title, as had sundry other senior executives, so I was really in no position to turn down their kind offer. But education and I were not really cut out for each other. I could never unravel all those circulars with complex numerical names which my rivals on other papers regarded as light bedtime reading. (But I did get to meet Margaret Thatcher, then Education Secretary, for the first time. At her Christmas party for the education lobby, in her office at the DES, I was deeply impressed by the amount of government gin she dispensed while reeling off free milk statistics.)

So it was not long – having won my spurs with juggernaut axle-weight surveys and other such *Sunday Times* obsessions – before I was shunted off to Northern Ireland. This was regarded in the newsroom as a mixed blessing – a status assignment, next rung on the intrepid ladder to the Insight office, but absolute hell while you're there. For all its prestige, I was not sure I really wanted to join Insight; on the *Sunday Times* of that day it was heresy to say so, but I didn't much enjoy team journalism. I did, however, desperately want to be a hard-nosed 'heavy' like all around me, so off I went. The effect was ruined when Cyril Connolly, having reviewed my translations of Greek Pastoral Poetry, wandered into the newsroom one day to discuss the relative merits of Theocritus and Bion. David Blundy, with whom I shared a desk, never looked at me in quite the same way again.

Strange to relate, I enjoyed my three years in Ulster. It *was* hell at the time: lonely, nerve-racking and very depressing. But there were few more challenging or important news stories for a British journalist, as alas remains true today. It was only after much agonizing that I decided not to include any of my work there in this book. It still means a lot to me, but it is all now so dated: a melancholy catalogue of death and disarray which could scarcely interest, let alone entertain, the reader.

Similarly, the big occasions always brought out *Sunday Times* team fever; and it seems to me correct to include only solo work in this book. The major milestones of those years (except the hideously complex Assembly elections, where I was left alone with my slide-rule) I reported in tandem with others. At the height of the Ulster Workers' Council strike, which brought down that same Assembly, Blundy and I toiled all night by gaslight in the bomb-shaken Europa Hotel. At David's insis-

tence – quite rightly, he never leaves people's clothes unchron-
icled – we filed a vivid description of the 'bulges' beneath the
armpits of some Protestant thugs we had encountered. It came
out in the paper as 'bugles'.

Some years later I had occasion to tell this story to a
celebrated concert pianist, having discovered over a private
dinner table the unlikely fact that he is an avid collector of
newspaper misprints. At his London home he has whole scrap-
books of them. Delighted though I was to meet the maestro, I did
not wish to know this about him. I have never since been able to
listen to one of his recitals with quite the same uncomplicated
admiration. So I had learnt another useful early lesson: never
meet your heroes.

It was to come in handy during my two heady years editing
Atticus, the *Sunday Times* diary column – then still in a
wonderfully prominent position on the back page of the paper's
front section. Readers turned to it first, thinking it was the
sports page, and with any luck got stuck there. When the
Queen's official Silver Jubilee photographs were published, she
was – rather amazingly – pictured reading a copy of the *Sunday
Times*. So that the paper's name could be clearly seen, HM was of
course reading the back page. I was not slow to draw my readers'
attention to the discriminating company they were keeping.

The mantle of Atticus, previously donned by such other
personal heroes as Ian Fleming and Nicholas Tomalin, was the
passport to a high old time hobnobbing with princes and
potentates. Almost anyone would say yes to a rendezvous, in the
hope of some favourable publicity among the upper crust. The
'noes' began to mount up when my vignettes became more
barbed. Which was just as well. The dangers of diary writing are
evident in a *Punch* piece in this collection (p.291). And my
encounters with the mighty only confirmed my resolution to try
and avoid meeting people I *really* admired. It could prove so
disillusioning.

Which is not, of course, to say that Jim Callaghan, Margaret
Thatcher, Edward Heath or the Prince of Wales come into that
category. Between them, they provided my own personal
highlights of those Atticus years, as well as the chance to visit
China and India for the first time, and renew my long romance
with the United States. After I returned from India, and was off

3

work for a month with mumps (p.13), a 'get-well' note from the editor gently expressed the hope that I might one day bring Atticus back to Britain, where it belonged.

On taking leave from the paper in 1978-9 to complete a biography of Prince Charles, I bid farewell to Atticus readers, who had proved a very friendly bunch, in heroic couplets (p.318). The object of this exercise was to own up to having felt a bit of an imposter throughout my time as a diarist. I see no reason to deny a devout fascination with celebrity *per se*, but I have never felt at all at home among certain of Britain's *demi-mondes*, notably that hooraying its way around those areas of London S.W. which are supposed to be a newspaper diarist's regular beat. I confess I also felt every journalist's constant anxiety that he ought to be doing something a trifle more, well, substantial.

It was during my sabbatical that Donald Trelford, editor of the *Observer*, offered me the job I coveted most: Washington. After a tense meeting with Evans at the Royal Automobile Club, I reluctantly severed my links with the *Sunday Times* and led the ever-expanding Holden family west, where we all took to our *vita nuova* with an enthusiasm worthy of the Pilgrim Fathers.

The American section of this book amounts to a brief look back at the 1980 presidential election, and makes chastening re-reading in this, the next US election year. My time there was also haunted by the Iranian hostage crisis, which dragged on well beyond all initial expectations, and provided a dramatic backdrop to the home stretch of the race for the White House. It was, I suppose, inevitable that the *Observer* should occasionally wheel out its Washington correspondent, somewhat incongruously, to pronounce on the Prince of Wales's progress towards domestic bliss. But he felt much more at home chronicling presidents than princes, and even had the drama of an assassination attempt (p.71) to mark his last week in the job – which he was to leave with the greatest reluctance.

The morning of 24 February 1981 was one I will not easily forget. A few days after Rupert Murdoch had announced the appointment of Harold Evans to the editorship of *The Times*, Buckingham Palace announced the engagement of Prince Charles to the Lady Diana Spencer. In the midst of writing an impromptu Review Front for the *Observer* (p.196), gearing up to finish in three weeks a little hardback celebration of the wedding, and preparing to welcome the Prime Minister to Washington next day (p.141), I had a call from Evans inviting me to be features editor – and one of his assistant editors – at *The Times*. The previous weekend I had been discussing a long-term Washington contract with Donald Trelford, and my wife and I had started looking at houses for sale. We were contemplating raising our children there.

Harry didn't know this. Nor did he know that the night before I had had another transatlantic call – from Ron Hall, editor of the *Sunday Times* magazine, who had been promoted to deputy editor. Would I be interested in returning to edit the magazine? The following morning's literary exertions were interrupted by touching calls of encouragement from sundry old *Sunday Times* chums.

It wasn't long before Harry had got wind of it all, and was phoning three times a day before meals, pressing for an answer. I was still hesitating.

'Are you saying you'd rather be editor of the *Sunday Times* magazine than assistant editor of *The Times*?'

'No, Harry, I'm saying I'd rather be Washington correspondent of the *Observer*.'

But that night we decided it was an offer I couldn't refuse. I still, I can't deny, harboured vague hopes of one day editing a newspaper. And the prospect of joining Harry to 'kick *The Times* up the bum', as both he and Murdoch put it, was irresistible. I hated returning to England (p.193), but faced exciting times. I couldn't have known quite *how* exciting. Just a year later they were suddenly over, and I was blowing the cobwebs off my typewriter.

Most journalists are at some point tempted away from writing by the lure of executive status; but it's usually a mistake. Editors these days spend more time cutting costs, placating print unions and stroking belligerent egos than they do editing their newspapers. There's no denying it's much easier to get other people to write things than it is to write them yourself – and you get paid more for it, too. Writing, in Michael Frayn's marvellous phrase, is 'rather like breaking rocks'. If it is, as seems likely, a form of masochism, I regret to confess I'm an addict.

In a Christmas greeting Evans sent me while we were at *The Times*, he wrote: 'Producing a newspaper is a serious business, but it should also be fun.' Throughout that year, he kept a close eye on what we called my fun index. 'Let me know', he would say, 'when it stops being fun.' It often did. Refereeing the *prima donna* squabbles of Britain's most pompous journalists was not my idea of fun, nor indeed my idea of journalism. On the other hand: all the travelling, watching, noticing, questioning, thinking and deciding that went into the articles in this collection was always fun; attempting, at the end of each adventure, to write some cohesive account of it was always torture. I suppose it always will be. My trouble is that I don't know how to do anything else.

Anthony Holden
London, 1984

Witness

Down the Mississippi with Jimmy Carter

St Louis, Missouri

'It has nothing this-worldly about it, nothing to hang a threat or a worry upon,' wrote Mark Twain of the Mississippi. 'It is always as tranquil and reposeful as dreamland.'

It wasn't last week. With what wild surmise would Huckleberry Finn have surveyed the scene as the President of the United States dropped by to solicit his vote? The Jimmy Carter re-election bandwagon, he might well have thought, keeps on rollin' along.

It was supposed to be a vacation. If any normal human being spends his summer holidays making six speeches a day, kissing babies, shaking thousands of hands, holding public meetings and radio phone-ins, then it was a vacation. Jimmy Carter chose to spend his week off this summer sailing through the three states holding crucial early primaries next year.

A few months ago, some 140 normal human beings did book themselves a pleasant summer vacation – sailing the 700 majestic miles of the Mississippi from St Paul to St Louis aboard an ancient sternwheel paddle-boat, the *Delta Queen*. Among them were the John Bakers and the John Works of St Paul, two friendly couples sharing a retirement celebration.

Two weeks ago, having shelled out $980 per person on their 'second honeymoons', the Bakers and the Works learned that they had been pitched out of their grade A cabins. Fifteen other couples were chucked off the boat altogether. They were making way for the President, his wife and daughter, a 'skeleton' White House staff of thirty, and a rotating daily pool of eight Washington journalists.

Those left aboard the *Queen* enjoyed a somewhat disrupted week away from it all. The boat made many an unscheduled stop along the way so that the man in cabin 339 could seize the newly installed public address system and cry to the crowd on the

riverbank : 'Don't you think we live in a great country ? Together, we can make it even greater. Will you help me ? Thank
you. I love you.'

From a distance the *Delta Queen* looked a truly romantic
vision : the last of the old Mississippi paddle-steamers, Stars and
Stripes flying, the steam organ belting out 'Old Man River',
'Dixie' and other such appropriate golden oldies, the giant rear
wheel churning through the placid sheen of the mile-wide river.

When it approached the riverbank, however, the atmosphere
changed. The Calliope, still endearingly out of tune, began to
play 'God Bless America', 'The Stars and Stripes', even 'Hail to
the Chief'. On the white wood-frame roof stood those sharp-
suited men in dark glasses, with walkie-talkies, giant binocu-
lars and bulging hips. Large bullet-proof cars gathered on the
quay.

Bullying coastguard patrol boats kept the accompanying
flotilla at bay. 'Three hundred yards minimum distance' bel-
lowed the Tannoy, 'Mister, will you move your boat away, or
shall we ?'

Fierce sunlight alternated with thunderous rain as the slight,
familiar figure edged along the walkway to the microphone.
'Hello, Keokuk, Iowa. Thank you for coming to greet us today.
We've got the greatest country in the world, and if you'll help
me . . . '

Carter was at it night and day. Advance launches checked the
size of waiting crowds to see if they were worth an unscheduled
stop. Most nights, the publicity people would get him out of bed
to shout a passing greeting to a gaggle of the curious grassroots.
'This is a non-partisan trip,' he insisted. 'People have come out
to see the President, not Jimmy Carter.'

It was tempting to agree, if only because it was hard to believe
that this grinning, rain-soaked figure in T-shirt, blue jeans and
sneakers was the President of the United States. 'Hello, Fort
Madison, I love ya,' shrilled his disembodied, sing-song voice
through the gathering darkness. Could this be the leader of the
free world ?

The first morning, he was up jogging – as usual – at 6.30 am.
There were, for the first and only time, complaints from the
other passengers, rudely awakened from their holiday sleep.
Thereafter, the President stopped the boat, stripped down and

went ashore at dawn each day to run his statutory five miles in thirty-five minutes – faster, he told his doctor, than he could manage when running for his naval college a generation ago.

At fifty-four, Carter was one of the youngest passengers aboard. Mississippi riverboat rides, for some reason, are the preserve of senior citizens, which means that the entertainment aboard the *Delta Queen* consists of checkers, bingo, whist drives and sing-songs. The President, by all accounts, proved a poor contestant.

Daughter Amy, however, joined in with a will, organizing the few other children on board, and kicking up a fuss when the purser refused to call back for her the one library copy of *Tom Sawyer*.

The First Lady, Rosalynn Carter, seemed even less on holiday than the President, seizing the microphone from him when he ran out of platitudes, and delaying the boat for two hours in Burlington, Iowa, so she could have her hair done.

Her husband, to beguile the time, went fishing again – and returned, as he did every day, empty-handed. 'I'm a better President than I am a fisherman,' he declared to the citizens of Burlington, a straw-poll of whom appeared to think this a matter for debate.

Carter had been addressing them on the subject of his energy campaign, the official pretext for the trip – which meant that the taxpayer, rather than the President or the Democratic Party, was footing the bill. 'Yes, Amy's violin-playing has improved' and 'No, there is no more beautiful countryside in America than you folks have here' were typical answers to questions on the oil shortage.

Palestine and its place in the growing Middle East crisis seemed far, far away as the detested but inescapable Washington press corps kept plying him with questions about the real world. What, for instance, about Ambassador Bob Strauss's ill-humoured return from his abortive talks in Jerusalem and Cairo ? 'You'd better ask the Vice-President about that.'

'We welcome President Carter,' said the *Quad City Times*, as did every newspaper along his route. 'But, to put it bluntly, we wish he had remained in Washington. There is much to be done there.'

Back aboard the *Delta Queen*, 1980 around the next corner,

Witness

Jimmy Carter played chopsticks on the Calliope as Lebanon burned.

Observer, 26 August 1979

With Jim Callaghan in India

Delhi-Rawalpindi

When someone of my humble station in life gets a bout of the blasted mumps, it is not common for him to receive the condolences of the Prime Minister and the attentions of his personal physician. Such, however, was my mixed fate on Wednesday, as the Callaghan roadshow left India for Pakistan en route to see Sadat at Aswan.

The grim announcement was made by the PM's flying doc – not David Owen, but Monty Levine, MD – in the air between Ahmedabad and Bombay. The Prime Minister at once came back to commiserate, and told me he had not himself had mumps. I got up to move further away from him, not wishing to alter the immediate future of British politics, and he recoiled across the aisle, thinking I was moving closer.

Dr Levine assured Mr Callaghan that if I was going to infect him, I would probably have done so already. I had been incubating the disease for a fortnight, and my victims would not reveal themselves for perhaps ten days. This made the PM blench, and set me to thinking. In the past week I had not only spent my entire time around the Prime Minister and his most senior staff (not to mention the cream of Fleet Street), I had shaken hands and conversed with General Zia-ur Rahman, President of Bangladesh, and eighty-two-year-old Morarji Desai, Prime Minister of India. In between came countless diplomats and senior politicians of all three nationalities. What might I have done to the new-found stability of South Asia ?

Decisions were hurriedly taken at the highest levels. A special meeting of the Kitchen Cabinet resolved that I should remain aboard the prime ministerial VC10, in as much isolation as possible. The Prime Minister – here comes that tired but rather dramatic formula – asked to be kept informed of my condition. I resolved to keep my own company at Aswan, not wishing to foul up his Middle East peace initiative.

In my cosy little office at the back of the jet, the bolder spirits paid regular visits. Dr Bernard Donoughue, the Prime Minister's senior policy adviser, who was not sure whether he had had mumps, lent me a book about Indian independence to while away the isolated hours. Tom McCaffrey, the Prime Minister's Press Secretary, told me he had not had mumps, and understandably decided to issue all future statements from a safe distance. The cream of Fleet Street, with cries of 'Unclean', retreated to file stories about me to their newspapers. I achieved a life-long ambition by making page one of the *Daily Express*, under the headline PM IN MEDICAL ALERT.

As I languish in my Rawalpindi hotel room, and the cream stand in the cold, grey Pakistan morning outside the latest round of talks, I can see I'm going to have to tell you the story so far. If you haven't had mumps, be sure to hold the paper at arm's length.

'The in-flight movie', announces one of the Prime Minister's personal staff, 'will be Emanuelle Goes to Bangladesh.' We are rubbing the windows of a Heathrow VIP hut, gazing through the filthy London morning at the plain grey RAF VC10, wondering in quite what style we are to travel those 16,000 miles. The PM's arrival permits us to board and find out. No movie, as feared, but first-class accommodation and catering to be shared between only two Callaghans (who have their own state rooms), twenty-four Downing Street and Whitehall staff, and twelve pressmen. On the thirteen-hour first leg to Dacca the time, as it were, flies by.

Before a sixty-minute refuelling stop at Bahrain, the PM summons us up to his sofa-lined suite for a rare on-the-record briefing. Why is he going to the Indian sub-continent? 'Because I was asked. Besides, I thought you'd like to see some sunshine.' He is reading a fat new life of Harry Truman, which reminds him of his wartime days in those very parts for which we're bound : he reminisces expansively. Back down the cabin, the typewriters of three Downing Street secretaries chatter out messages of greetings to each country we 'overfly'.

At 7.30 am local time, after a sleepless day and night by our body clocks, we arrive in Dacca. It is immediately clear what an ego-trip awaits Jim, the first British prime minister to set foot in Bangladesh. Not merely the President but the entire Government is on the tarmac; there are guards of honour to be inspected, salutes to be taken, national anthems and speeches to be exchanged, before we motorcade into town through cheering, flag-waving crowds, beneath arches bearing our leader's familiar (if slightly younger) features and such slogans as 'Welcome to the great leader of a great nation.'

The price he has to pay, here as elsewhere, is a truly punishing schedule. Within a few hours, we are on the bumpy road to the interior, to meet some wide-eyed villagers and lay a wreath to Bangladesh's freedom fighters. Jim is then straight into two hours of jet-lagged talks with President Zia. Another hour, and there is the first of many state banquets. The British press, bag-eyed and bed-bound, generously elect me to represent them.

Next day, the PM is miffed with the daily papers. His morning news summary from London says they've been going on about immigration. It may be the last subject he wants to get entangled in, but he hasn't exactly given them much else to write home about. With this in mind, he begins to wax lyrical about harnessing the waters of the Ganges, a project for which he's offered Zia lots of money. There are problems attached, but for now the enthusiasm is so intense that one No. 10 man tells me: 'The waters of the Ganges have been raised in depth.'

We have our own private session with President Zia, a soft-spoken, shrewd, defensive little man who looks nothing like the fierce military dictator he is. Jim, he tells us, has been giving him a few tips on parliamentary democracy, which he hopes to introduce in his country. There's no doubt this visit has done Zia a lot of good. He can scarcely believe his luck that the British Prime Minister has dropped by to offer him public endorsement. Nor, come to that, can we.

What but goodwill do such visits as this achieve? The truth is, of course, that for all the backbreaking diplomacy behind them, they are not designed to produce much else. Half our time here, in fact, has been spent mucking about in boats in deference to Jim's naval origins. All very pleasant; but no one can pretend anything important is going on when the whole of today, our last here, is consumed by flying down to Chittagong to board another boat, take the salute at a naval academy, and sail back up-river for a pleasantly boozy lunch aboard the Bangladesh Navy (one sometime-British frigate). At least Bernard Donoughue has got his run this morning: a cool thirteen minutes for the one-and-a-half miles round Dacca's main park.

When we get to India, we see why we went to Bangladesh. The welcome at Delhi airport is twice as lavish: half Parliament is here, and the band even plays in tune. For Callaghan, this is clearly a very emotional moment, Bangladesh and Pakistan are the entrance and exit to an Aladdin's cave of adulation – certainly some sort of climax in Jim's political career.

You can tell by the way he keeps going on about chairing Krishna Menon's India League meetings in London in the 1930s. The thing is that Jim cut his political teeth on the fight for Indian independence: his greatest pride, he tells the Indian Parliament in the major speech of the trip, is to have been a junior minister in the Attlee Government that saw it through. Now he is the first Labour prime minister to visit India, and no Briton can have been received with such rapture since the end of the Raj thirty years ago.

He is even managing to upstage Jimmy Carter, who has only been gone two days. To give you just one statistic: Carter's advance party of security and administrative staff numbered 184, Callaghan's three. But there's no doubt whom Morarji Desai regards as more important. Their chat in the official Mercedes, during the triumphal entry into Delhi from the airport, is so intense they carry it on after reaching the presidential palace. Harassed and sweaty protocol men despair as forty-five whole minutes are hiccuped out of the schedule.

Six am next morning, and dawn rises over the imposing red-stone avenue between the presidential palace and the India Gate. A lone figure in sweat-shirt and track shoes is seen jogging through the incongruous morning bagpipers. Yes, it's Dr Bernard Donoughue, out to beat thirty minutes for the five-kilometre circuit (he's gone metric). He does so.

At the High Commissioner's residence Callaghan is at his ease on the verandah, fingering a set of smart brass worry beads he got 'somewhere in the Gulf'. He says I am not to read too much significance into them, 'I just put this suit on this morning and found them in the pocket. When I put the suit away tonight, I'll be putting the worry beads away too. Nice, though, aren't they?'

Jim's in a good mood. Morarji is his kind of guy, and they're doing each other proud. Later that afternoon, in the stunning setting of the Red Fort at dusk, Jim is again garlanded and showered with gifts as Desai pays him more tributes. To ice the cake, Jim ends his own, rather dull, speech about urban blight with a few words in Hindi. In translation they mean: 'To be in Delhi is a source of great happiness.'

Sunday is a day off: down in the VC10 to some sightseeing in Agra, a photogenic stroll round the Taj Mahal, a picnic lunch (complete with Indian dancing girls) in an abandoned Moghul fortress, and a helicopter trip to a spooky bird sanctuary. Audrey Callaghan is more in evidence than usual today. At the Taj, she's a bit sharp with Jim about his dynasties, and won't let him hold her hand for photographers. When the BBC and ITN political heavies both ask him, on camera, if he's having a nice day, Jim responds rather more eloquently by quoting Tagore: 'The Taj Mahal is a teardrop on the cheek of destiny.'

Next day, he's up at seven to write today's Parliament speech, or rather to discuss it with his writers. 'I just put in the twiddly bits,' he candidly confesses. Nevertheless, a press conference that morning is postponed – a flap for Tom McCaffrey – because the PM is not happy with the draft. In Parliament that afternoon, it goes down better than it deserves. Callaghan advances down the aisle at Churchillian pace, but his technical chappies can't write him Churchillian scripts. He goes on about 'a new framework of Anglo-Indian relations', which apparently means he'd like to meet Desai every year instead of every other year.

We have a private session with Desai while Callaghan has his with Mrs Gandhi. Desai tells us nothing, and attacks us for asking perceptive questions. We meet Mrs Gandhi leaving Callaghan's suite: she too tells us nothing, rather more charmingly. Inside, Callaghan is angry that we asked Desai perceptive questions. He has read a transcript of our private meeting. We wonder how. When we ask him about his meeting with Mrs Gandhi, he quotes what she said to us as we came in. 'Which one of us have you got bugged?' asks David Holmes of the BBC. Jim chuckles 'Yes, I'm the Nixon around here.' The phenomenon remains unexplained.

In the morning, Desai comes aboard the VC10 to show Jim round his native state of Gujarat. They're such good pals now I can't see how we're going to part them. The day is spent visiting the Gandhi Ashram, receiving honorary degrees, taking tea with governors, visiting milk and fertilizer plants. We fly off to Bombay, for a sail around the harbour. Then the VC10 climbs towards Pakistan; at its front is a conquering hero, at its rear a gloomy pariah.

The full resources of a prime ministerial safari are wrapping me up in cotton wool. At Islamabad I am whisked off to isolation, but not before watching the arrival ceremony, the most impressive, most military, indeed most frightening, yet. Our motorcade speeds into town through the empty night streets. Even through my glass darkly, I can sense the grip of General Zia-ul Haq's martial law.

My colleagues go off to see him, and return with the news that ex-President Bhutto's wife and daughter are to be kept under house arrest during our visit. So, it seems, am I.

The Bhutto women, says the General, have been bringing politics to the cricket field. He wishes the British Prime Minister, who is to look in on the one-day England-Pakistan game, to 'watch his cricket in peace'. It's a pretty elaborate gesture, as Jim is only at the ground for one hour. The protocol boys have cut short the cricket to get us off to Aswan, and we only have four hours there before jetting off home.

UPI is by now monitoring my mumps. The Pakistan papers said Jim had probably caught it; the Egyptian press fears Sadat will catch it from him. As the two meet beneath the Arabian stars, I watch from a discreet distance, chilled by the most awesome thought of all. Might I, through Jim, have given mumps to Geoff Boycott?

For all these risks our kind-hearted Prime Minister repeatedly endangers his own health by approaching to inquire after mine. His parting words to me are: 'Well, we'll see in ten days if I've caught it. If I have, I hope it strikes just before question time.'

Sunday Times, 15 January 1978

With Prince Charles in Canada

Calgary, Alberta

Tuesday: His Royal Hysteria

It is 4 pm London time, 11 am local time, and I am flying over Prince Charles Island, off the coast of Greenland. Nothing too remarkable about that, except that I am doing so in the company of Prince Charles.

He is in the first-class compartment of an Air Canada jumbo jet, flight AC853, with his private secretary, his press secretary, his private secretary's private secretary, his equerry, his air attaché, his police officer, his valet, and the Premier of Alberta. I am back in the economy section with 300 package tourists, four malfunctioning toilets and a headache. We are bound for Calgary, Alberta.

His Royal Highness and I are both blissfully unaware of the eponymous island beneath, as we are both engrossed in a particularly dreadful in-flight movie by the name of *Logan's Run*. 'Frightful' is his verdict in conversation later, and I cannot quibble. He tells me, however, that he stuck it out because he is something of an admirer of Miss Jenny Agutter. I wonder whether to start rumours of a new royal romance.

But Miss Agutter all too soon fades from our sight, to be replaced by the rugged landscape of central Canada. As I scan my fellow passengers for potential hijackers, assassins or even security men, I am told by the stewardess that we have been escorted by jet fighters all the way from Heathrow. So flying with royalty does have its compensations. We left London, and reach Calgary, bang on time, despite an air traffic staff dispute which delayed many other flights. As we taxi towards the reception committee, a hostess opens a flap in the roof and holds aloft a tiny royal standard. The Prince is back in his suit and tie, out of which he had changed shortly after take-off.

By now, word of his presence has spread among my fellow-travellers. They crowd to the windows for a glimpse before being whisked on to Vancouver. 'He might have popped back to say hello,' complains one large, loudly dressed matron, just as the royal face pops through the curtain and says 'Hello. Everyone all right back here? Food all right, was it?' There is an enormous cheer. Strong men weep, and the large matron blushes to the roots of her coiffure. The head disappears again.

Then, a gun goes off. There is a moment of total, appalled silence, before we realize it is the start of a twenty-one-gun salute outside. Prince Charles inspects a guard of honour from Lord Strathcona's Horse (Royal Canadians), of which he is Colonel-in-Chief, as I join the customs queue, of which I am at the back. We are staying at the same hotel in downtown Calgary, in which he is safely installed before I have even been reunited with my suitcase.

I am the only journalist to have arrived on the same flight as HRH, as all the itineraries call him. He and I have missed a two-hour briefing explaining the week's schedule to countless officials and 'accredited media personnel'. But we meet up with them all at a mid-afternoon cocktail party, during which he tells a rather funny story about his father and a busby headdress. The laughter is hysterical. And with 200 journalists gathered together in one place, the words Marie-Astrid are bound soon to fall from a passing lip. 'Oh, you don't believe all that stuff, do you?' is the royal comment. 'It goes to show that you journalists are all romantics at heart.'

Reaching me, he expresses surprise at my presence: 'I didn't think the *Sunday Times* bothered with this sort of thing.' There's no answer to that. And so, jet-lagged, to bed.

Wednesday: Charles Kills a Scoop
'OK, move it out. C'mon, let's move. *Move.*'

I am beginning to understand what it is to cover a royal tour. Thirty of us have been whisked by helicopter, in convoy with HRH, to a remote stretch of Indian prairie land called Blackfoot Crossing. We emerge to discover another 150 journalists waiting, plus as many Mounties, and two or three thousand Indians. They have taken days to get here. Our quarry vanishes into their midst, the focal point of an ebb tide, surging this way and that on a tight schedule. Just occasionally, you bump into him, unmistakable in his (it has to be said) rather scruffy safari gear. He will be discussing the finer points of tepee construction with

Chief Nelson Small Legs Jr, or indeed disappearing into one with Chief Pretty Youngman.

We are shepherded along a special press path, to watch at a distance as HRH mounts a horse, rides a hundred yards, and dismounts again. In my head, I am polishing a phrase about being herded like cattle, when once again I am told by a Media Liaison Officer to 'move it out', and we are driven, quite literally, into a corral. From this dubious vantage point, we watch the ceremonies marking the centenary of the signing of Treaty Seven.

In 1877, the chiefs of the Blackfoot Confederacy signed away their land to Queen Victoria's representative, in return for promises of various types of support. Those chiefs' descendants are here today, as indeed is Queen Victoria's, to see how it has all worked out.

It is soon clear that the Indians are far from pleased. Only in the last ten of those 100 years have they received a vestige of that support, let alone their own self-government, as promised by the white man. Sensing the significance of Charles's presence, Chief Jim Shot Both Sides has hired a public relations firm to get the Blackfoot message across to the watching world.

So the first ceremony is a highly photogenic Smoking of the Peace Pipe, from which HRH seems to have difficulty extracting any smoke. This is followed by two hours of speeches. Copies of each are handed to us, immaculately printed, which is just as well as several of the chiefs have difficulty reading their own words. HRH appears unmoved by the curses being rained down on the white man – a hasty reaction, it transpires, as those curses soon convert punishing sunlight into a truly Saharan sandstorm, presumably some kind of cosmic smoke signal. Then it pours with rain.

HRH gets drenched. For once the press are better off, awaiting him in the shelter of the Entertainment Tepee. As he shakes himself down, entertainments commence. These turn out to be traditional Indian dances – of a quality, the MC assures us, to be seen only once every 100 years. They consist of colourfully dressed Indians mooching round in circles, scarcely acknowledging the distinguished presence in their midst. The world's press persuades its bus driver to leave early, abandoning HRH to his fate.

Cunningly, I remain behind, to find myself within war-cry distance of a world scoop. The MC announces, clearly to Prince Charles's surprise, that HRH will now join the throng in a celebration dance – in which he will be partnered by the nubile Princess Tina A. Youngman. 'At least she's not a Catholic,' murmurs a well-read young brave at my side. I look around for a camera to borrow. But HRH announces, clearly to the MC's surprise, that he's having none of it, and remains firmly in his seat.

Rushing to fill the diplomatic breach, the Federal Minister for Indian Affairs, the Hon. Warren Allmand, volunteers to take the Prince's place beside the Princess. He joins the dance with some gusto in his federal suit – and looks, appropriately enough, a proper Charlie.

Thursday: the Prince of Blood

Summertime, and the weather is worsening. Winds are rising and the chopper is high.

Today, we are bound even further afield, to the Blood Indian reserves at Stand Off, Southern Alberta, where HRH is to be made an honorary Kainai chieftain. First, however, Chief Jim Shot Both Sides – he of yesterday's fiery tongue, now all sweetness and light – must show him the Shot Both Sides building, and the Prince must unveil a statue of the legendary chief of the Bloods, Red Crow. Attempting this feat in a high wind, he suceeds rather in veiling himself.

The paucity of what we see, touring the Kainai reservation, confirms yesterday's denunciations of whitie. Ninety-five per cent of the Blood Indians are on federal welfare; we visit the modular homes factory, in which some of the remainder work, a farm and a village school. With the press cameras a safe two minutes behind him at one point, I notice HRH – for a brief, heady moment – sink his left hand into his trouser pocket. With the arrival of the media charabanc, it is safely restored to its partner behind his back.

There follows lunch. I watch from a balcony above as Chief Jim and Mrs Shot Both Sides, on either side of the Prince, tuck into their salads for some time before noticing that he hasn't even got a plate. A plate is summoned, but it is yet longer before the chief is delicately prompted by HRH to pass him the salad bowl. I marvel at the scantiness of their meal, as I wolf my media sandwiches, before learning that the tribal catering department has failed to show up with the main course.

There is no time to wait. Charles downs his lettuce, and departs for his installation as a chieftain. The first to be so honoured was his late great-uncle, the Duke of Windsor; among the subsequent were Douglas Bader and John Diefenbaker, the former Canadian Prime Minister, who is on the rostrum in full Indian regalia. The winds drop; the sun grows hot across the plain; the clouds gather against the Rocky Mountains in a dramatic prairie skyscape; and the charming ceremony is at last under way.

Chief Medicine Man Arthur Healy paints the Prince of Wales's face in dramatic red and yellow stripes. The Prince dons an enormous head-dress of eagle feathers, which the wind persists in blowing forward over his face. He is presented with a peace pipe, with an eight-year-old pinto horse called Cross Bell, with a hand-made leather saddle, and with the proud name of Red Crow. He disappears for half-an-hour to put on the complete buckskin outfit, and returns to join – albeit reservedly – in a rhythmic Indian dance. The world's press is so beside itself it breaks through the Blood Indians' sacred barrier, and has its names taken by the tribal police.

Friday: Stampeding the Colour

'Howdy, Charles and Andrew,' enthuses the neon sign outside my hotel window. 'Welcome to the Calgary Stampede.' Prince Andrew – at seventeen taller, more relaxed and much more of a dash-cutter than his brother – has arrived to join in the fun as the scenario changes from Indians to cowboys.

What is the Calgary Stampede? Well, along about 1912, a cowpoke name o' Guy Weadick rode into Calgary with a dream as big as the Albertan sky. He borrowed 100,000 smackeroos and staged the biggest frontier show the world had ever seen. People sho' liked it, and it's been goin' ever since. Leastways, that's what it says here in my programme, adding that the Stampede Story isn't one of your regular once-upon-a-time tales. No siree. It's a 'Granpappy's knee-slappin' yarn o' the Ol' Wild West'.

I am awoken by the sounds of yips and yahoos outside my

23

window, and blink out to see my future King – whom I last remember dressed as a Red Indian – in a wide-brimmed stetson hat, cowboy boots and a tan western suit. He is astride a nut-brown, non-bucking bronco, at the head of a parade which turns out to be five miles long. The whole of Alberta, wads of oil dollars in its denim pocket, is headed for the Stampede.

I struggle through to join the Princes on a rostrum overlooking bouts of steer-wrestling, wild-cow-milking, bareback-bronc-riding, calf-roping, wild-horse-racing, and chuckwagon-racing. Soon after our arrival, a bronc bucks its rider into the wall of the royal stand, and he is carried out semi-conscious. No one takes too much notice. Alongside his ignominious zero zero score, the electronic scoreboard flashes TOUGH LUCK.

The Princes are joined on their perch by their local counterparts, the Stampede Queen and her princesses, all studded buckskin, tasselled skirts and eye-shadow. Not eager to be too much photographed with them, Charles plunges into a mêlée of attendant cowpokes, whose slouches suddenly emphasize his own formal mannerisms. He has several nervous habits, does HRH; he licks his lips a lot, he fiddles with the gold three-feathered signet ring on his left little finger, and the right-hand corner of his mouth has a nervous tic which frequently drags it down towards his chin. While anatomizing, I notice today that the substantial bags under his eyes are heavier and blacker, which must mean his job is almost as tiring as mine.

Nevertheless, the royal show must go on. In the evening, he declares the Calgary Stampede open, quite rightly pointing out that he thought it was already open. Fierce daytime heat has, now familiarly, given way to heavy rainstorms, and Charles is again quite right to cut his remarks short, surmising: 'I'm sure you'll all want to go home as soon as I've declared the Stampede open.' The electronic scoreboard, which has been flashing such encouragement as 'Fantastic' and 'Wow' during the chuckwagon-racing, chooses the onset of utterly torrential rain, with everyone fleeing for cover, to light up 'Are you having fun?'

Charles, for one, is beat. He's back in the hotel before the fireworks begin. Tomorrow he will leave this strange land, with its executive cowboys and professional Indians, and return to Blighty, reliable sunshine, the Silver Jubilee and the Second Test Match. I shall seek alternative sanity elsewhere on this continent. But I must finally report, after my first encounter with real live Red Indians, that His Royal Highness Prince Red Crow is the only one I have heard all week to say: 'How?'

Sunday Times, 10 July 1977

With Margaret Thatcher in China

Peking

'Women', Chairman Mao Tse-tung was fond of observing, 'hold up half the sky.' Last Thursday morning the woman who wants to hold up half the Western sky winged out of it into Peking, preceded by her Russian reputation as Britain's Iron Maiden. The Chinese may have some difficulty pronouncing the phrase, but Margaret Thatcher is giving them every opportunity to believe it.

Everywhere she goes, Mrs Thatcher is carefully making anti-Russian noises of the kind her hosts want to hear. Her manner, meanwhile, is not unlike that of the Queen on a state visit. In conversation with Vice-Premier Li Hsien-nin, she referred to 'my people', having swept regally into the room pursued by a flotilla of attendant males. Her twenty-three-year-old daughter, Carol, who is along for the ride, also behaves remarkably like Princess Anne. The Chinese are clearly impressed.

Mrs Thatcher's keynote speech in the Great Hall of the People, at the banquet in her honour on Thursday night, was not as stridently anti-Soviet as might have been expected – although she herself insists it was 'no less fiery' than anything she might have said at home. She is clearly keeping her options open for further foreign trips. But the speech was reprinted in full next morning in the *People's Daily* – an honour normally reserved for visiting heads of state – and went down well with party chiefs present at the feast.

Much better, in fact, than the eight-course meal went down with Mrs Thatcher. She appeared to draw the line at sea-slugs (course number six). When the time came for the famous toasts, she avoided the 150-proof maotai which caused Richard Nixon such trouble, and toured the room raising a tiny glass of China's sickly-sweet red wine. She had, she told me, been into the protocol, and discovered to her relief that it is acceptable for ladies to sip from their glasses rather than toss each of the many toasts back in one gulp, as is the Chinese way. The journalists in the party, she noted, did not seem to be experiencing too much difficulty.

Mrs Thatcher has come to China with only two escorts – John Stanley MP, her parliamentary private secretary, and Douglas Hurd MP, the Tory Party's China expert, who also came here two years ago with Edward Heath. The Chinese know enough of British politics to avoid asking after Heath's well-being. Mrs Thatcher might as well ask Chairman Hua Kuo-feng how he sprang from nowhere to become Mao's resolute successor, quickly erasing Mao's widow, Chiang-ching, and her 'Gang of Four' from the scene.

The Thatcher party are staying in a government guest house, complete with small lake, while the rest of us are installed in the comfortable Peking Hotel. Right from the airport, where she was met by Huang Hua, the foreign affairs minister, Mrs Thatcher has headed a twenty-five-car motorcade, which in effect means we have a car each. The parade sweeps all before it, under the curious gaze of the bicycling masses.

Her visit coincides with that of President Ould Dada of Mauritania, who as a head of state seemed at first to be taking precedence. He was met at the airport by Chairman Hua himself, and was guest of honour at a banquet for several thousand in the state banqueting hall. Mrs Thatcher's dinner was held in a small ante-room and attended by some sixty people, half of whom were British. Yesterday, however, honour was more than satisfied when Mrs Thatcher became the first Western politician to meet Chairman Hua, though he kept her waiting for an hour before they approached each other from opposite ends of a corridor in the Great Hall of the People.

Also in town is an American congressional delegation, including President Carter's son, and a deputation of Glasgow businessmen, led by the Lord Provost, whose secret hope is to take home a panda for Scotland.

Mrs Thatcher's first day here was consumed by extremely formal political talks. Only six hours after the gruelling sixteen hour flight – which China Airlines failed to alleviate with movies, music or, indeed, liquor – she was starting a two-hour session with Huang. 'We expect and hope', she told him 'to be worked very hard whilst we are here.' He replied that China was undergoing a great political revolution at the moment, and urged her to go and look at it. He had just started saying that rumours of instability in China had been 'greatly exaggerated' when journalists were unceremoniously bundled out of the room.

The same happened later, at her pre-dinner chat with China's number two, Vice-Premier Li Hsien-nin. Li told Mrs Thatcher that she had expressed many political views with which he agreed. 'They were very firm views,' said his guest. He said he had met 'other members of the British Government'. Too tactful to correct him, Mrs Thatcher asked 'Who?' 'Mr Julian Amery,' he said proudly. 'Ah', said Mrs Thatcher. 'Did you meet Edward Heath when he was here?' Li said No, he had not met Heath. Had he met 'our other great statesman, Sir Alec Douglas-Home'? Exit journalists before the question was answered, and before the chat – one assumes – got slightly more interesting.

Next morning, Mrs Thatcher had an audience with Chou En-lai's widow, Teng Ying-chiao, who is now vice-chairman of the standing committee of the People's National Congress. Said Madame Chou: 'I see from your appearance that you have high spirits and strong stamina.' Said Madame Thatcher: 'I just wear well.'

During the flight, at a one-hour stopover in Karachi, I asked Mrs Thatcher if she intended to walk further than Edward Heath along the Great Wall. Much to the relief of those present, she said she didn't. 'We've come an awfully long way, you know. There'll be a lot else to do.' And she's certainly doing it. Up at seven on her second morning, she was out in a Peking market soon after eight, buying stocks of tea, chocolate and preserved fruit. Each session of talks is punctuated by a bit of sightseeing, during which she is an assiduously inquiring tourist. And when the time came, she walked as far along the Wall as Ted did, as far as Alec even, and further than either Ford or Nixon. 'We climbed right to the top,' she told Chairman Hua proudly. 'It was a lovely day.' To which the Chairman replied, with a quotation from Mao: 'He who fails to reach the top of the Great Wall is no true man.' Mrs Thatcher laughed and the translation was quickly changed to 'no true leader'.

In the forbidden city, where we toured the magnificent imperial palace, Mrs Thatcher was stumping the Minister of Information with detailed questions about dates and styles. She also visited the neighbourhood committee of Fu Shiu Ching, where she asked a pointed question about female representation, to find that eighteen of the twenty-seven committee members were women. 'Where are they all, then?' she asked the all-male reception committee, and was instantly whisked off to a 'typical' household which had been laid on. 'I bet she goes for broke to get in the kitchen,' said one of her escorts irreverently, just before she asked where the kitchen was. The family of nine, she discovered, had one Calor-gas stove in their tiny, scrupulously clean kitchen, and two bedrooms between them.

Then it was on to the neighbourhood kindergarten, where strictly disciplined rows of three-year-olds sang a song of welcome and jumped up and down with excitement. Their six-year-old brothers and sisters laid on a song-and-dance show, which included a group of tiny armed pilots shooting down the form's non-dancer, who represented a Russian Mig. A pretty four-year-old girl sang in praise of Chairman Hua.

Yesterday, Mrs Thatcher talked with Chairman Hua, flanked by Vice-Premier Li Hsien-nin and Huang Hua, for just over an hour. Beside each armchair in the semi-circle was a table piled high with nuts and fruit. Chairman Hua said: 'I hope there will be second, third and fourth visits.'

'I hope so too,' replied Mrs Thatcher, looking very nervous and ill-at-ease. 'There's so much to see. It's all so very exciting.'

Journalists and Mrs Thatcher's staff were then ushered out of the room, leaving the Tory leader and the British Ambassador, Sir Edward Youde, to continue the talks.

Mrs Thatcher will not reveal what happens each time the journalists exit, except to say that talks range 'right round the world', and to stress that the Chinese are 'very, very well briefed'. She herself is extremely well briefed – she was the only Briton not to sleep during the flight. She ploughed through books, Foreign Office briefings, and as she puts it, 'even newspaper articles'. Everything in China, she says, turns out to be just like it is in the books and the cuttings. 'Except that things must be rather different when you actually see them in practice.'

Last night, she hosted a return banquet in the Great Hall, with invitations on Conservative Party cards saying the Opposition Leader would be 'At home' in the Great Hall of the People.

The Conservative leader and her guests are continually harangued with denunciations of the Gang of Four who are currently undergoing 'intensive interrogation and instruction'. Nobody knows where they are. But the expected rehabilitation of Teng Hsiao-ping, the moderate expunged after last year's 5 April riots, will apparently not come as soon as has been rumoured.

Despite the overthrow of the radicals, and the discrediting of all their leaders stood for, Chairman Hua still appears to regard Teng as some kind of threat to his own position. This year's 5 April celebrations – dedicated to the memory of the dead – were cancelled for the first time since the declaration of the People's Republic. This can only be because Hua feared demonstrations in favour of Teng, whom he accused of organizing last year's unruly scenes in the Square of Heavenly Peace. At seventy-three, Teng is seventeen years Hua's senior; he has a massive following among the people, who cannot understand what rivalry there could be between them. This is all that can be gleaned from random encounters with the Chinese, who cower with fear if you try to discuss such matters.

The China entertaining Mrs Thatcher, therefore, is either a secure and forward-looking politburo, or a shaky government seething with internal strife. It is extraordinary how little the most astute and attentive observer can glean. Resident journalists regard Mrs Thatcher's visit as a passing irritant, but are delighted to accompany her to schools and factories – having applied to visit such places many times without success, even without reply.

Mrs Thatcher, meanwhile, is withholding all verdicts, intent merely on appearing as aware as the Chinese of the Soviet menace. As one 'preparing to take part in the government of Britain', she told them, she shared their views on Europe as a crucial defence grouping. Vice-Premier Li warmly quoted her previously voiced concerns about detente, and added a Chinese proverb: 'As we say, there is great disorder under heaven, and the situation is excellent.'

That seems to be the limit of the views actually being exchanged. For the rest, Mrs Thatcher is intent to appear both sturdy and charming. In a country whose most prominent woman politician, Chiang-ching, is now in disgrace, a woman successor to Home and Heath is transparently regarded as a curiosity. Confucius, whose thoughts included 'Women are backward', is also of course in disgrace, but the uniformly dressed Chinese are clearly fascinated, for instance, by Mrs Thatcher's wardrobe. In her first forty-eight hours here, I counted no fewer than six different outfits. Alas, I am not qualified to describe them, but they all seemed eminently sensible.

Incongruities crowd the eye. To see Mrs Thatcher, an English rose with her newly-cropped blonde hair, sandwiched between portraits of Mao and Hua, is in itself arresting. To see her struggling with chopsticks is cheap entertainment, especially in view of one's own limited skills. To see her nodding sagely as a neighbourhood chairman explains, 'When the Gang of Four was smashed in one blow, this was declared an area of jubilation', is to understand diplomacy. To hear her fulsome tributes to the Chinese revolution is worth a cable to Central Office.

She herself will contribute. One of her many suitcases contains only Crown Derby china and House of Commons ashtrays to be liberally distributed to her hosts. But this incongruity pales besides the greater irony it prompts. Mrs Thatcher was invited to China a year ago, before Mao's death and the upheavals of the subsequent power struggle. The recipients of her gifts will not be those who invited her, and she will leave China no wiser about how their succession took place.

Sunday Times, 10 April 1977

Postscript
Shanghai

It is well after midnight in a Chinese provincial hotel. Margaret Thatcher, prospective British prime minister, is wandering up and down the corridor looking for her daughter. She pauses outside a bedroom door, unsure it is the right one. 'Carol dear, are you there?' Silence. Carol, sensibly enough, is fast asleep.

As are most of the rest of Mrs Thatcher's entourage. After their umpteenth exhausting Chinese banquet – two hours of ten courses and more toasts, hosted this time by the Hangchow municipal revolutionary committee – they have attended a bring-a-bottle party thrown by Mrs Thatcher for her travelling companions. Everyone is weary but her. She bounces from one group to the next, her enthusiasms ranging over the cleaning of

Chinese silk paintings, comparative living standards in China and India, the beauty of Chairman Hua's hands. And the delights of Hong Kong. 'It's a market economy, dear boy.'

In passing, she makes a startling admission which her British political opponents may care to note. 'To find out what someone is really like,' she says, 'I normally look very carefully at their eyes.' The technique has proved somewhat unproductive in China, as Oriental eyes are none too revealing. Chairman Hua, however, had 'rather ruthless' eyes.

One journalist, somewhat the worse for wear, crashes against the Opposition leader on his indirect course to the drinks table. She politely appears not to notice. As others fall by the wayside, she seems disappointed. Her insatiable capacity for activity and argument, coupled with her minimal need of sleep, leaves her the last standing. Stout men slump and watch as she tidies the room, humping enormous armchairs back to their proper places.

Next morning, I go shopping with Mrs Thatcher at the friend-ship shop in Soochow. Impressed with her expertise on the sub-ject, I ask her to recommend a silk painting. She offers detailed criticism of each one on display, finally advising against a purchase. She scrutinizes the jade with withering eye, as I des-perately hunt for an antique Chinese figure within my price range, yet up to her standards. I find one with, as I put it, a hint of the Michelangelo about it. 'It's frightfully ugly, dear boy. Put it back at once.' I obey. The evening ends with each of us carry-ing a silk painting under our arm. She bought hers on a dif-ferent floor, and I took advantage of her absence to snap up one she had ruled out. Neither of us asks about the other's acquisi-tion.

All such pleasant excursions take place amid the lunches, banquets, speeches, visits to factories, schools, communes, revolutionary committees and notables of which you will have read in your daily papers. In Hangchow we go boating on the lake, still in protocol-order convoy; in Soochow we take tea in the Garden of the Futility of Politics, where imaginative jokes are made. The two worlds come together in the ornate, anach-ronistic observation car of a train from Hangchow to Shanghai. Mrs Thatcher – looking, as she puts it, like Victoria en route for Osborne – gives us an off-the record, unattributable, unquot-able, lobby-basis briefing on her views of Chinese communism. I am, therefore, not allowed to repeat them.

I can say, however, that I understand from sources close to Mrs Thatcher that there is not much about China of which she approves. She believes that the 'spark of human spirit' – by which she means the spirit of free enterprise – will be the undoing of the People's Republic. Some communes are more prosperous than others, workers are not allowed to move from one commune to another, thus follows jealousy and discord.

Mrs Thatcher, alone of her party, believes living standards in India are higher than those in China. She finds it difficult, as a Westerner, to perceive what a Chinese is really thinking, but she does not believe they all accept the clichéd propaganda they interminably trot out. She, again alone of her party, gives the impression of believing the Chinese revolution cannot last. She also gives the impression of having believed all this, and made up her mind about it, long before she left London.

Sunday Times, 17 April 1977

With Ted Heath in Manchester

The time is 3.15 pm last Wednesday, the place Platform Twelve of Piccadilly Station, Manchester. I am standing alone in a darkened railway carriage, looking down on the prostrate form of our former national leader, the Rt Hon. Edward Heath MP, who is stretched out on a British Rail sofa, fast asleep. (Yes, since you ask, he *is* snoring slightly.) Outside, a crowd jostles for a glimpse of the visitor, come among them to sign copies of their Christmas presents. He is, alas, beneath their line of vision. They peer at me curiously, as the station-master struggles through to perform his official duties.

For a moment, the station-master too is puzzled. He has entered the darkling gloom of what is supposed to be Supertrain, and has a letter to deliver, quite apart from his own formal greetings. The potential recipient of both is, however, still asleep, still purring gently. Both the station-master and I are wondering whether to save everyone's dignity by giving him a shake, when Providence intervenes. With a grunt, and a cry of 'It's cold in here', he is awake. He looks up at the station-master, who welcomes him and hands over his missive, for all the world as if it were the Summons to the Palace. The visitor mutters something and puts the brown envelope aside unopened without stirring. The station-master, his world falling quietly about his ears, murmurs his thanks, hesitates, then turns and leaves.

Suddenly the lights snap on again, and the steely Heath gaze catches me, not for the first time, with a glass of Gewürztraminer 1973 in my hand. Well, I am in my duly discreet corner, at the rear end of Supertrain's central carriage, separated from the still occupied sofa only by the Queen Anne desk and chair (specially hired for the week) at which my host will in a moment again be greeting his customers. The vase of red carnations (changed every day) spares my blushes. For beside me is the luxurious bar, specially stocked with such local favourites as Bollinger champagne and Glenfiddich malt whisky – but the rest of all that is off the record.

Besides, the hordes are heading in again. Heath is quite alert now, and dashes off a couple of radio interviews before unscrewing the Cartier gold pen given him by Lord Longford at his 100th signing session, and getting back down to business. This afternoon, he will sign his 50,000th book. Publicists await the unsuspecting customer with a presentation pen (this one, I fear, not from Cartier's).

The queue stretches out from the central carriage to the entrance coach, lined as in a bookshop with shelves creaking beneath *Travel, Music, Sailing, Carols* and the author's six LPs. To pass from one to the other, the customer must obey the large signs on the walls: 'Pay for your books and records before having them signed by Edward Heath.' To be ushered into the presence, he must pass between two red-hot cash registers, guarding like Cerberus the entrance to the signing coach. Most enter into the spirit of the thing, some clutching a complete set (a cool £30 worth) for signing; a few slip through the net, mostly schoolboys carrying scraps of paper. One is a postman who presents his overtime docket for signature. The author obliges reluctantly; the postman leaves with a cry of 'He's signed me off!'

Behind the entrance coach is a guard's van. To enter it you must watch your step, which descends a few inches, so great is the weight of books and records it contains. The train manager is quite worried about it; indeed, it accounts for the earlier darkling gloom, for an electricity cable came uncoupled between Liverpool and Manchester. I stand in wonderment beside Mr Heath's suitcase, peering around at the 20,000 books and records which also bear his name.

We have been in Manchester one hour, and the cash registers have taken £750. Sidgwick and Jackson can hope to pull in one hundred times that this week, which makes light of the (rumoured) £10,000 hire fee for the train. The cause of it all, if you mention money, mutters about Denis Healey and 83 per cent. He is, as you will have heard him say on departure from Paddington, selling for Britain.

Back in the signing coach, there is a lull. Not, however, at the desk. When the queue evaporates, the author continues to sign, as if transfixed. Beside the bar behind him are a cache of Manchester booksellers, whose vans wait on the platform to carry off crates of signed copies for their shelves. Stephen du Sautoy of Sidgwick's, the driving force behind the Heath pen, puts another stack of *Carols* on the desk. Their author looks up wearily. 'What are these for?' he asks irrelevantly. 'Signing,' says Mr du Sautoy smartly. I offer to make Mr Heath a Christmas present of a wax model of Mr du Sautoy, to stick pins in ; neither seems to think this very funny. Stephen tells me he has a leather sheath ready for his author's right little finger, which occasionally gets sore from its movement across so many pages.

It's now after five, and there's an hour and a half to go. Heath is wearying, though he keeps saying how much he enjoys it all, and indeed appears to do so. But I have already watched the performance for three hours in Liverpool that morning, and beside me at lunch (that's in the next carriage, the one before the sleeping car) his conversation was not bright. He scarcely seemed to notice the charcuterie, pot breast of chicken with green salad, pears in red wine with creamed rice, cheese and coffee, let alone that '73 Gewürztraminer, described by the caterers as 'his usual diet'. Amid desultory answers to my small talk, he stared out of the window at the bleak, rainy Lancashire landscape, as if a man possessed by a single, nagging thought – and that, I suspect, not much to do with books and records.

He did perk up briefly when the talk turned to another author-signer, Harold Wilson. 'Fancy thinking Roosevelt was at Potsdam!' Heath laughed. 'I can't understand what that man thinks he's doing these days.' Wishing to intimate that many wonder the same about *him*, I asked if he thought it fair to suggest that his present activity demeaned his former office. 'No,' he said. 'What's the time?' It was 2.59. 'Wake me up at 3.29.'

With which he was off to his sofa. Which is where we came in.

Sunday Times, 11 December 1977

With Princ od Velsa in Yugoslavia

Belgrade

Princ od Velsa, alias the Prince of Wales, is out shooting in Liechtenstein this weekend, recovering from his first glimpse of life according to Karl Marx. Five days in sunny, non-aligned Yugoslavia – the first two spent sightseeing in those very fleshpots where the last Prince of Wales went canoodling with Wallis Simpson – is scarcely the most rigorous introduction to state communism. But the style was not quite that to which Prince Charles is accustomed.

The banquets were smaller than usual, the motorcades longer, the security much tighter. His hosts were careful not to remind Charles, while showing him the benefits of Marxist self-management, what they had done to their own monarchy only thirty years ago. The visit had not been announced in advance, so there were none of the familiar hysterical mob scenes (except, of course, among the travelling photographers). 'Eet ees the Preence of England?' asked one Croatian matron excitedly, only to wander away dejected when told no, it was the Prince of Wales.

The visit was confined to four of the federal states, and carefully avoided Macedonia, for fear of offending the Bulgars. There were, alas, no delicate trade deals for the Prince to clinch, as he did in Brazil. There was little likelihood of his persuading Yugoslav industry to build a factory in the Rhondda, as he did Sony in Japan. Even his pre-lunch talks with President Tito were confined, according to the official statement, to 'family matters' – and with Mrs Tito strictly not on the agenda, let alone on the premises, there was only one family that could mean.

But the (six-course) lunch was different. Over the foie gras, caviar, spit-roasted duck, veal medallions, bombe surprise, champagne and local wines, Tito gave the Prince a wide-ranging, perhaps somewhat avuncular view of the world as he sees it. Prince Charles, apparently, gave as good as he got – on Camp David, Eurocommunism, the North-South dialogue and the Russian advance through Africa. His political views tend to the conservative, but he has a great admiration for Tito as agitator, resistance fighter, peacetime leader and architect of the federation.

Tito in turn bears a special affection for the British Royal Family. His first trip outside Yugoslavia was to London in 1953, before the coronation, and he was here only last March. Prince Charles's visit was made at his personal request. Musing on all this at the gates of Tito's country retreat, overlooking the spectacular Adriatic coast, I concluded that Tito is in many ways the first communist monarch.

There were many more in the Press party than usual, as British newspapers grind up to their thirtieth birthday tributes next month. This seemed to unsettle the Prince somewhat. It also unsettled the Yugoslavs, who constantly refused the press admission to the most interesting events. No, the photographers were told, they could not see the Prince, because he was looking at a secret helicopter. Yes, they were told, it was the same helicopter as those flying in convoy over their heads.

Such caution became obsessive, and by day three the Prince himself had been declared a state secret. The travelling press were aroused at six, taken to an undeclared destination, and told after an hour's wait that the Prince was not there. By the time they discovered where he was – after listening with ill-concealed impatience to a lecture on the efficiency of Yugoslav industry – the bus had disappeared with their cameras. By the time it returned, and the Prince was run to ground, the photographers were embarked upon militant action.

The Prince of Wales had the unusual experience of entering a building through an arcade of silent photographers, their cameras on the ground at their feet. 'What's this?' he asked. 'You on strike?' Yes. 'What, *Again*?' Nervous laughter. 'Are you going home then?' 'No – we ain't got no pictures and we're staying till we do.' HRH looked distinctly annoyed.

His press secretary smoothed over a potential diplomatic incident and, two hours later, the Prince gave the photographers what is known in the trade as a facility. High on a bleak, wind-swept mountaintop, the scene of fierce partisan resistance to the German and Italian advance in 1943, he posed for pictures with Sir Fitzroy Maclean – something of a national hero in Yugoslavia for his work as Churchill's emissary to the partisan cause. The pictures were never used, of course, but the lads were happy again.

Such, on these trips, is the Prince's fate. A goodwill mission to Yugoslavia is measured in terms of a four-year-old British child nibbling his finger on day one, his refusal to stand on a weighing machine on day two (CHARLES WORRIED ABOUT HIS WEIGHT), and the photographers' 'strike' on day three (though none of them thought of taking a picture of the others not taking pictures).

His official visits abroad achieve little more than goodwill – apart from the occasional commercial initiative – but the toll they take on the Prince is considerable. As the press argue on their bus about the monarchy's dependence on the media, he is making laborious conversation through interpreters with the officials in Car Number One. The strain of a day being formally polite to hosts, while every nervous tic is being recorded for posterity, has him struggling to keep awake during the ethnic cabaret after the evening's official dinner.

One occasionally wonders if he can know what life is like aboard a bus containing forty short-tempered pressmen all wanting to go in different directions. But they can certainly never quite know the strains of being in Car Number One. On his official visit to America last year – eleven cities in fourteen days – Prince Charles lost a stone in weight. Thanks respectively to Karl Marx and to the British press, he left Yugoslavia last Friday a wiser and a thinner man.

Sunday Times, 29 October 1978

With the Pope in North America

New York

He might as well have descended from heaven in a fiery chariot as from the urban smog in a TWA jet christened Shepherd One. John Paul II, this most human of Popes, tonight leaves America convinced that it has brushed with the divine.

Earthly matters contributed to the other-worldliness of his progress. The security presence around him was, even by American standards, unprecedented. His white vestments would catch the light and glow in the centre of massive crowds, illuminating that kindly, at times rather impish smile.

TV lights would dramatically signal his emergence onto a cathedral's steps or a cardinal's balcony. In New York's Shea Stadium, to universal delight and papal amusement, the sun actually did break through merciless rainclouds at the very moment of his entrance.

After a final Mass in Washington today, expected to attract another crowd of more than a million, Pope John Paul returns to Rome established beyond all doubt as a major voice in international affairs. It was one of the purposes of an otherwise pastoral trip, and it has succeeded beyond the expectations even of the Catholic hierarchy.

The hysteria with which he has been received, however, has tended to obscure the true nature of his message. Everywhere he has travelled, all week, the Pope's remarks have been tailored to the local scene, and he has chastened and admonished much more than he has offered thanks or praise.

The only audience which appeared to sense this was the General Assembly of the United Nations, whose applause after a sixty-minute shortened version of his published speech was distinctly lukewarm. Clouds passed over the brows of various delegates, several of them from Catholic countries, as the Pope took the UN on a guided tour of human rights around the world.

In other appearances in New York City, John Paul made headlines by saying 'Shalom' and 'God bless New York'. The gist of all his speeches, however, was that the rich conurbations of the world were forgetting the less fortunate in an unconditional surrender to mammon. The emotional cheers were none the less unanimous.

In Philadelphia, whose reputation as the city of brotherly love has of late been somewhat dented, he pointedly reminded people to love their neighbour. Mayor Frank Rizzo had just knelt to kiss the papal ring in front of a million people. But John Paul's words left no doubt of his awareness that Rizzo is currently under federal indictment for 'condoning systematic police brutality'.

In rural Iowa, where he travelled in a helicopter dubbed Angel One, he urged the farmers of America to share the fruits of their labour with the rest of the world.

As Shepherd One approached Washington, domestic politics were less to the fore than had been expected. Rosalynn Carter, to be sure, had virtually pushed the Pope past Senator Edward Kennedy during the arrival ceremony in Boston: after a very brief word, Kennedy was to be seen uncharacteristically hovering on the edge of someone else's crowd, straining for a glimpse.

By the end of the week, the Pope had skilfully raised his presence high above merely presidential politics. Various of his messages – his continued stand, for instance, against abortion – will no doubt be seized as political ammunition, but he was doing no one any campaign favours.

John Paul's appeal to America was that of a serene leader, moral and non-partisan, visiting a country sorely in need of one. His instinct for the human touch, for sharing intimate moments with huge crowds, only heightened his stature. Newspapers wheeled out psychologists to declare, in this case quite correctly, that people like their leaders to be one of them as well as set apart and above.

In St Patrick's Cathedral, New York, he stopped his procession to take out a handkerchief and mop the brow of the choir's soloist; in Madison Square Garden he lifted a child from the audience and set her on the roof of his custom-built Jeep – known even to his entourage as 'The Popemobile'.

At solemn moments, after a prayer or a blessing, he would say in his broken English 'very nice, very nice'. At times he appeared humbled, even baffled, by the immensity of his reception, putting his hands to his ears against the noise and shaking his head in disbelief.

Perhaps the most touching moment came during a celebration in New York with 20,000 children, whose enthusiasm would not permit the silence he evidently needs before he can begin a speech in English. For nine minutes he sat rapt, listening to their unfamiliar high school chants, responding over the public address system with a repeated cry of 'Woooo', 'Woooo' – the Polish equivalent apparently of 'Wow'.

At length Cardinal Cooke, the Archbishop of New York, had to rise and implore him with open arms to get on with it. 'You know what it is,' John Paul confided to the hushed children. 'We are destroying the programme.' Everywhere he went, inevitably, he got further and further behind schedule.

Knowledge of John Paul's past – his support of the Jews in Nazi-occupied Poland, his Church-and-State struggles as Archbishop of Cracow – drew as many Jews, Protestants and heathen as Catholics to fight for a place in the papal glow. One side-effect of his visit has been to endanger the tradition of Polish jokes in America, where the Poles – like the Irish in England – have long been the butt of patronizing humour.

Will America, in the meantime, have heeded John Paul's pleas for harmony and self-sacrifice? 'It won't make no difference,' said one black woman in Harlem, New York, soon after the papal motorcade had passed over the newly surfaced streets. 'This street will soon be full of potholes again, as sure as they'll be selling drugs again tomorrow right over there where he stood.'

Pope John Paul's American pilgrimage has confirmed him as a figure to whom the world will have to listen. It remains to be seen, alas, whether his words can bear much fruit.

Observer, 7 October 1979

The Italian Earthquake: Inside the Stricken Villages

Udine, N. Italy

The little north Italian towns of Buia, Gemona and Osoppo, with a population of some 10,000 between them, each mourns nearly a hundred of its citizens this weekend. At the epicentre of last Thursday's earthquake, these three farming communities took the brunt of the sudden horror.

Miraculously, some say, the ancient bell tower of Buia's Church of the Madonna still stands, veined with wide cracks, tilting and swaying perilously. The twelfth-century cathedral of Gemona lies in utter ruins, its noble cupola buried beneath its walls. But in Osoppo, soon after yesterday's sunrise, there was a sight far more moving than the fall of any great cathedral. After more than thirty hours of waiting, a defiant old man finally learnt for sure that his only son was dead.

Since Thursday evening, when the main fifty-five second tremor reduced his son's home and half of Osoppo to rubble, the old man had – against all the odds – kept alive some hope. He even hung on to it at first light yesterday, when summoned by soldiers clearing the ruins of the home. But protruding from the rubble they had found an outstretched hand.

As the troops picked away, stone by stone, the old man peered in, weeping, but still refusing to face the truth. Gradually a shape emerged, and the final brutal thrust of a bulldozer revealed his inescapable loss. With a long wail he broke down, and a few of the soldiers, young enough to be his grandchildren, wept with him.

The son's body was one of fifty already recovered from what remains of Osoppo. At least as many more are thought to be still hidden beneath the mountainous debris, which will take perhaps another week to clear. In a circular area north of Udine, covering some forty square miles, as many as 500 people may have died in those fifty-five seconds. Those who survived, the thousands of injured and crippled, shocked and homeless, have fearsome tales to tell.

It was just before nine at the end of a warm, still summer day. Most families in the area were watching television. In the north, some were greeting a new landlord to the local inn; further east, a few were at a restaurant birthday party.

The first shock came at 8.55, a short, sharp tremor which rattled a few pots and pans. The second followed five minutes later, rather stronger, but causing no damage. People began to run on to the streets in alarm.

Then, after two more minutes, came the major shock. It lasted fully fifty-five seconds, destroying whole towns, ravaging country farm houses, tearing roads and toppling bridges.

To one driver, the road suddenly began to move 'like the sea'; his car was thrown into a field, but he escaped. Another man, standing in his town square when the shock came, said: 'At first, it was like being drunk. It was hard to stand up. Then my friend and I were thrown to the floor, and we thought the earth was going to open up beneath us.'

A child was thrown from a third-floor window; a falling beam split above the boy and held off the weight of the rubble. He survived.

Most who describe what they remember of that night use the same phrase: 'It was like the end of the world.' The sight of their towns now, the open homes left as they were abandoned, others turned inside out by the blast, shows above all how horrible death by earthquake must be.

Sides of houses have sheared off, leaving upper-floor kitchens, living-rooms, bedrooms exposed. A torn and scarred double bed hangs over a severed third floor, pointing to where its occupants were thrown to their death. Cars, scarcely visible, are crushed like balls of paper beneath the fallen masonry. Torn and tattered clothes hang, wind-blown, from the piles of rocks.

Those left behind wander the streets in a daze, wrapped in blankets which cocoon their state of shock. They look on almost impassively as neighbours and friends are dragged from the wreckage of their homes.

Further, minor shocks have continued. As many as twenty-nine have been reported since Thursday night. A damaged river bridge, over which photographer Bryan Wharton and I drove on

Friday evening, fell during a slight tremor ten minutes later.

The towns are still dangerous to be in. As the huge search-and-clear operation goes on, with volunteers arriving from all over Europe, many rescuers are risking their lives.

On Friday night, we followed a Swiss military team led by tracker dogs to sniff out bodies, down Osoppo's Via Dominico Fabris, forbidden territory until lit up by army floodlights. Overhead, loose gutters hung menacingly, gradually nearer to falling. Tiles and masonry collapsed continually.

In this street, the roof of No. 9, which until Thursday was the Communist Party headquarters, was dangerously askew. No. 7, the tobacconist's, was the only building still standing on its side of the street. The whole building creaked. On its third floor, we could see a woman's dressing-table open to the winds. Before the front door, the tobacconist's little Fiat had been buried beneath the fallen roof.

Beyond, at the back of Via Leonardo Andervolti, a young farmer picks his way through what was his tiny plot. Those of his few hens that have survived cluck around him, eager for food. His dog mooches after him, sniffing the rocks for food.

The farmer does not notice them. For a long time, he stares disbelievingly at the house in which he lived, some of whose rooms are crudely exposed to the passing gaze. He spies a sock at his feet, tugs at it, and gradually unfolds an entire metal washing line from the debris. Carefully, in the midst of the desolation, he removes each sock, puts them away in a white plastic bag, and wheels them away slowly on the saddle of his bicycle – his only remaining wordly goods.

A cat has a brief skirmish with a rat. As the light grows, a bewildered Alsatian, too shaken to threaten human trespassers on his patch, peers around pathetically from beside his kennel – intact in the stone wilderness, and absurdly labelled Dick. A canary, bright yellow amid the scene of dusty grey, flits past him from an open door. It comes to rest on the old chapel bell, which toppled with its tower last Thursday evening, and lies upside-down amid a maze of broken tombstones. There is no sign of human life.

Sunday Times, 9 May 1976

Invading Spanish Sahara

Agadir, Morocco

At ten o'clock last Thursday morning a triumphal arch was erected above the makeshift barrier which marks the military border between Morocco and the Spanish Sahara. At its crest was a huge portrait of King Hassan, in whose name 100,000 chanting, flag-waving Moroccans, each clutching a copy of the Koran, half an hour later swept across the border towards an abandoned Spanish fort.

They swarmed over it like ants, fighting to be the first to hoist the Moroccan flag. Within seconds it was up, and the mass of humanity, now a mile wide and soon to be several miles deep, surged on into a gathering sandstorm. They had no water, little food and carried their beds on their backs. Behind them another quarter of a million were preparing to march. Beyond the horizon lay unknown Spanish resistance.

Their King had compared the march to the glorious re-entry of Mohammed into Mecca in AD 630. He had once promised to be at their head, but now he sat in Agadir's sumptuous royal palace, in council with his ministers. His brother-in-law, Ahmed Osman, the Prime Minister, was at the border only long enough to see the marchers vanish into the desert.

King Hassan had called Spain's bluff, but he knew no more than did his army of peaceful marchers – one in fifty of his subjects – what lay ahead in the Sahara.

At seven the previous evening the King had tugged his ear nervously and flicked a fly from his nose as he announced on live television that the march would go ahead.

In the desert the King's words were received with rapture. Thousands of open trucks at once began ferrying the first of the 350,000 volunteers along the bumpy ten miles from their encampment at Tarfaya to the frontier. The operation continued all night, and Thursday's dawn revealed a vast crusader-like array of pinnacled tents at the border post.

Army jeeps dragooned the hundred thousand into tidy squares for a noisy prayer meeting. The desert air was filled with an incessant Arabic chant: 'The struggle, the struggle, the Koran is the arm of the struggle.'

Moroccan spotter planes criss-crossed, monitoring the huge operation by radio. A couple of miles to the south, inquisitive Spanish helicopters took periodic looks at the extraordinary scene, always keeping a safe distance. The word was that the Spanish had retreated thirty kilometres, half way to the Saharan capital of El Aaiún.

But senior Moroccan officers knew of a Spanish line of resistance some twenty-five kilometres away. Either the Spanish Foreign Legion or the Algerian-backed guerrilla underground group, Polisario, had built hills of sand in the desert. Behind them lurked Spanish tanks and cannons. Around them lay perhaps as many as 70,000 mines.

All that was tomorrow's or the next day's problem. For the first day the front marchers were to proceed ten kilometres, all of which had been abandoned by the Spanish and quietly checked by Moroccan troops. The rest would follow in waves.

The marchers knew vaguely of the threats ahead, but remained noisily euphoric. Besides, they had their orders from their King: 'If you meet a Spaniard, be he civil or military, greet him and embrace him. Even if the Spanish open fire on you, arm yourselves with your courage and your faith, and march on. But if you are attacked by anyone other than Spaniards, be sure, dear people, that your valiant army will come to your rescue.'

Wind-whipped sand stung the eyes and clogged the throat as the march moved off. Delegations from Jordan, Saudi Arabia, Sudan, Libya, Oman and the United Arab Emirate took up the centre through the arch, with four American students carrying a Stars and Stripes, the largest of many flags.

The huge phalanxes of Moroccans packed them in on each side, themselves an ocean of red flags. Scattered amid them were colourful detachments of women, many of them barefoot. All waved and embraced the harassed international press, who had snatched a few hours' sleep in tents pitched on cobblestones at Tarfaya.

Nothing like it has been seen in the desert, as one ecstatic Arab put it, since the filming of *Lawrence of Arabia*. Even that, however, could scarcely compare with the astonishing sight which unfolded on Thursday morning. Tents, trucks and swarm upon swarm of Arabs stretched back as far as the eye could see. Conditions in the morning heat soon became appalling as sudden sandstorms attacked savagely. But once the marchers were off and covering Spanish territory at a cracking pace – exultantly rubbing the conquered sand in their faces – their euphoria could take everything the desert might throw at them.

For this sea of humanity, the day was the climax to two weeks' patient waiting in the desert. They had been ferried to the border, 250 miles south of Agadir, by the same trucks which now followed them, many commandeered by the Government, others donated by industry on the King's orders. More than a million of Morocco's seventeen million people volunteered for the march when the King first announced it on 16 October. The 350,000 chosen were all seasonal workers, unproductive until the orange harvest. Civil servants, academics, factory workers, anyone contributing to the economy, were excluded, as were students for cosmetic reasons.

At the King's behest, all Moroccans are donating a week's pay to the cost of the march, estimated by the Finance Minister to approach $8 million. 'It is', he commented, 'cheaper than a jet plane.' But for weeks the Moroccan economy has been disrupted to support the march.

Reclaiming 'Our Sahara', as Moroccans talk of it, would win the country another 100,000 square miles of desert territory to which history gives them a deeply emotional tie. It would also, however, win the rich phosphate mines at Bu Craa, giving Morocco a world monopoly in phosphates, making Hassan a phosphate sheik to rival the oil sheiks and enhancing his status in the Arab League. And somewhere in that vast tract of emptiness, Hassan knows, there must be oil.

The King has ruled with an iron fist since he succeeded his storm-tossed father in 1956. He has never allowed elections, twice postponing promised ones. One reason he did not lead the march is that the long drive to the border is immensely arduous. The Prime Minister flew to an airstrip built in forty-eight hours at Tarfaya, but the King has not flown anywhere since dissident pilots tried to shoot down his jet in 1972. Then he grabbed the microphone himself, radioed to the attackers that the King was dead, and landed safely.

He survived another attempted coup the following year, when troops stormed a party at his coastal summer palace and killed ninety-eight guests. The leaders were taken out and shot on the spot. Hassan has left the country only once since then, to visit President Boumedienne in Algiers. He travelled by boat.

The King, his court and his Government stayed in Agadir on Thursday because the country's concentration on the south makes it vulnerable to another coup, despite the support of all political parties for the Sahara march.

To save his 350,000 loyal subjects from a desert massacre, Hassan has to hope Spain will keep its troops withdrawing from the advancing hordes. He has to trust that Prince Juan Carlos will wish to emerge to the world as a liberal monarch by peacefully yielding Spain's last colony in Africa. He believes, say his officials, that Juan Carlos will not wish to found his rule, as Franco did, on blood.

Moroccans regard Algeria as a greater threat than Spain. Already this weekend there are unconfirmed reports of skirmishes on Algeria's narrow border with the Sahara. Boumedienne said little last week, but has recently armed and encouraged the Polisario, and is determined to allow the Saharans a referendum to decide their own future. An enriched Morocco, in Algerian eyes, might prove an uncomfortable neighbour. But how, argue Moroccans, could some 70,000 desert nomads ever constitute a serious independent state? The same number on the march are themselves Saharans, exultantly returning to the desert after a reluctant exile in Morocco.

As the diplomacy continues, and appropriately curt notes arrive from the United Nations to a swift rejection, little is announced to the Moroccan people beyond the progress of the march towards the Spanish.

King Hassan, once the international playboy of the Riviera set, this weekend appears a strong and popular monarch in Morocco. Wednesday's broadcast was the climax of fourteen year's hard work by the forty-five-year-old monarch at shedding his playboy reputation and, in his own words, becoming 'a King to suit the pride of Morocco'. He appeared before the cameras flanked by his son, the twelve-year-old Crown Prince, and his royal cousin Moulay Ali, whom he also despatched to the desert in his place on Thursday morning.

As Hassan sits and hopes in Agadir, perhaps his biggest trump card in the negotiations sits with him – Sheik Hadj Katri Ould Said Al Joumani, leader of the Spanish Saharan tribes, and a member of the Spanish Parliament by Franco's personal appointment. The sheik has sworn his and his people's allegiance to Hassan, which effectively undermines Algeria's talk of self-determination. Both repeatedly quote the ruling earlier this year of the International Court at The Hague: that Morocco had significant historical ties with Spanish Sahara.

From Agadir, the official view is that no one will dare challenge the march, that it may not even need to travel the full fifteen-day distance to El-Aaiún before Hassan can order a massive celebration party in the desert.

But the official view smacks more of official optimism than real confidence.

The next few days will decide, as Juan Carlos wonders whether to flex his new-found muscles. The irony for Hassan is that suddenly this is a confrontation of two nervous monarchs. Had the march gone ahead against Franco's Spain, as was the original plan, Hassan knew his deal with Franco would ensure the marchers a safe passage, and a contented Spanish withdrawal.

Now instead he is up against a new ruler anxious to please his people. Hassan has pushed his gamble to its limits. Morocco's place in the Arab world, perhaps Hassan's throne and certainly the fate of the innocents marching across the promised land, now depends on an unknown monarch whose first test may prove his toughest.

Sunday Times, 9 November 1975

The British Poker Championships

Birmingham

It was supposed to be Las Vegas, but it seemed more like Death Row.

Grim-faced, tense, silent and sweaty, seventy-one men and two women sat in groups of four around an other-worldly sub-terranean cavern. Their movements were few: a nervous twitch of the hand, a despairing shake of the head, the occasional long, hard stare at the ceiling. Intermittent sighs could be heard. Everyone strove to avoid everyone else's eye. Now and then someone would rise resignedly, reluctantly, put on his coat and quietly disappear through the door – never to be seen again.

In a way, it *was* Death Row. All that stood between each of us and extinction was a little pile of plastic (alas, not silicon) chips, which accounted for the twitches of the left hand. In some cases, as the pile grew, the twitch in time became a satisfied, protective riffle. Those of the right hand were reserved for the bits of pasteboard, which came at you in pairs. The more flamboyant (like myself) would actually lift them – bodily – from the table, hug them close to the chest, then sink the chin into the neck for a quick, unobtrusive peep. The more stylish would leave them where they fell, consider them blankly, then take the nearest corner between finger and thumb and raise them for minute inspection. In those bits of pasteboard lay the decrees of the Grim Reaper.

It was in the company of a poet, a painter and a professor, a playwright, a printer and a punter that I took myself off last weekend on the long trek to the fogbound Midlands. Birmingham seemed an unlikely venue for the first-ever British Poker Championships, but we soon forgot where we were. In the numinous atmosphere of that underground cell, padded with deep-pile and plush with green-baize, we might as well have been in Heaven or Hades.

The poet and I arrived to find our friends already there, stone cold sober at a Saturday lunchtime, their eyes ranging critically over the assembling opposition. A few London pros had been spotted: lounge-lizards who hugged the walls and crept into corners to avoid recognition. The amateurs were easily discerned: affable characters who actually came up to introduce themselves, simple souls who offered to buy drinks, smiled, even laughed and wished you luck. They seemed to think the idea was to *enjoy* it all. You could tell them by the way they actually put on the green eyeshades distributed by the management.

First sign of any action was the auction. Players could buy each other, or indeed themselves, with the prospect of a fat percentage if they purchased a winner. Even by auction room standards, the gestures of bidders were scarcely discernible. Prices grew outlandish; it was everyone's first taste of everyone else's money. The pot grew to nearly £2,000. The auctioneer introduced me as 'Babyface', which appellation I was still pondering when someone bought me for £105. I never found out who he was, the joker.

Play began sharp at two. I was up against a sophisticated London American whom I knew – and feared – by repute, and two smart local lads. We each had £200 in chips, the object being to garner all £800. (It's known in the trade as a 'freeze-out'.) It seems so long ago now that the games – all analysed in the minutest detail at the bar that evening – have since merged into one. Suffice it to say that the Yank was the first to go, to my astonished relief, and the local lads put up stern resistance. But, to my even more astonished relief, I won. Suddenly, just as I had to go and telephone a calm report of the proceedings to my newspaper, I was a nervous wreck. I was through to the semi-final – the last twenty – of the British championships.

The paper didn't seem too impressed by my achievement. They refused to hold the front page. They were even reluctant to consider a PS (known in *that* trade as a 'blob par'). All that mattered to them were the subs' queries about the game we were playing, Hold 'Em, a variant of seven-card stud. Well, I'd said it was a high-only seven-card game, two dark ('in the hole') to each player, then a communal flop of five rolled three-one-one, with betting intervals between each stage, bullets high, and antes rising with each quarter-hour to £50 and more at pot limit. Surely that's as clear as a stripped deck?

Having dealt with that – and told the painter, the prof, the playwright, the printer and the punter that their picture was to dominate the front page next morning – I shaped up for the semi-final. This time the oppo was a bit less clear. Three completely expressionless faces of utterly indeterminate age, speaking only to shush the spectators. I could scarcely see my cards for my cigarette smoke. My head was beginning to ache. All my friends had been knocked out in the first round, and were already sitting down across the room to play for real money. On a reasonable straight, I put myself all in.

(Which in translation means: on a mediocre hand, I risked the lot for a quick kill. Which in turn means I cocked it up.)

Out of the main event; into the consolation chase. In the meantime, however, there was Saturday night – an all-night orgy of heavy side-games in Birmingham's unsuspecting Grand Hotel. The Buckingham Suite, which I occupied at a drastically reduced rate, had never seen anything like it. A poet, a playwright, a painter etc. filling the rococo ante-room with smoke, sandwiches, *soft* drinks, playing cards, money, oaths, insults and demonstrations of considerable mental agility until well past 6 am. The hotel had lowered its prices for poker-players, the dumdums. Any of the Buckingham Suite pots could have bought the place.

Down, an hour later, to breakfast, where someone ordered roast beef in the certain knowledge that it was dinner-time. The conversation all around was enlivening. 'So I had these two pairs, aces up. All in; the bugger called, and pulled trips on the last flop. I mean, what can you do? It's not poker, is it?'

Or, alternatively: 'So I had this pair, to his bullets and trays. I got the sucker in, knowing – I mean, I just *knew* – I'd smeg the trip on the roll. That's poker, isn't it? That's the name of the game.' And so on. The Prince of Wales's thirtieth birthday and Edmund Dell's resignation from the Cabinet were not matters of heated debate.

All over the hotel, down the street and through the casino, all you could hear was people saying: 'So I got blah blah blah, bet, call, call, raise, backraise, call, flop. . . ruined. I mean, who'd *believe* such luck?'

On into the consolation, where I was up against a sinister Greek with a monosyllabic pseudonym, and the championship organizer. Sailed through. I mean, I pulled a house to his flush, bluffed the back-call and Bob's your bankrupt uncle. Consolation semi-finalist: no problem getting the first two out, then head-to-head with a macho merchant of my long acquaintance known to his intimates as Bullethead. He was wearing a tweed cap, which attracted the television cameras. Cunningly, I psyched him by refusing to play while the cameras were rolling, demanding a fat fee if they wanted to film me. That got rid of them. I eventually got rid of Bullethead, too, by suckering him in on a well-read king pair against my concealed bullets in the dark. A lot of pride was at stake. Afterwards, he was sorry the best man hadn't won. 'I mean,' he kept saying, 'you really screwed up that hand you beat me on.' Boy, was that guy's ego in some twist.

Mine, of course, was rampant. Phone the wife, friends, people I've never met before, dial random numbers. Through to the consolation final. Guaranteed at worst a place in the Top Ten. About to play my fifth game in thirty hours.

Blew it. Lasted ninety minutes, but by that time on automatic pilot. Felt for my chips and found there weren't any there. Made graceful exit, in something of a dream. Still and all, stumbled into official who said I'd come ninth, handed me £60 and a miniature bottle of champagne. Someone else had worked out that if the money had been real, I'd have cleared £2,000. Too numb to take in enormity of statement.

Reeled across room to poet, prof, painter etc. All agreed we were looking forward to Tuesday night, as usual, and a real game of poker.

Punch, 22 November 1978

The World Series of Poker

Las Vegas, Nevada

Suppose you got heavily into debt at the poker table. Suppose, just suppose, you decided to run out on those debts and join the French Foreign Legion. And suppose – well, it would be *inevitable* – you got lost on an exercise in the desert, crawled for days without water, and came up against a mirage, a classic MGM mirage. You'd be looking at Las Vegas.

Las Vegas has to be a mirage. It's the kind of place that exists only when you're looking at it, that disappears, surely, the minute you turn your back. That one main drag slapped down in the Nevada Desert, approachable by car only through Death Valley, towered over by ornate, fantastical fun palaces bizarre enough to make Hieronymus Bosch blink, to make Coleridge wake up and find himself in Xanadu.

This is The Strip, where man's wildest, most splendidly vulgar architectural fantasies have come to life to the clatter of fruit machines. On one side, Caesar's Palace, a surreal extravaganza of Greco-Roman confusion, where mobile walkways sweep you through the air to a wonderworld of giant circular waterbeds, where you can get lost in the pile of the carpets, where the dry martinis are mixed and served by the Muses. On the other side, the Aladdin, whose bulbous Oriental towers conceal a magic realm in which you can rub your lamp and see Raquel Welch dance and sing.

But there is another Las Vegas, known simply as Downtown. This is where the serious people go – and by serious people, in Las Vegas, you mean serious gamblers. On The Strip, you walk through a maze of crap games, blackjack tables and roulette wheels to reach your hotel reception desk: Downtown such frivolity is frowned on, and the gambling salons are properly set apart from the mere mechanics of eating and sleeping.

Check in at the Golden Nugget, and you'll soon forget about Raquel Welch. Your bed is a four-poster, a decent concession to the bankrolls presumed to be about your person, but you aren't going to spend much time in it. On your bedroom wall are a few pictures of the old Wild West, notably a portrait of Wild Bill Hickok being shot in the back of the head at the poker table. The detail is scrupulously authentic. In his hand Bill holds two pairs, aces and eights – from that day to this known as 'dead man's hand'. Nobody ever looked at Bill's fifth card, and the artist quite properly refrains from speculation as to its identity.

We are not spending long admiring the scenery, however, as we're in town for poker's main annual event, the Professional World Series, played right across the road from the Nugget in Binion's Horseshoe Casino. Over the next four days we're going to cross that road three or four times a day, at each of which moments we will suddenly remember that there is a world outside, that the sun shines here at 110 degrees, and that at a certain point in events it seems to disappear, to be replaced by a balmy darkness which we understand is known as night-time. Can't understand why it bothers, really: don't make no difference to what goes on inside.

Binion's is a dark and bustling place in which you can actually smell the money. You quickly get used to the noise: a constant clack of chips, whether they're being scooped in by the house croupiers, or riffled incessantly by nervous gamblers. You see row upon row of vast, hungry computerized fruit machines; the craps tables, where the action is constant and noisy; and the roulette and blackjack tables, where people part with their money more quietly, and with a certain dignified resignation.

The poker is being played in a small room at the back. To help you find it through the cigar smoke there is an apt landmark: $1 million in real cash displayed in a giant, see-through plastic horseshoe. If you take too close an interest in the sturdiness of the plastic, large men materialize from behind pillars to divert your attention.

No great problem for a Tuesday night poker player from England, entering a room full of his lifetime's heroes. The thing about professional poker players is that they never retire: they grow old, certainly, as if they were merely mortal, but they don't really seem to die as much as other people. For fellow cricket enthusiasts, for instance, it is like entering a room where Jack Hobbs is mixing a whisky sour for Gary Sobers; where W.G. Grace is chewing a Kentucky chicken bone with Geoffrey Boycott; where Don Bradman is engaged in a fierce disagreement about handle lengths with Hammond and Hutton; and where nobody is talking to Tony Greig.

There is Doyle 'Texas Dolly' Brunson, the twenty-stone intellectual giant and specialist theoretician of the poker world, the man who has won several million dollars playing the game (and lost maybe a few thousand of them). There is Amarillo 'Slim' Preston, as lean as Cassius but not as hungry, the man who occasionally arrives at the table on horseback and is assumed to sleep in his stetson. There is Walter Clyde 'Pug' Pearson, his sunken nose sniffing his opponent's every move, ever talkative, a bit of a braggart, his cigar seemingly an extension of his epiglottis. There is the grand old man, the W.G. Grace of poker, Johnny Moss, known simply (and in hushed tones) as 'The Man': now seventy-one, he defies the existence of the word dotage, his face remaining impassive even when convulsed with laughter. Former world champions all.

The Ian Botham of the scene is Bobby 'The Owl' Baldwin, last year's world champion at just twenty-seven, the leading representative of a rising young generation of calculating, methodical university graduates who are threatening to whip the deep-pile from beneath the feet of the oldsters. Johnny Moss is not enthusiastic: 'Me,' he says, 'ah'm a gamblin' man' (the effect on your correspondent being much as if Enrico Caruso had said 'Me, I kinda sing sawngs'). 'I don't hold with this computer approach. These guys ain't gamblers, they're mathematicians.'

Not but what Mr Moss has a healthy respect for the mathematics of poker, his own gut version of mental arithmetic having made him a very, very rich man.

Before they do battle for the 1979 title, there is a momentous ceremony to perform. CBS television is here to network it, and the immortal Minnesota Fats is here to compère it (or 'emcee' it, as they say hereabouts).

Benny Binion, seventy-six-year-old founder and proprietor of Binion's Horseshoe Casino, has decided to inaugurate a Poker Hall of Fame. Seven immortals are to be admitted this first year, their portraits to be hung in the poker room with as much ceremony as those of presidents in the White House. Only one is still playing: the aforementioned Mr Moss, acknowledged by his rivals to be 'The Man' for the rest of his allotted span. The others are the aforementioned Mr Hickok (1837-76); Edmond Hoyle

(1672-1769), the 'Wisden' of all card games: and four eternally remembered practitioners of the art; Felton 'Corky' McCorquodale (1904-68), 'Sid' Wyman (1910-78), J.H. 'Red' Winn (1896-) and Nicholas 'Nick the Greek' Dandolas (1883-1966). Brief homage is paid, then the action begins.

Fifty-four players are seated at seven tables, each with $10,000 in front of him (or, in two cases, her). This is their 'buy-in'. The game is a 'freeze-out', which being interpreted means they play until one of them has won all $540,000. As soon as a player loses his Ten Grand – known around here as 'Ten Big Gs' – he retires, gracefully or otherwise.

The game is Hold 'Em, a variant of seven-card stud. It is a game in which vast amounts of money are wagered before anybody knows very much at all: in other words, while each player has two cards revealed to himself alone, before anyone has a clue what the other five communal cards ('the flop') are going to be. It is an ascetic, deep-dyed American variant of poker, though Britons aspiring to Las Vegan stature played it in the first British national poker championships, staged last October in Birmingham.

For the next three days and nights, these fifty-four people retire from any semblance of contact with the outside world, oblivious to the fact that the sun circles the earth, that people are drawing guns in Las Vegas petrol queues, that Bert Lance is being indicted for fraud, that Raquel Welch is just down the road.

Over three days and nights they grind each other down. They break each other. There are many different ways of doing it. Amarillo Slim, one of the first former champs to fall, finds the action a trifle slow: he calls for a *Reader's Digest*. Nobody in Las Vegas has heard of so cerebral a publication, so he contents himself with reading *Gambling Times* while his opponents agonize.

Ken Smith, a twenty-five-stone giant dressed as an undertaker, surmounted by the top hat in which Lincoln was shot, cries, 'What a player!' each time he scoops a pot. The select all-time greats, Brunson, Pearson, Moss and others, discuss hands between tables, making light of the opposition. 'That guy's in outer space,' they cry as an antagonist flukes a big win. But they fall, they all fall. Their time has come and gone.

Moss is the only veteran pro to remain at the final table. Another is Crandall Addington, of whom even the multi-million-dollar-winners will tell you: 'Crandall, he's kinda loaded.' Crandall is a Texas wildcat oilman, which means he's an independent owner of oil wells. He's extremely good-looking and a very snappy dresser. He plays for three days and nights, coming back from the dead several times, without loosening his Dior necktie.

Crandall is followed by poker groupies. He is also, as is true of several of these finalists, shadowed by a bodyguard. He wears, as is true of all of them, exotic jewellery. Diamond rings flash as chips are pushed forward. For no reason other than to admire their worldly goods, players constantly check the time on gold-encrusted watches with computerized digital dials, capable no doubt of surviving all that Jacques Cousteau might choose to throw at them. Time is utterly irrelevant to the proceedings.

By night three, and into the wee small hours of day four, just two players are left – with $540,000 between them. All the former champs have gone, but they crowd the ringside among hushed spectators. In the blue corner Bobby Hoff, the local favourite, a Las Vegas professional who knows the title is his for the waiting. Up against him is Hal Fowler, a not-so-tall dark stranger who just strolled into town to push his luck. Everyone is waiting for Fowler to crack.

The side-betting is huge, all of it against Fowler. 'Who *is* dis guy?' ask the pros, needled that an amateur is getting all this TV time. 'The money ain't nothing,' says last year's champion, Bobby Baldwin. 'I'd pay quarter of a million right now to get back in there.'

Intensive inquiries reveal that Fowler is a public relations man from Los Angeles. 'A *whaaat*?' howls Pug Pearson when I tell him the bad news. He passes it on to Brunson, Moss and others, who exchange gloomy glances.

'Go, Bobby,' they cry, closing ranks against the amateur. But Bobby's looking sweaty. The amateur just bluffed him out of a quarter-million dollar pot, then threw his worthless cards face up across the table to add salt to the wound. They've been head-to-head for six hours.

The 160th hand between them is decisive. After the deal Hoff bets $30,000 and Fowler calls. The first three communal cards are the five of hearts, three of clubs and jack of spades. Hoff bets $40,000 and Fowler calls. The four of spades comes up. Hoff goes all in: he pushes his remaining $43,000 to centre table. Fowler calls. The fifth card is the ten of diamonds. Hoff shows his cards: a pair of aces. After a delicious pause, Fowler shows his: the seven of spades and the six of diamonds. He has a straight. He is the new world champion.

His face remains, to the last, immobile. He has beaten the pros at their own game. They're in a state of shock, I tell him. 'They've got a right to be,' he says. 'They let me whup 'em.'

The world series has never before been won by an amateur. The amateur, as it happens, is also somewhat disdainful. 'So I could turn pro tonight,' he says. 'But who needs it? It's chicken today, nuttin' tomorrow.'

The pros have lost a little of their swagger. On The Strip Raquel Welch still attempts to sing, but Downtown will never be quite the same again. A holidaymaker has just won $280,000 on a fruit machine. Can the amateurs be taking over? The pros are prepared to forgive and forget – they'll come back and spank the young puppy next year – until Fowler delivers the *coup de grace*. 'Is there an Internal Revenue man round here? I'd better tell him about this half million.'

The pros scatter.

Observer magazine, 18 November 1979

Bobo, Bigfoot and the
Future of the West

Washington

Could John Connally beat Ted Kennedy? That was the question besieging fashionable dinner tables when I pitched camp in Washington in April 1979. I thought I had arrived in time to cover the 1980 presidential election. But it had clearly – some months, if not years, before – started without me.

Britain was just going to the polls, and friends were moaning down the transatlantic phone about the four long weeks of the campaign. Over here, eighteen months before election day, more than a dozen candidates were already at one another's throats.

Americans would assure me how keenly they deplored the length of the modern American campaign. But it was an open-and-shut case of protesting too much. The more they complained of growing electorally punch-drunk, of domestic and foreign policy being hamstrung for a year and more, the clearer it became that they loved every minute of it.

The hoop-la, the balloons, the lapel buttons – above all, the Machiavellian scheming – now provide the adrenalin of American political life. Given the influence of ethnic lobbies and special interest groups, all issues are weighed and pursued through a quadrennial cycle of electoral self-interest. It is the era of the permanent campaign.

'You've got here just in time,' I was told by one of those same Machiavels, the political strategists, Washington's new elite. 'The last two years have been real dull.' The half-way mark of a president's first term, it seems, is now institutionalized as the time to start looking for a new one.

This, of course, has not gone unremarked by the present incumbent, the modern master of electoral politics. 'It didn't start without you,' I was told by one of the President's men. 'It never stopped.' Was I to infer, I asked in shocked tones, that the prime objective of the President's first term was to secure a second one?

His answer was to point out of the window. There, across the road, just a block from the White House, a humdrum, unmarked office building concealed the director and staff of the discreetly named Carter-Mondale Presidential Committee. 1976 posters filled the walls, as it would be another six months before the President publicly declared it his intention to seek re-election. The chain of 1976 campaign headquarters around the country, however, had never really closed down.

In California, so-called 'exploratory' committees were nursing the machinery set in place last time round by Ronald Reagan and Governor Jerry Brown. Bronzed, wide-eyed West Coast amazons manned a bank of Brown telephones in a poky office near Los Angeles airport as their master came and went, talking of 'Spaceship Earth'. Despite their hero's daily disavowals, 'Draft Kennedy' movements were already active in twenty-seven states. Elsewhere, there were committees promoting people who didn't even know if they wanted to run.

A clutch of out-of-work millionaires – Bush, Reagan, Connally – had between them sewn up the Republican Party's grass roots. Like Jimmy Carter after 1972, when he left the governorship of Georgia, they had enjoyed time and money enough to spend a few years criss-crossing the country, pumping hands, kissing babies, making after-dinner speeches, leaving in place a growing network of devotees to promote their presidential aspirations.

Any mere senator with thoughts of higher office had already left it too late, as the estimable Howard Baker was to discover. No one has been elected directly from the Senate to the White House since John F. Kennedy in 1960. That year there were six primaries before the nominating conventions; this year, there were thirty-six.

The present system is custom-built for unseated congressmen and retired governors. A full-time job on Capitol Hill, otherwise known as experience in federal government, was once a qualification for the presidency. Now it is a handicap. Given the length and exigencies of the campaign trail, the idle rich have a head start.

A string of political upheavals, forcing changes in the electoral system, has made this the age of a new breed of American politician: men driven more by the quest for power than by its exercise, more adept at the management of a campaign than of the government machinery which is its reward. Few Americans of truly presidential timbre are any longer prepared, in the prime of their lives, to enter the jostling, demeaning marathon which now comprises the obstacle course to the White House.

American elections have always been the apotheosis of personality politics. As the campaign began, candidates were assessed in terms of their style, their charm, their television presence, anything but the odd principle or belief they might claim to represent. One by one they came to Washington, to the bar of the National Press Club, to talk waftily about visions and dreams.

They were fallow days, those first few months of my sojourn. President Jimmy Carter's hopes of re-election had already been written off. A few impartial observers whose opinion I respected, notably James Reston of the *New York Times* and Peter Jay, then still the British Ambassador, kept making an eloquent case for Carter's integrity. I should watch, they told me, as he pressed home his battles against imported oil and for the SALT treaty, regardless of electoral advantage.

But establishment Washington, then as now, hated the man. He had made it to town as an outsider, and he had remained one, rarely venturing outside the White House, spurning the invitations of society hostesses. More than two years after his inauguration, peanut jokes were still very much in vogue.

Carter was deemed to lack the one quality Americans look for in their chief executive: leadership. With inflation unbridled, and a recession on the horizon, the nation was in depressed mood. The President's own pollster, Patrick Caddell, found ill omens in the entrails. For the first time in American history, people did not believe that their children would enjoy a better life than they had.

Also unprecedently, a third of Americans were pessimistic about their own future. A majority of the nation thought it would make no difference whom they elected in 1980. A majority felt that government put corporate and special interests before those of the people. The American dream was beginning to fray at the edges.

As I tagged along on the President's Mississippi riverboat

cruise that summer, through the heartland of small-town Middle America, I talked with people the pollsters never get anywhere near. To my surprise, they echoed big-city disenchantment. 'We've turned out', they said on the riverbank, waiting in their Sunday-best, 'for the President of the United States. It's the first time a president has been through our town. We're not waiting here for Jimmy Carter. What's he done for us?' Despite Jimmy Carter, the man who was going to hand government back to the people, Americans were more disillusioned, more cynical than they were at the height of Watergate.

My first glimpses of the President were disappointing. Like most journalists arriving in Washington, I was prepared to be seduced by the trappings of power, to chronicle the sleepless nights of the leader of the free world, to bask in the aura of the man combining the offices of head of state and chief executive of a contemporary super-power. Fortunately, perhaps, Carter did not provide the chance.

'The only President', declared one old Washington hand, 'who has visibly shrunk in office.' Carter did not display the vision of recent giants of the presidency – Roosevelt, Kennedy, Johnson – and, in his way, Nixon. There were merely petulant, shifty responses to day-to-day problems, the eye for fine details of the engineer. (He once admitted he had spent some time studying parking allocations at the Bureau of Indian Affairs.) The first time I saw him in action, the President of the United States was denying that he maintained personal control of the schedule for the White House tennis courts.

The furnishings of the Oval Office seemed to reflect Carter's character: austere, workmanlike, colourless, haughty. The only symbol of any political philosophy was Harry Truman's famous slogan, which Carter had dusted down and returned to the presidential desk: 'The buck stops here.' Bert Lance, Andrew Young, Cyrus Vance and Billy Carter – along with many others, including half the Cabinet – were soon to have reason to question that.

Visiting Kennedy's Senate office at that time was far more exciting than wandering around the White House. To reach the Senator you passed imposing portraits of him arm-in-arm with his brothers, the President and the President-that-might-have-been; you negotiated your way through the largest staff on

Capitol Hill, handling the demands of a constituency much larger than Massachusetts; and you finally reached the office of a senator of seventeen years' standing, chairman of the power-ful Judiciary Committee, the scourge of big business and the champion of the underprivileged.

Kennedy, at forty-seven, was older than either of his brothers had lived to be. As far as Washington was concerned – and Washington, where the action is, knows best – the White House was his for the asking. But Kennedy, grinning behind his huge cigar, would insist that he 'expected' President Carter to be renominated, and 'expected' to campaign for him in the fall. He was running two-to-one ahead of him in the polls, but he was biding his time.

So, across the nation, was Ronald Reagan. 'The Governor', as his devoted staff still call him, was to be found digging ditches and building fences at his ritzy ranch north of Los Angeles. He too was ahead in the polls – but, at sixty-nine, he was being portrayed as too old for the presidency, too conservative to win a general election, too simplistic to stand up to the scrutiny of the campaign. It was anyway, surely, some passing American fantasy that cast a Hollywood cowboy in the role of president.

Back in the White House, there were surprisingly confident smiles. The permanent campaign was on target. On 17 January 1979, almost two years before election day, the President had received a long, confidential memo from his Chief of Staff, Hamilton Jordan, outlining a strategy for renomination and re-election. Leaked only this summer, when the nomination was locked up, it proved in devastating fashion that the handling of US policy for the previous eighteen months had been geared primarily to a second Carter term.

It says something about the mentality of those around the President that they chose, in a spirit of self-congratulation after bringing their boss back from the dead, to make such a damning document public. American politicians tend to talk with astonishing candour about tactics, manipulations of popular perceptions, 'image factors' and the like; but the Jordan memo amounted to a manual expertly showing Carter how to fool all the people all of the time – for example, by fixing the dates of primaries to his own advantage.

The fundamental premise of Jordan's entire strategy was that

Kennedy would be harder to beat to the nomination than any Republican in the subsequent general election. 'The absolute worst thing we can do', wrote Jordan, 'is to behave in a way that suggests we fear a Kennedy candidacy. We should proceed publicly on the same course we have been on recently, that of praising him, minimizing differences, etc.'

So Carter ignored Kennedy until 11 June last year, when he told a White House dinner guest: 'If Kennedy runs, I'll whip his ass.' One Democratic congressman present, startled at such Nixonian language from a born-again Baptist, asked the President to repeat himself. He did so, in so many words, and later got his staff to call the congressman, urging him to repeat the remark to the press.

The press duly obliged, though it didn't always have it so easy. Cocooned with one candidate for the duration, American journalists envied the freedom of their foreign brethren to bob from one campaign to another. Stuck with the same man on bus and plane for months on end, they were all going quietly mad.

Each campaign had its own teddy-bear mascot, to ensure safe take-offs and landings. The Kennedy bear was Bigfoot, sworn rival of Ronald Reagan's Bobo. A fifth columnist aboard Reagan's plane once hid Bobo, grounding the campaign until the candidate himself found him in the lavatory.

In this adventure playground of the air, the campaign could and did get significantly misreported. Travelling with the same candidate and colleagues day after day, week after week, journalists tended to compare notes, file identical stories to their respective papers – and, knowing they'd be seeing the great man again in the morning, pull their punches. A few developed delusions of grandeur, envisaging White House assignments at the end of the trail; they would write their man up, qualify his errors, urge him on to victory.

As a healthy antidote, you could gauge a candidate's success by the size of his aeroplane. Kennedy's chartered Boeing 727, his status symbol in the early weeks, was soon dispensed with. His state-room up front, where lobsters and champagne had been the order of the day, was swapped for economy seats on scheduled commercial aircraft. Once you're marked as a loser, campaign funds dry up fast.

With the President skulking in the Rose Garden, Air Force

One remained grounded at Andrews Air Force Base, to the annoyance of its crew. 'It's covered with cobwebs,' they told me as we climbed aboard its little sister, Executive One, to accompany the First Lady to Pittsburgh. We were served a presidental breakfast, then charged $4 a head, cash on the nail.

For a British journalist, with no votes to deliver, the trail could prove uncomfortable. One week in January the Bush campaign, to my astonishment, refused *Time* magazine's demand that it should take over my seat on his tiny aircraft. Flattering, but foolish. The following week, the Reagan camp swiftly acceded to the self-same request, leaving me without transport, with no place to rest my weary head, in snowbound, sub-zero Vermont. Now there's a winner for you.

Travelling with Reagan did have its compensations. The Governor rarely showed his head before 11 am, leaving plenty of time for a lie-in and a leisurely breakfast before easing into the day. With Bush, by contrast, it was up betimes for a dawn jog, followed by a furious spate of breakfast meetings. On the aircraft – it was now a 727, with room for all – Mrs Reagan would distribute chocolates to the weary scribes. Rejuvenated by his success, the candidate would be disarmingly witty: 'If they show any of my movies on TV during the campaign, I'll demand equal time.'

A month before, when Bush was ahead, Reagan had had the shuffling gait and drop-jawed aspect of an old man. In Alabama, I once had to ask him a question four times before he heard it. Was the Governor going deaf? He'd had trouble with that ear, he explained, since his Hollywood days, when someone had let loose a Colt 45 right next to it. At that stage he would do anything, anything. Ask him if he dyed his hair, and his head would sink between his knees, with an invitation to run your fingers through it, looking for clues in the roots. Ask him if he'd had a facelift, and down it went again. 'Look behind the ears for those tell-tale scars.'

Reagan used to do TV adverts for a laxative. Now he's a walking advert for the physical benefits of political success.

A week after arriving in Washington, I had asked James Reston about John Connally's prospects for the Republican nomination. Well, he was a turncoat, he bore the taint of Nixon, there was the little matter of the milk fund scandal. 'But that man is so dynamic that when he walks into a room, the lights flicker.' And Reagan? 'Dwight Eisenhower, the oldest president in American history, left office at seventy. Reagan would be seventy a month after his inauguration.'

No disrespect to Mr Reston, but just about everybody else got it just about as wrong. The polls, which come at the American people in tidal waves, showed Kennedy ahead of Carter, Connally remorselessly catching Reagan. So what happened? How did American voters inflict on themselves the two candidates they appeared, a year ago, least to want?

Carter and Reagan both owe their nominations, Carter almost wholly, to skilful manipulation of a complex system which is the legacy of the late 1960s and Watergate. Post-Watergate reforms were designed to take clout from the hands of party bosses, operating in the notorious 'smoke-filled rooms', and transfer it to the people. They have transferred it rather into the hands of the non-smoking, jogging political strategists and public relations wallahs, who shrewdly manipulate public perceptions of the candidates.

Reforms of electoral finance laws were intended, by restricting individual contributions to $1,000 a head, to do away with big corporation politicking, and those million-dollar backers out to buy themselves cosy ambassadorships. The limits on campaign spending have, by contrast, enhanced the electoral influence of television and the media advisers. They are a candidate's best investment.

John Anderson, that most confessional of candidates, admitted he would cancel three meetings and drive 300 miles for the chance of a spot on a local TV show. (He may be an extreme example. After the first Republican debate in New Hampshire, I recall seeing the other candidates climb into their limousines as Anderson tried in vain to hail a taxi.)

But the American electorate is peculiarly susceptible to televised politicking, particularly the slick 'negative' advertising which goes surreptitiously for the opponent's jugular. Carter's privately commissioned soundings show that Kennedy's late resurgence was contained, in April and May, by a series of ads which ran along similar lines to this one:

A man brings two things to a presidential ballot. He brings his record and he brings himself. In the voting booth, the voter must weigh both character and record before deciding. Often it's not easy. And this voter winds up asking [unfortunate picture of Kennedy]: 'Is this the person I really want in the White House for the next four years?' [Cut to magisterial portrait of Carter, gazing, with visionary zeal, at some distant presidential horizon.]

Reagan is now in for the same treatment. This autumn's campaign will be conducted almost entirely on television. Apart from the pivotal debates and the invaluable 'free advertising' on the network news, each side will be devoting more than half its budget to national and local TV advertising.

Television's major role has already been seen in its exhaustive coverage of the two party conventions, four consecutive all-evening TV shows in which a united party is out to bewail its opponents' shortcomings. Each of the three major networks spent more covering each of this year's conventions than did MGM making *Gone With The Wind*.

Television exposure is indeed now the major reason for holding party conventions at all. Their function used to be the choosing of a candidate. This has now been pre-empted by the scale of the primary campaign, where so many delegates are mandated that the conventions are left merely to rubber-stamp a long predetermined choice.

Thanks also to television, and its love of a good political scrap, the last thing Carter will campaign on this autumn is his own record as president. As his all-powerful media adviser, Gerald Rafshoon, told him in another White House memo: 'The only person who can beat Jimmy Carter is Jimmy Carter.' In other words: don't let the conversation get around to you, or you're done for.

Carter's skill at implementing such instructions is seen at its most chilling, its most cynical, in his use of the American hostages in Tehran. By making them the overwhelming issue of the early primaries, he successfully cast his opponents as rude intruders into the President's busy time. Skilful White House news management led to a moratorium on criticism of the President – a moratorium, believe it or not, which political candidates felt obliged to observe about one of their own number.

The hostages were a national obsession, symbolized by the national Christmas tree still standing behind the White House. As the months went by, however, and their plight began to rebound on him, the President mentioned them less. They no longer dominated the TV news. They were, if not forgotten, swept under the carpet. At the Republican convention in Detroit, each evening began with a moment of silence in support of the hostages Carter had failed to free; at the Democratic convention in New York, they went unmentioned.

Given one more week before polling day, runs a received political wisdom, Gerry Ford would probably have beaten Jimmy Carter in 1976. It was that close, and the tide was turning. One more week – after a campaign of more than a year? There is the same feeling in 1980. Much has happened since those Kennedy-Connally days of early last year. The length and complexity of the primary campaign, its susceptibility to chance events, the subliminal skills of the candidates' media men – all conspired this year to benefit Ladbroke's more than the political system of the world's most powerful democracy.

Even at this late stage, a gaffe in a presidential debate, a stirring speech by John Anderson, the redeployment of a Soviet combat brigade, a chance whim of the Ayatollah – any such single incident could still sway the American people's long-draw-out decision.

In any case many of them, so many, don't care. It will be a surprise, on 4 November, if Americans improve on their barely 50 per cent turnover of 1976. Washington may thrive on it, but the rest of the nation is weary. As I ended this summer's vacation, to return for the start of the campaign, one New Englander offered this not uncharacteristic endorsement of the incumbent: 'If it's a choice between two evils, maybe it's better the devil you know.'

After all those months of manoeuvring, of realigning government policy, after all those bruised egos, those insults and warcries, after all the fancy phrases and promised dreams, after the expense of some $250 million of public and private money, that, for John Doe, is all it comes down to.

Observer, 14 September 1980

The Shooting of President Reagan

Washington

Withdrawn, a loner . . . unable to work steadily in the last year
or so before the assassination . . . white, male . . . chooses a
handgun as his weapon . . . selects a moment when the
President is appearing among crowds.

The description is that made in 1968, by President Johnson's
violence commission, of the likely profile of 'the next assassin to
strike at a president'. It is a chilling sneak preview of John W.
Hinckley Jr, the man accused of attempting to kill President
Reagan for love of a teenage film star.

In one haunting sentence, it distills the feeling here all week
that there was something wholly predictable, almost inevitable
about this 'latest' (for so it is billed in the newspapers) attempt
on a president's life. A common remark from bystanders,
ineluctably drawn to the scene, was: 'I thought it would happen,
but not this soon.' Even the President's brother, Neil Reagan,
said: 'I expected something like this.'

I was lunching a few blocks away. A waiter, knowing my
companion and I were both journalists, passed by with apologies for interrupting our conversation: 'Sorry, but I thought you
might like to know that the President has been shot.' We left at
once; but nobody else did. People got on with their lunch – there
was even some laughter – as the news passed around the room.

Later in the day, as the ritualistic messages poured in from
foreign leaders, the words 'shocked' and 'stunned' seemed
mechanical and inappropriate. Nobody here was feeling that
way. Depressed, yes, disgusted, sick at heart, but not surprised.
There was none of the dazed horror, the disbelief, which greeted
the news from Dallas in November 1963. Just a deep world-
weariness, a mood of baffled introspection.

The executive vice-president of Handgun Control Inc.,
Charles J. Orasin Jr, was out of town when he heard the news.

71

He immediately called his office – and was astonished to get straight through. When John Lennon was shot dead in New York last December, the switchboard had been overloaded for hours.

'What is it?' Orasin wondered aloud. 'Are people just exhausted by all this violence? Are they so inured to violence in their neighbourhoods that they expect it? Are they so used to seeing national leaders fall that they don't react anymore?

'What's going to get them angry enough to pick up the phone, call their congressman and demand they pass a gun control law now and stop this madness?'

Over at the Citizens' Committee for the Right to Keep and Bear Arms, its chief lobbyist, John M. Snyder, gave the appropriately ironic reply: 'Reagan is the best friend we've had in the White House for generations.' He went on: 'What has happened to him proves we've been right all along' – by which Snyder means to say that the 'answer' lies in exploring the motives for crime and imposing steeper penalties, rather than in tighter restrictions on handguns.

But even a new round of gun control debate seemed too banal a response. Senator Edward Kennedy, who offered to modify his demands 'to get some legislation through', was immediately given secret service protection. Written and telephoned threats against Reagan's life tripled in twenty-four hours. Suddenly, it was open season for maniacs. As Kennedy's brother John once said while president: 'No amount of protection is enough. All a man needs is a willingness to trade his life for mine.'

There are plenty of such people about, as America now knows all too well. Of the last nine presidents, six have been fired upon – only one, Harry Truman, by assailants with an identifiable political motive. The solitary, obsessive gunman, wandering from cheap motels with his weapon in his pocket and malice in his heart, has become an American stereotype.

It came as no surprise when Hinckley's friends began to recall his reading *Mein Kampf*, when he was discovered to have a 'history of mental illness', when letters turned up betraying his own dire intents. It all fitted the pattern. There is now even a phrase used by secret service psychologists: 'The Bremer Type', named after the man who shadowed and finally gunned down George Wallace in 1972. It was used publicly for the first time in

Nashville, a film about a 'Bremer Type' who shadowed and tried to gun down a politician.

Nashville – again, as always, these chilling coincidences – was the town in which Hinckley was arrested last October for trying to board an aeroplane with three handguns in his possession. When asked why the arrest was reported only to the FBI, not to the secret service, the airport police said last week it had 'not occurred' to them to link the incident with the presence in Nashville that day of the then President Jimmy Carter.

It was another movie, *Taxi Driver*, which appears to have given Hinckley his idea. Robert De Niro, withdrawn loner, etc., attempts to kill public figures to impress a teenage hooker, his love for whom is unrequited. The hooker is played by Jodie Foster, to whom John Hinckley wrote at approximately 1 pm last Monday: 'By sacrificing my freedom, and possibly my life, I hope to change your mind about me. This letter is being written an hour before I leave for the Hilton Hotel.'

Ninety minutes later, after Hinckley had performed what he himself billed as his 'historical deed', Reagan was much nearer death than was initially acknowledged. Jerry Parr, the secret service man who bundled the President into his car, at first ordered the driver to head for the White House. He then saw a trickle of blood coming from the President's mouth and ordered a diversion to George Washington Hospital.

It was the nearest. Had Parr decided to make for Walter Reed Hospital, where presidents are traditionally treated, Reagan might not have survived. An eyewitness leaving the emergency entrance as the President 'walked in' said: 'He was gasping for air. He looked like he was in shock . . . then his eyes rolled upward, his head went back, his knees buckled and he started to collapse.'

Once a tube was inserted between Reagan's chest wall and collapsed left lung, two quarts of his blood – between a third and a half of his total blood volume – flowed out at what a doctor present described as 'a rather brisk rate'. His blood pressure was low enough to signify shock, a condition which could prevent a man of seventy from recovering.

Reagan has since, as Ed Meese joked on Wednesday, made 'great progress for a fifty-year-old'. The President's now famous wisecracks – to the surgeons: 'Are you guys Republicans?', to a nurse: 'Does Nancy know about you and me?' – seemed deliberately designed to bolster national morale. There was much reminiscence about Theodore Roosevelt in 1912; shot while making a speech, he insisted on finishing it before receiving medical attention.

Meanwhile, back at the White House, the Secretary of State, Alexander Haig, had taken it upon himself to reassure the nation and the world. Those with him in the 'situation room' two hours after the shootings, when he decided to take to national television, said his intent was 'to assure the allies that everything was under control'. That was not the impression Haig gave the nation.

Not only did he promote himself in the 'chain of succession' – an unpardonable error from so high an official, especially after last week's controversy over 'crisis management' – but he sweated profusely, his voice choked with emotion, and his hands shook as they gripped the lectern. He had reacted the same way, said a friend, after the attempt on his own life in Belgium in 1979. It was not the demeanour looked for in a man declaring that it was his finger temporarily on the button.

The button, in fact, was elsewhere. Television viewers may have seen the famous 'man with the black bag' – the military officer assigned to stay within six feet of the President at all times, carrying the coded devices needed to order a nuclear attack or retaliation – sprinting desperately after the fleeing motorcade. He made it; and he stood doggedly in the operating theatre throughout the two hours that the President underwent surgery.

When Haig returned to the White House nerve-centre, there was a brief 'tiff' with the Defence Secretary, Caspar Weinberger, who knew that *he* should have been in charge. But colleagues later paid tribute to Haig's calmness under pressure – and the entire proceedings were tape-recorded for posterity to judge. The consensus afterwards, with the Russians hovering on the Polish border, was that an incapacitated president made them less – not more – likely to invade. 'They won't do anything rash', said one of those in the situation room,'when they don't know who'll be responding.'

Haig did himself damage by his unwarranted usurpation of power, while Vice-President Bush was en route back to Washington from Texas. Bush and others were careful, as the week wore on, to be seen rehabilitating the Secretary of State; this was not the time for the Cabinet to disintegrate. But Reagan, even from the intensive care unit, was adamant that Haig should go ahead as planned with his visit to the Middle East – despite the Secretary's evident reluctance to leave town just now.

When news of the shootings had first reached the White House, an old Nixon hand named Herb Klein happened to be hanging around the Press Office. Klein immediately recalled the days Nixon dubbed one of his 'Six Crises' – when, as vice-president, he had to take over temporary command in 1955 after President Eisenhower's heart attack. It was vital, Nixon noted at the time, 'to appear neither brash nor timid'.

Klein remembered Nixon telling him that even a casual facial expression in a photograph could be disastrously misinterpreted in such circumstances. 'My problem', said Nixon, 'was to provide leadership without appearing to lead . . . . It would have been dangerous to make any move that might be interpreted as an attempt to usurp the powers of the presidency.'

At Klein's dictation, White House speech-writer Tony Dolan immediately wrote a memo to Ed Meese, the President's counsellor. It began: 'During the Eisenhower Administration, the Administration kept to the theme of business as usual.' It continued:

1. Officials noted in their public statement that President Eisenhower had established a Cabinet-style Government – 'The Ike Team' – and had carefully delegated authority which had prepared the Government for just such an eventuality.
2. The Administration kept to previously announced schedules of government activities, even to trips abroad by Cabinet officers.
3. The first Cabinet meeting after Ike's attack was opened with prayers for his recovery.
4. Nixon noted the incredibly heightened sensitivity of the press during this period. . . . It was a time for carefully guarded words and actions, especially for the Vice-President.

Dolan's memo set the tone for the week, in which Vice-President Bush was at pains to stress the business-as-usual theme. Acting President without full presidential powers, he conducted Cabinet meetings from his own chair, leaving Reagan's poignantly vacant. But he was, according to those present, none the less forceful for that.

Second, of course, to Reagan, Bush has been the hero of the week. He had a characteristically American reward by Thursday, when an instant ABC *Washington Post* poll showed 68 per cent of Americans saying yes, Bush could 'handle the job of president, if he has to'. Reagan's popularity, in the wake of the assassination attempt, jumped eleven points in forty-eight hours, with 73 per cent saying they approved his performance as president.

It is expected on Capitol Hill that the attempt on Reagan's life and his relaxed, courageous response to it, will extend his legislative 'honeymoon' by anything up to six months. By midweek the jubilant Majority Leader, Howard Baker, was openly defying such Democrats as Senator Howard Metzenbaum to stand up and repeat their charges that the Reagan economic and social programmes were 'cruel' and 'inhumane'. They stayed mum.

Some congressmen went so far as to recall the passage of Lyndon Johnson's 'Great Society' programme in the wake of President Kennedy's death. A sometime Johnson aide, Loyd Hackler, now a lobbyist, said: 'Reagan was beginning to lose the real good momentum last week and was in bad shape on the tax bill . . . now I think he's going to get it all back because of this. Even if he can't get out there himself, conveying his wishes from the sick-bed will be powerful stuff.'

It was, indeed, on his sick-bed on Tuesday morning, some sixteen hours after he had been shot, that Reagan signed into law his first piece of legislation as president. The signature was a mite wobbly, but there it was on network news for the nation to see and take comfort from. Plans for a photograph of him to be released on Wednesday were postponed for forty-eight hours. The official explanation was that he still had unsightly tubes emanating from his arm and chest; talkative hospital staff were saying that he in fact looked much less well than he would like people to think.

The aftermath of Monday's dramatic scenes will be with us for some time yet: most notably in the shape of the invulnerable, macho President, who hopes to leave hospital next week and be back at his full powers 'within the month'. Told by his doctors he couldn't ride for at least two months, Reagan apparently raised one finger in silent reply.

But he has apparently agreed that he will in future wear a bullet-proof vest on some public occasions – there is a new, lightweight variety sometimes worn by Carter and his staff – though it is unlikely that such protection would have helped much on Monday, when the bullet entered his left armpit. (The .22 'Destructor' bullet had in fact ricochetted off the President's limousine door before hitting him.)

With that in mind, the secret service are also aware that these attacks tend to come in spates. It was only ten days after Sara Jane Moore's bullet whistled over his head in 1975 that Gerald Ford was attacked by Lynette 'Squeaky' Fromme. Said a chastened Ford last week: 'If we can't have the opportunity of talking with one another, seeing one another, shaking hands with one another, something has gone wrong with our society.'

It was a universal sentiment. Another such attack on a public figure in the near future would have this country on the edge of a collective nervous breakdown. President Reagan's humour last week, for all its John Wayne bravado, always verged on the macabre – but never more so than when a nurse told him he must 'keep up the good work'.

'Why?' said the President. 'You mean this is going to happen again?'

Observer, 5 April 1981

With Prince Charles in Australia

Sydney

Were I the Prince of Wales's private secretary – which I am not, nor am ever like to be – I could not advise HRH to pursue his undisguised hopes of one day governing Australia.

As a Pom at the end of his first visit to this country, made in the company of the heir to its throne, I have come to a very different conclusion. The Prince should hope to mark Australia's bicentenary in 1988 by presiding over the independence celebrations of a new republic within the Commonwealth.

In the past two weeks I have seen the Australian Prime Minister fawn all over Prince Charles, almost as if he were a voter. I have seen schoolgirls faint away at his mere approach, as if he were an honorary Bee Gee. I have seen Anglo-Saxon high society, elderly matrons and even the polo set fight to touch him, as if he possessed supernatural powers.

But I have also seen students in Melbourne jostle him, brandish beer cans and call him 'parasite'. I have seen polls concluding that only some 20 per cent are actively in favour of his becoming governor-general. I have heard Greeks, Italians, Irish, Chinese, Vietnamese, Slavs – Australians all – seethe with rank indifference.

'Prince *who?*' I've never heard him called that before. To travel around Australia with Prince Charles is to travel around with Britain itself – to receive an up-to-the-minute print-out on current attitudes to 'the old country', as it stands personified before them.

Unlike the Prince, however, a fellow-traveller also gets the chance to meet the heart and soul of the country, rather than merely its ruling elite. And I beg to report, Sir, that the natives are getting rather restless.

07.00, 9 April: Below me is my first glimpse of Sydney Harbour. Though arriving by a somewhat different mode of transport, I can see why Arthur Phillip called it 'the finest natural harbour in the world' when he landed Australia's first 'settlers' here on 26 January 1788. From up here, the famous Opera House looks like an oyster fight, the bridge not much bigger than that between Runcorn and Widnes. But the coves, inlets and lagoons seem to go on forever.

Down there is Botany Bay, where Phillip and that first wretched shipload of convicts had fetched up a week before. This is what Australians are supposed to be 'celebrating' in January 1988. In the words of an avowedly Republican writer, Geoffrey Dutton, 'We will be celebrating the invasion of Australia by British troops and their pathetic captives, the rejects of British society . . . patriotism cannot be linked with such infamous origins.'

After thirty hours in aeroplanes, we are compelled to wait another thirty minutes while strip-cartoon Australians – swarthy, jocular figures in shorts – spray us with insecticide. We are given an ill-humoured lecture on the ecological disaster Australia is courting by letting us set foot in the place. We are searched for mouldering food, disease, farm-stains on our boots, then queue to have our passports reluctantly stamped by officials suspicious of our every pore. Welcome to God's own country.

16.30, same day, Canberra: After a visit to Parliament House, which looks disappointingly like a provincial post office, I have the first of many such encounters. My bus driver whisks me a mile past my hotel, jet-lag and all, then concedes – in what almost becomes a fist-fight – that he's done it because 'I'm a Pom-hater.' This is a caricature; it can't be true. Friends at dinner, alarmed by my first impressions, assure me that it isn't, so we fall instead into a violent argument about the forthcoming Test series.

13 April: If you can compare a pitch-and-putt course with the Royal and Ancient links, St Andrews, then you can compare Canberra with Washington DC, on which it is supposed to have been modelled. Though equally spacious and green, it seems even more out of touch with the rest of the country than is the American capital. You cannot properly govern a democratic society by sitting in a luxurious, air-conditioned office all day before returning to a luxurious, air-conditioned suburban home.

While HRH lays a wreath and unveils a plaque, I pay a call on Professor Manning Clark, Australian of the Year 1980, now half-way through volume five of his monumental *History of Australia*. Balliol-educated, another avowed Republican, he would like to see all formal links severed 'so that we can have normal relations with Great Britain, without the echoes of past overlordship'.

Clark advocates a system like that in India, with an indigenous president and prime minister, and recognition of Britain as head of the Commonwealth. Less than half Australians are now of British descent, more than a third from non-English-speaking countries. A quarter of the population is Asian, a third Catholic. 'How many other countries in the modern world have a foreign head of state?'

Melbourne, after Athens and New York, is now the third-largest Greek city in the world, Sydney the fourth. Not for the first or the last time, I hear it suggested that ex-King Constantine would make as logical a choice for governor-general as Prince Charles.

As the Professor waves me off, my cab driver takes one look at him, then spits out: 'Bloody Red'. On making further inquiries, I am sternly lectured on the growing 'revolutionary' movement in Australia, and the benefits of stability and dignity under the Crown. There seems to be an emerging consensus that 40 per cent of Australians would take Clark's view, 40 per cent my cab driver's, with 20 unmoved either way.

I have learnt, in this egalitarian society, to sit in the front of a taxi, but I have not yet learnt not to tip. My proferred coins are brusquely waved away as the harangue continues. Yes, of course he's of British stock – but 'you're not going to quote me, are you?' This has been the first off-the-record taxi ride in the history of journalism.

14 April: HRH has gone on to Sydney to inspect the cathedral, meet some newly naturalized Brits, and visit the Transglobe Expedition. I stay behind in Canberra for a Press Club lunch with the Leader of the Opposition, Bill Hayden. His theme today is American defence installations in Australia, and the quest-ions peter out all too soon.

The television cameras round angrily on me, I am booed, and there are cries of 'Bo-o-oring' as I stand to raise the question of Prince Charles's local aspirations. Hayden responds, with a sigh, that I've now wiped his defence speech off tomorrow's front pages.

He then reveals, interestingly enough, that his wife sat next to the Prince at dinner last night, and was repeatedly told that he is the son of the Queen of Australia, and therefore an Australian citizen. Hayden describes this argument as 'well-developed', which raises a cheap laugh. He then goes on, even more interestingly, to stress that his opposition to it all is purely personal, not Labour Party policy. To start a political row over the Prince, it is clear, would lose Labour more votes than it would gain.

At 4 pm the previous afternoon, I have learnt, the head of the Prime Minister's department, Sir Geoffrey Yeend, met the Prince's private secretary, Edward Adeane, to talk turkey. There emerged a plan for the Prime Minister, Malcolm Fraser, to win an election in early 1983, then immediately install the Prince in Government House for as long as he could guarantee political stability – with luck, three years.

I know why Prince Charles is so keen on all this, but why Fraser? His staff too are rather baffled. There is some political mileage for him in being seen to enjoy so close an association with the Royal Family. In Commonwealth terms, netting the Prince would amount to a technical knockout over Canada. But everyone keeps coming back to the same refrain: 'Well, you know, Fraser is from one of *those* families.'

15 April: I've caught up with HRH in Sydney, a dramatically beautiful city, and enjoy a pleasant stroll through the Royal Botanical Gardens, where he plants a tree. A flash of the royal wit, which so often eludes the pen: 'Wherever I go in the world, I find trees planted by my parents before me. I notice that my mother's seem to flourish, while my father's tend to droop rather wearily. Which leads me to assume that trees must be snobs.'

As he retreats in triumph to Government House, I lunch with a Liberal MP, an hour after the Foreign Secretary's dramatic resignation. Fraser, it is assumed, will tough out this latest crisis. Operation HRH still looks intact. The MP believes the monarchy an indispensable sheet-anchor for so politically volatile a country. Even he, however, stresses that no other non-Australian – no other member, indeed, of the British Royal Family – would be acceptable as governor-general.

We compare Australia with the United States, whence I have come, and with which I see many potential parallels. The same debilitating conflict between federal and state governments. A nation of immigrants, with the same motives for bedrock conservatism: entrepreneurship, the acquisition of property and the spread of middle-class affluence as the Australian/American dream. Australia has the world's highest percentage of home owners. Its population is approaching fifteen million – 84 per cent of them city-dwellers – in a land mass almost the size of that of the United States (population approaching 250 million).

But Australia is 70 per cent self-sufficient in oil, and a net exporter of food. Despite an 80 per cent drop-off in agricultural trade with Europe since Britain joined the Common Market, it has developed more than adequate markets elsewhere, notably in the Middle East, for meat, wheat and wool exports. 'If we stopped exporting wheat to Egypt,' an Australian diplomat told me, 'Egypt would starve.'

Its domestic markets are less content, making it increasingly an economic colony of Japan. One hundred and fifty million potentially cut fingers, for instance, did not prove enough to keep Elastoplast in business here. And one of the reasons for strict population containment is the alarmingly low water supply. For the 60,000-odd a year admitted, however, the living is refreshingly easy.

16-17 April: Melbourne, home of the Melbourne Club – where, I am told, can be found twenty-five of the fifty people who 'really run Australia' (only three of whom are politicians). But it is Good Friday, and the club, like the city, is closed. I visit the deserted Melbourne cricket ground, with misty imaginings of the Centenary Test, Derek Randall – and another Pommy defeat.

Out to Monash University, Australia's most progressive and

most radical, where HRH is to receive an honorary degree. The novelist Patrick White, winner of the Nobel Prize, declares himself 'particularly surprised' by this offer; he calls it 'a cunning ploy' to disarm the Republican movement and dismisses the monarchy scathingly as 'those tireless commuters'. Monash students seem to agree. As HRH exits there ensues what the tabloid boys term a 'riot', the rest of us a 'disturbance'.

Left to my own devices awhile in the office of the editor of *The Melbourne Age*, otherwise known to *Observer* readers as Michael Davie, I take out volume one of *Encyclopaedia Britannica* (1965 edition) and look up Australia. 'The long delay in the discovery and settlement of Australia', it tells me, 'was caused by many factors – predominantly its geographical remoteness', and, finally, 'the lack of any sign that the land possessed anything worth having.'

Leap to the index to identify JFC, the author of this article, who turns out to be James Ford Cairns, lecturer in economic history at Melbourne University, MP for Yarra and Gough Whitlam's Deputy Prime Minister in 1974-5. Well, well.

Australia is now known, of course, to sit on perhaps the richest supply of natural resources on earth. It can legitimately regard itself as one of those nations likely in the future to be least vulnerable to downward economic world trends. This fact is hammered away at by Republicans, who want to see Australians harness this potential, and take control of their own destiny.

But his fellow-countrymen, says Patrick White, are still encouraged 'to snuggle up to the British and Americans' – in which process he equates the welcoming of Prince Charles with that of US defence installations:

> Everything is done today to distract us from reality. Reality is the rape of this country for its material wealth, regardless of the shambles we'll be in when we've appeased foreign interests and the dollars are burned. . . . Reality as it could and ought to be is justice, moral and material, for all classes.

Unless politicians 'stop considering their own interests only', Australia will become 'a quaint collection of relics from an abortive culture'.

17 April et seq: Myth v. Reality. Another recurring theme. On the flight back to Sydney I am deep in another myth, that of the Greek island in *The Magus*, when John Fowles inadvertently jolts me back to reality. 'You know what Australians are like,' says the novel's protagonist. 'They're terribly half-baked culturally. They don't really know who they are, where they belong... very gauche. Anti-British.'

Is the boorish, Pom-baiting, Fosters-toting ocker stereotype the myth that Republicans claim? In an attempt to disprove Fowles's cliché, I take in a *Hamlet* at Sydney Opera House, symbol of Australia's cultural renaissance. Aware of my Pom prejudice, I have to leave: 'to buy or not to buy' I just can't buy. There is ample consolation, however, in a spectacular Chinese exhibition at the art gallery of New South Wales.

A special supplement in *The Bulletin* (a weekly magazine) testifies to the liveliness of contemporary Australian writing. The Australian film industry, moreover, is booming, with 100 feature films next year in the wake of *Breaker Morant* and *My Brilliant Career*.

20 April: HRH has been getting in plenty of swimming, surfing and polo. He is spending the Easter weekend at the remote ranch of his millionaire polo coach, Sinclair Hill, while I am most hospitably received across Sydney Harbour by a British family who came here sixteen years ago, and who take me to a dozen beaches within minutes of their ocean-view home. 'Beats Brentwood, eh?' is the general consensus.

The family has two sons, the elder working on a doctorate in seventeenth-century British history, the younger a university dropout, unabashedly enjoying Australia's hairy-chested outdoor life, and cheerfully disowning the mother country. The first, it strikes me, is characteristic of those who eventually leave: the Robert Hugheses, Germaine Greers, Fleet Street's Australian Mafia – even the Olivia Newton-Johns and, at a pinch, the Rolf Harrises – to plunder riper cultural markets.

The second son represents the Australia of the future, the self-made 'lucky country', thriving on its own natural resources, aggressively regarding the monarchy, including the (Australian) governor-general, as an irritating irrelevance. I reflect that HRH might have had a more eye-opening weekend here than among the antipodean horsey set.

22 April: Geoffrey Dutton, I learn, was once assigned to take Prince Philip round an Australian art gallery. 'You're the Republican chap, aren't you?' inquired the Prince, well briefed. 'Well, when you want us to go, tell us and we'll go.' Says Dutton now: 'Without the slightest ill-will, and severing none of our other ties with Britain, we should tell them that 1988 is the year in which they should go.'

The 40 per cent who would agree with him are the youth and future of Australia, people much Prince Charles's age, many of whom have come here from countries which have overthrown their own monarchies, or which never had one in the first place. The only thing hampering a tidal wave of Republicanism, it seems to me, is another aspect of the Australian character: a particularly lazy species of 'good life' complacency, a laid-back contentment with the status quo.

23 April: HRH is off to Venezuela, by way of more plaques, trees and troop inspections in Hobart and Adelaide. Me, I'm off back to Washington (where I'll see him again next weekend) and thence, reluctantly, to London. From two countries looking alive to their future to one which, from both vantage-points, seems able only to take a decaying satisfaction in its past.

Observer, 26 April 1981

Reporting America

Aboard Ted Kennedy's Campaign Plane

Newark, New Jersey

He offered champagne with the crab, though there didn't seem to be much to celebrate. Number two in the polls for the first time in a decade, Ted Kennedy is watching helplessly as the presidency slips from his grasp.

Over dinner on his campaign plane last Wednesday, however, he assured me he still feels 'upbeat and hopeful and optimistic about this thing'.

What else can he say? We had just visited four New England states in twenty-four hours, an indication of Kennedy's own fears that even his family's homeland could fall to President Carter in the primaries ahead. In two extraordinary months, the Ayatollah Khomeini and President Brezhnev have between them yanked Carter back from oblivion and made a mockery of Kennedy's hereditary claims on the White House.

He calls the present presidential impasse 'unique in American history'. Would he have entered the race, had a staff soothsayer foreseen events in Iran and Afghanistan?

Oh, sure. The reasons for entering the race still stand, and in fact have been accentuated by the failures of foreign policy.

There's an obvious and natural concern among the American people about the safety of the hostages. That issue has subsumed the broader debate and discussion. But it's only a matter of time before we'll come to grips with the central domestic issues of the campaign – energy, inflation, the economy – on all of which I differ sharply from the President. I hope it'll be sooner rather than later, but I think it's only a matter of time.

Time is not on Kennedy's side. He is expected to suffer his first major setback tomorrow at the caucuses to select Democratic convention delegates in Iowa, the state which hoisted Jimmy Carter from nowhere in 1976. Some months ago, when things were looking good, Kennedy rashly called the Iowa caucuses 'the first real test of strength'.

The remark looks like backfiring. In the past three weeks Kennedy has spent sixteen days travelling 6,000 miles around Iowa, while Carter, pleading affairs of state, has sent thirty White House staff 'on vacation' there and thrilled wavering households with chatty presidential phone calls. Kennedy could even come third behind Carter and 'uncommitted'.

A Carter victory tomorrow will confront the Senator with a painful and very personal truth. The President's grain embargo against Moscow, obviously unpopular in so predominantly agricultural a state, has not driven Democrats into the waiting arms of Ted Kennedy. They have crossed to the Republicans, they have stuck with Carter despite it all, or they have simply stayed home. In a storm, any port but Kennedy's.

Why? Because they don't trust him. It all comes back to Chappaquiddick – which, contrary to most expectations, both the Senator's and the pollsters', just won't go away. 'I stand by my sworn testimony,' he says; 'I wouldn't have gotten into this thing if I thought any new evidence could come up to contradict it.'

The second remark is particularly heartfelt. Last week two major publications, the *Washington Star* and the *Reader's Digest*, came up with what they claimed was just such new evidence. The details were complex, involving tide tables, shifting land masses, and the speed at which cars travel through the air after falling off bridges. But, to the reading public, they proved in a vague sort of way that Kennedy was still lying.

In a fit of anger, he overreacted. For the first time in ten years, Kennedy called a press conference to rebut Chappaquiddick accusations, thus ensuring they received an even wider hearing. He had a good case, but it got lost amid the tables, charts and sworn depositions issued to the press. The Senator was protesting too much.

Later in the week, Rupert Murdoch's *New York Post* dusted down a 'beautiful, blonde Czech-born countess' and assorted other lovelies to talk of their fun and games with Kennedy on Chappaquiddick in the late 1960s, thus suggesting that Kennedy knew the island's geography rather better than he has claimed. This time, the Senator chose not to respond at all.

'The interesting thing', he says aboard the aircraft, chewing on his huge cigar, 'is that two investigating teams have studied this for several months and come up with completely conflicting stories. I know what happened and the independent assessments have substantiated my account.'

You could press him all night on Chappaquiddick without getting any further. But even having allowed him to wriggle off the hook, back onto sturdier domestic platforms, it is difficult to pin him down to any specifics. In interview, as in his stump speeches, Kennedy contents himself with bland generalities.

Asked for a foreign policy to rival the 'Carter doctrine', to be unveiled amid great fanfare this week, Kennedy is not prepared to go beyond 'What I believe should be the basic elements of a foreign policy.' He then talks unexceptionally about restraint, arms limitation, obligations to the Third World, and – as a conscious gesture to a British newspaper – 'the reaffirmation of our relationships with our allies'.

Suddenly he leans forward, as if he'd thought of something worth saying. 'Let me just say that besides the United States and its allies, and besides the United States and Third World countries, I think that there's an important responsibility for the US as a force within the world to try and help resolve these, er, you know, disputes.' His voice trails away again.

Campaign audiences are as dismayed as interlocutors by the sight of a Kennedy who appears to have given up. Each entry into each hall provokes all-American whoops and whistles, a brief whiff of Camelot which momentarily revives the flagging spirits of his attendant journalists. They, like the audience, then sink back with glazed eyes as the candidate's rhetoric fails to scale the nursery slopes.

His walkabouts, by contrast, are tumultuous – a daily agony for his secret service detail, thirty-six of whom, several armed with sub-machine-guns, guard the man they have code-named 'Sunburn'. It was awesome, on Wednesday evening, to watch the ferocity with which they overwhelmed three Newark Communists who sprayed eggs in the Senator's direction.

During the day he made twelve speeches: to small groups of enthusiastic party workers, to larger gatherings of students and the small-town curious, to labour leaders and local newspaper editors. All received the same bored homily, and all were expected to be swayed more by the presence than by any substance that might go with it.

The lacklustre performance has disappointed even his most ardent supporters. 'I waited twelve years for Kennedy to get into this race,' said one man emerging from the Claremont meeting. 'Now I'm going to vote for Carter.'

The Senator resists the thesis that recent trends in the polls have been as much anti-Kennedy as pro-Carter.

No, the debate is taking place at a unique time. On the one hand, one is restrained, to the extent that a person seeking office could undermine the position of the principal negotiator for the United States. On the other, one does want to see a constructive debate and discussion of the issues.

You have to strike a balance. I've tried to. You have to be sensitive to all those considerations. I've tried to be. You have to be responsible. I've tried to be. And I think I have been.

A note of desperation has crept in. Listening to him, you are reminded of the image dragged once again to the forefront of the American consciousness last week: that of the Senator struggling against the tide, being swept out to sea, thinking he was going to drown. It is an apt metaphor for his present political plight.

Observer, 20 January 1980

No Messiah in the Year of the Yo-Yo

Nashua, New Hampshire

'Up in the mountains of New Hampshire,' said Daniel Webster, 'God Almighty has hung out a sign to show that there he makes men.'

The Almighty's sign last week seemed due a few graffiti. In New Hampshire, with some relish, he also makes fools of prophets. And in recent years he seems to have endowed 'The Granite State' with the mixed blessing of making presidents.

Since 1952, when the state initiated its 'first-in-the-nation' primary, no White House aspirant has been elected without first winning in New Hampshire. By historical precedent, therefore, this tiny, rural patch of land, one of the least representative states in the Union, now offers its fellow-citizens Jimmy Carter or Ronald Reagan to guide their uncertain steps towards 1984.

Spare a thought for George Orwell. At a particularly low ebb in American fortunes, both at home and abroad, New Hampshire has presented a choice between the man held most responsible for causing the country's woes, and the man thought least likely to cure them.

Inflation in the United States is now running at 18 per cent, compared with 4.5 per cent when Gerald Ford left office in 1977. Interest rates are the highest in history, the prime lending rate having climbed from 12 to 16.75 per cent in the past twelve months alone. Last spring, motorists were queueing to buy gasoline at 75 cents a gallon; this summer, they are expected to be queueing for it at twice that amount.

Six months ago, the President said the presence of a brigade of Soviet combat troops in Cuba would never become 'an acceptable status quo'. Now, utterly forgotten, they go about their exercises in peace, as the presence of battalions of their

93

comrades in Afghanistan becomes, if not acceptable, the status quo.

Four months ago, the nation responded with dignity and restraint to what amounted to an act of war by Iran. Now an overwhelming majority favours unprecedented peacetime increases in defence spending, and scornful rejection of the Strategic Arms Limitation Treaty.

Today, their 120th in captivity, the American hostages in Tehran appear in less hope than ever of imminent release. After an interval of some weeks, Americans are again seeing their national flag burnt on the network news each evening, as a result of 'a gentleman's agreement' with someone few would deem a gentleman.

President Carter, having himself spent a fortnight gently raising America's hopes, last Tuesday chided the nation for 'excessive optimism'. That evening, after repeating that he would not leave the White House to campaign because of 'international preoccupations', he went to the theatre.

That day, the day of the New Hampshire vote, saw the announcement of the worst monthly inflation figures in six years. It was the day the White House had hoped to throw a party for the returning hostages. Carter managed nevertheless to dominate the morning's news, beaming triumphantly, by instead throwing a party for America's victorious Olympic skaters.

Somebody up there likes that man. The cold New England states, whose winter heating bills alone were once expected to see off the Carter presidency, have enjoyed their mildest winter for forty years. President Brezhnev and the Ayatollah Khomeini, meanwhile, have been serving as honorary joint chairmen of the campaign to re-elect the President.

Having trailed Senator Kennedy by two-to-one six months ago, Carter is now set to 'whip his ass' all the way to California. It should be said that the Senator's own flaws, as much as the President's supposed strengths, have accounted for his abrupt demise.

The Republicans, at the same time, have lurched from one front-runner to another and back again, by equally spectacular margins. In American politics this has been, and looks like continuing to be, the Year of the Yo-Yo.

One reason is the paucity of the electorate's choice. Dismayed and angered by events abroad – even more, it would seem, than by the economic chaos at home – they have no obvious place of refuge among this year's candidates.

'If only', sighed a friend the other day, 'there was someone to get excited about, someone to go out and work for.' There is no Jack Kennedy offering a glorious New Frontier, no Robert Kennedy or Gene McCarthy arousing liberal passions, no Barry Goldwater sounding the distant trumpets of war.

Come to that, there's no Jimmy Carter, promising a bright-eyed outsider's new broom to sweep through a discredited and unpopular Washington.

This at a time when American political fervour is high. The turnout in New Hampshire last week was more than a third up on 1976, as in the earlier Iowa and Maine caucuses. The electorate is brimming with questions, but the front-running candidates – those given any chance of actually winning – are carefully evasive in their answers.

Reagan, for instance, is on the record as proposing simply to be 'tough' towards the Russians. Beyond that, his one specific suggestion is to impose an immediate naval blockade on Cuba. The electorate, at the moment, is in the mood for toughness, but has equally few practical ideas for displaying it.

President Bush would also be 'tough', in his case by maintaining arms superiority. The trouble is he might actually use them, if we can judge from his blithe discussions of post-holocaust America, where 5 per cent of the population survive to re-create the Promised Land. And candidate Bush makes himself out to be a moderate.

The villain of the piece, and the reason the nation is squirming in confusion, is surely the American electoral system, the democratic world's most unwieldy method of choosing a leader. Each time round, it grows more protracted and more wasteful.

Despite recent revisions of electoral finance laws, it costs some $500,000 a week to keep a campaign on the road. Between them, the candidates spent $2 million in New Hampshire – or roughly $8 per vote cast. After spending more than $10 million, John Connally has won precisely one convention delegate, Mrs Aida Mills of Arkansas, whose vote must surely qualify as the most expensive in political history.

There is a growing argument that no American of any calibre would be prepared to go through the drawn-out, exhausting and demeaning hustle, consuming some three years of life at the height of one's powers, now required to win the presidency. The brand of man who once occupied the Oval Office is now accepting appointed government posts or retiring to Academe.

The voter is thus presented with serried ranks of smiling faces, be they out-of-work governors, former CIA chiefs or ambitious congressmen, all offering remarkably similar views. He makes his choice – and then keeps changing it – on largely cosmetic criteria.

Americans tend to vote, as one pollster put it last week, 'by feel'. The leading candidates, at this early stage, project themselves through slick advertising and platitudinous rhetoric, only vaguely representing political ideals. In choosing the party nominees, if not in the subsequent general election, the voter is prone to look and 'feel' rather than listen and think.

As a result, New Hampshire voters last week rejected those candidates with clear and carefully articulated positions – Kennedy, Howard Baker, John Anderson – in favour of two familiar faces with broadly jingoistic appeal.

Primary voters are also unduly susceptible to abrupt, media-blown incidents, wholly unconnected with the issues. New Hampshire was all set to propel George Bush along his line of momentum – largely because he had spent so much time telling them how he was going to win, rather than why he deserved to – when he fell smack into a trap of Ronald Reagan's devising.

Last weekend Bush arrived in Nashua for a one-to-one debate with Reagan, to find that his fellow front-runner had invited their five Republican rivals to join them. Loath to merge once more into the pack, Bush stood firm. Once the others were on the stage, shaking hands with Reagan and angrily thumbing their noses at Bush, he realized he had made a tactical error. Thus was it proven that George Bush panics in a crisis.

Amid the subsequent mêlée it was quite forgotten that Reagan, winner by a technical knockout, was the same man who had refused to debate with those same colleagues six weeks ago in Iowa. The Democrats, too, gave a handsome majority to the one candidate who has consistently refused to debate the issues with opponents from his own party.

When the Iowa debate invitations were issued in December, before Iran and Afghanistan had him leapfrogging up the polls, Carter welcomed the idea and accepted. A month later, a surprised front-runner, he was suddenly too busy with affairs of state. The Reagan saga is the same in reverse. Once again, the voters have been bamboozled by tactics.

The margin of Reagan's victory, however, suggests that last weekend's débâcle was merely the icing on his sixty-ninth birthday cake. Bush's mercurial appeal was that of a bright new face, singularly lacking in ideological conviction. Trying to woo all constituencies, he seduced none.

Bush had, in truth, tried to blur his highly conservative record, in a broad appeal to the moderate soft-centre of the party and the increasingly numerous independent vote. In retrospect, this is something of an irony. The New Hampshire results mark above all the deeply conservative mood of a troubled nation.

Against this background, it is small wonder the American mood is one of helplessness and pessimism. The voter in search of a candidate sees firm finger-wagging on the salient issues of the 1970s – abortion, gun control, the Equal Rights Amendment, national health insurance – but no one with a grand strategy encompassing the geopolitical issues of the day.

Not one of the electable candidates, for instance, speaks of energy in terms of foreign policy, of securing America's defences while ridding the nation of its dependence on imported oil. None can improve on Carter's current piecemeal response to Soviet belligerence.

Barring unforeseen events – which, this year, few do – Reagan and Carter should have the nominations sewn up when the primaries end in California on 3 June. Thus will the hapless American electorate, in its hour of most need, have been offered a choice devoid of men of truly presidential timber – including, by majority verdict, the incumbent.

Observer, 2 March 1980

The Candidate from Main Street, USA

Detroit, Michigan

On location in Detroit this week, Ronald Reagan begins work on the most ambitious role he has ever tackled. The production team is enormous, the financial backing assured, the studio unusually united in its enthusiasm. Special effects are being kept under wraps for a while, but box office returns already look promising.

Reviewing Reagan's long career, it remains a bizarre piece of casting. In his thirty years on the silver screen, he was never much of a big studio money-maker, still less an Oscar nominee. After half as long in politics, only half again of that time in elected office, he will, this Wednesday, receive the ultimate accolade of his new profession, a nomination even more coveted than Hollywood's.

Yet Reagan seems, throughout both careers, to have been playing potentially the same part. In his movies, as in his politics, it was always 'us' against an ill-defined 'them'. The small-town good guy tangling with destiny, seeing the local citizenry through, now aspires to do the same for the nation. Plain old-fashioned virtues will triumph, and the world will be set to rights.

So goes the scenario to be televised from Detroit this week, at a Republican convention so devoid of internal dissent as to promise a mere showbiz extravaganza. The likes of James Stewart will upstage the likes of Henry Kissinger, the one being on hand to prevent the nation's viewers switching off the other.

A big production number is in prospect for Wednesday, when the familiar state-by-state roll-call will climax in Reagan's anointment. The one element of suspense will be carefully sustained until the convention's dénouement, twenty-four hours later, when the candidate will unveil his chosen running-mate.

'One day, my boy, all this will be yours,' the script might well run at this point. Reagan has had to wait until his seventieth year for his name to climb at last above the title, and there is a general, rather morbid assumption that on Thursday he will be naming his successor – and thus, quite possibly, the forty-first president of the United States.

Whoever joins the ticket – George Bush still heads party popularity polls, with Senators Lugar and Laxalt the late tips from the stables – he is likely to have more obvious qualifications for the presidency than Ronald Reagan. Even folks in California, that eccentric Republican stronghold, concede that no other state in the union could ever have elected him governor.

In the past few weeks and months, however, Reagan has succeeded in what many a year ago thought impossible: he has convinced the American people that he is a credible candidate for the highest office in the land. In this, as in many other departments, old 'Dutch' (his parents' nickname still sticks) has been sorely underestimated.

Like Jimmy Carter in 1976, Reagan has won the presidential nomination in spite of, rather than with help from, the party machine. Once Gerald Ford bowed out, having dithered too long, Reagan's popular constituency could not be challenged.

In this Reagan was fortunate to belong to a party which, like the British Conservatives, puts its thirst for office above its ideological differences. In Detroit this week, there will be no evidence of the Republican establishment's desperate efforts last year to find a moderate candidate to see Reagan off. Conservatism is suddenly the mood of the hour, and he its hero.

It was not always thus. Reagan grew up a New Dealer, the son of the only Democrat in Republican Dixon, Illinois. His mother, like Jimmy Carter's, was a Sunday school do-gooder. His father was a drunk trying to be a shoe salesman, rescued from bankruptcy by a job in Roosevelt's work programme – precisely the kind of job his son is now eager to abolish.

Reagan didn't even join the Republican Party until 1962, when already past his fiftieth birthday. Two years later, he was co-chairman of California for Goldwater, his first political job. Two more years, and he was Governor of California;

another two, and he made his first bid for the presidency.

As second careers go, it was a model of rapid success, stalled in 1968 only by the political resilience of one Richard Nixon.

Throughout his early career as a radio sports commentator, through Hollywood, the war, and his two periods as president of the Screen Actors' Guild (1947-52 and 1959-60), Reagan remained a registered Democrat.

His swing to the right dates from the early 1950s, when two events altered the course of his life. Already divorced from Jane Wyman, whose screen career had left his behind, in 1952 he married Nancy Davis, daughter of a wealthy Chicago surgeon, an actress of sufficiently modest talents to be desperate for the role of housewife. (Reagan would be the first divorcee to become president in United States history.) Nancy's views were, and remain, even more conservative than her husband's.

In 1954, when his Hollywood career was nose-diving, Reagan became host of General Electric Theatre, a half-hour weekly TV series sponsored by the giant conglomerate. The $125,000-a-year contract was a handsome foundation for a career in politics: he was seen each week on network television, and he travelled the country expounding GE's big business, free enterprise politics to its executives and employees.

Thus began Reagan's years on what he still calls 'the mashed potato circuit', where he now commands $10,000 a speech. In the process he became rich, accumulating hefty investments and a series of increasingly large California ranches. Like so many before him, Reagan's abandonment of social democracy came with his own arrival in the upper tax bracket.

In 1948, he had voted for Harry Truman. In 1950, he supported Helen G. Douglas in her famous US Senate race against Richard Nixon. By 1960, he was a Democrat for Nixon. Two years of Jack Kennedy, and he signed up with the enemy.

Ten years later, Reagan was among the last, thin rank of Republicans urging President Nixon not to resign. His bold stand, in retrospect, was not entirely without self-interest. With Spiro Agnew gone, Nixon had no ordained heir. To challenge a temporary, unelected vice-president for the 1976 nomination would have incurred no charges of party disloyalty.

For Reagan was by now a professional politician of national stature, a two-term governor of California whose record in that office had not yet undergone close scrutiny. He himself was busy rewriting it, in two or three speeches a week around the nation – playing his own John the Baptist, and getting paid for it.

For all the tangle of argument now surrounding Reagan's time in Sacramento, one central picture emerges: he was a nine-to-five governor, heavily reliant on his large staff, with a mastery of compromise.

This last had been seen in his early days running the Screen Actors' Guild, when he appeared as a friendly witness before Joe McCarthy's UnAmerican Activities committee, only to defend his members' right to their political views. It was seen time and time again in his bartering with California's Democratic state legislature, where he trimmed his ideology to the size of the deals he could cut.

It is here that those alarmed by the prospect of President Reagan find a crumb of comfort. He professes to understand 'not only the power but the limits of the presidency', and would clearly be a delegating chief executive in what he sees as United States Inc., the ultimate multinational corporation.

The US would enter the era of government by mini-memo, a process Reagan pioneered in California, by which his aides summarize an issue for decision in four pithy paragraphs. President Reagan would be the complete antithesis of President Carter, the engineer with a love of fine detail.

There are those, of course, who believe that the future of US-Soviet relations, of the American economy, nuclear warfare and sundry other issues cannot be summarized in four pithy paragraphs. Not so Ronald Reagan, who does it day after day in speech after speech. It is this down-home, folksy appeal to traditional American values which has got him this far, and may yet see him further.

'I'm a Main Street Republican,' says Dixon's favourite son, espousing the Middle American values definitively mocked by Sinclair Lewis. On the stump he often recalled the simple verities of his childhood, the bygone age he seeks to restore, and the actor in him can choke his voice, bring forth real tears, as he does so.

Reagan the politician is still very much a role-player, a master of television in an age when it can elect presidents, heavily dependent on his Hollywood training to capitalize on his visceral ideological appeal. It was his ability to communicate his belief in simple homespun truths of a conservative persuasion which prompted a wealthy friend to put up $4 million for his unlikely gubernatorial bid in 1966. The trick worked by a landslide, and it could again.

'I completely underestimated him,' said his then opponent, the incumbent Democratic Governor, Edmund G. Brown (father of Jerry, California's current governor and another would-be president). So may Reagan's latest opponent, another incumbent Democrat, another master of electoral politics, who enters the fray as the most unpopular United States president since people started taking polls.

Reagan is hogging the first reel, and you can be sure he'll be pulling out all the stops during the epic ahead. There's just one more role he wants to play before taking that final ride into the sunset.

Observer, 13 July 1980

The Unmaking of a
Vice-President

Detroit, Michigan

Soon after 8 pm on Wednesday evening, his fate still publicly uncertain, an unusually downbeat George Bush mounted the podium of the Republican National Convention in Detroit. There followed the loudest and best-organized demonstration of an already very noisy week.

For fifteen minutes Bush stood helpless, as his supporters yelled for his name to be placed alongside Ronald Reagan's on the Republican presidential ticket. At last he spoke, rather more briefly, then scuttled from the stage, leaving behind the kind of delirium known only to Welsh Rugby matches and American political conventions.

Backstage he left hurriedly for his hotel. Bush had eloquently pledged his unqualified support for Reagan, but he had in fact cut short his prepared remarks. A publicly emotional man, he had been frightened of betraying his true feelings. He already knew he was not going to be Reagan's choice.

Ten minutes before his speech, as he waited beneath the podium, Bush had received an emissary from the Republican presidential candidate. Negotiations with Gerald Ford, he was told, were just about clinched, and Ford would be sharing the ticket. Bush went white. Then, in front of half a dozen people, he vomited.

A mile away, in his Detroit hotel suite, Reagan had just concluded one of many snatched meetings that day with Ford and his intimates. He turned to the TV to watch Bush's performance – and knowing the circumstances under which it was made, was rather impressed. But even he was convinced at that stage that he had persuaded a former president – for the first time in American history – to become his running-mate.

There were a few worries. Ford was imposing stern conditions, most of which Reagan was happy to accommodate. He would give the former commander-in-chief the Cabinet post he

103

sought, and do away – perhaps for all time – with the merely ceremonial role of a vice-president. That was something for which history would thank him.

But he was uneasy about bringing Henry Kissinger into a central role in his Administration, as Ford was insisting, doubly so because Kissinger was leading Ford's negotiating team. The former Secretary of State, architect of detente and the SALT II treaty, is anathema to the right-wing Republicans crucial to Reagan's election. And, characteristically, he had made no secret all week of his lust to return to power.

When it became clear on Wednesday morning that Ford would contemplate a negotiated offer, Kissinger leapt at the opportunity presented him by Reagan's campaign manager, Senator Paul Laxalt, to act as intermediary. The Reagan team, it became clear, would concede almost anything to get Ford on the ticket.

As the day wore on, the demands grew copious. Ford wanted power of appointing many of the National Security Council, the Domestic Policy Advisory Group, the Office of Management and Budget, and veto power over all Cabinet appointments. He wanted to be a quasi-president with full operational powers, subject only to the final policy decisions of the actual chief executive.

What it amounted to was a plan for a 'co-presidency' (another Kissinger invention), which Ford himself had brought up in a 7 pm TV interview with Walter Conkite, the colossus of network news. Reagan had touted himself as a nine-to-five president, keen on delegating his powers, but all this was getting out of hand.

He was, moreover, annoyed that Ford had gone public on the Cronkite show at so sensitive a moment in their dealings. His aides, many of whom were for neither Ford nor Bush, began to protest. Ford was demanding 'too much', and wielding too public an upper hand. Reagan was displaying grace, but not presidential firmness, under pressure.

For another hour after Bush's speech they agonized. At 9.30 pm Reagan called Ford in his suite one floor above, and told him he needed a decision that night. Time was running short, and their deliberations were constantly interrupted. At the high point of his uncertainty, Reagan had to admit TV cameras to his suite, to record him relaxing happily with his family as the state of Montana put him 'over the top' for the nomination.

At the heart of it all was the unassailable fact that Ford, a remarkably popular man in both major parties, would maximize Reagan's chances of election in November. He would stifle any argument that the ticket lacked Washington experience. Though only four years out of the White House, he was already a symbol of the lost days when America was a force to be reckoned with around the world.

But Reagan's lawyers, a pivotal force in the discussions, had begun to have their doubts. There was nothing in the Constitution to limit a vice-president's powers, indeed to deny anything Ford had sought. But Ford was insisting on a written contract, to be publicly proclaimed by Reagan. 'In the event of a dispute between president and vice-president,' as one of them put it, 'who in hell is going to arbitrate?'

At 10.50 pm their dilemma was resolved for them. Former President Gerald Ford returned to Reagan's suite, with the simple message – 'Ron, I don't think this thing's going to work out.' Pride, in the end, had overcome Gerry Ford's unparalleled readiness to put his party's interests before his own. The 'Treaty of Detroit' had come unstuck.

Across town, a weary and despondent George Bush had one eye on the TV as he got ready for bed. From the Joe Louis arena, he watched scenes of crazed euphoria over the man he had spent three years trying to beat to the nomination. Three times he had been runner-up for the vice-presidency: for Richard Nixon, when he chose Spiro Agnew and Gerald Ford, and for Gerald Ford when he chose Nelson Rockefeller. Now Reagan had won his revenge by making it four.

Bush was already in bed, at 11.35 pm, when the phone rang. There was a brief discussion of the party manifesto and its two most controversial planks, against abortion and the Equal Rights Amendment, on both of which Bush was on the wrong side. But his acceptance was never in doubt. He was too stunned for Reagan's final words to spoil his finest hour. The nominee was going to break with tradition by going to the convention to announce his choice of running-mate – alone.

Back in the arena, the formal proceedings had long since ended, but the scenes of jubilation went on. There was a rumour that Reagan was going to make an appearance, though it was already approaching midnight. Senior party figures had confirmed with authority that Gerry Ford would be on the ticket. Maybe Ford would be coming too.

At twelve it was confirmed that Reagan was on his way. TV screens showed the headlights of the motorcade dramatically, presidentially, picking its way through the muggy night. But Ford was on a boat in the middle of the Detroit River, taking questions on a radio phone-in show. Confusion turned to pandemonium as the cry gradually went up: 'It's Bush.'

One British newspaper editor present declared it 'the most exciting night in a hundred years'. Dan Rather, Walter Cronkite's anointed heir at CBS, proclaimed it 'the most extraordinary night in American political history'. Both, in the heat of the moment, may have allowed their journalistic excitement to run away with their better judgement. But Reagan certainly had urgent need to put an end to the chaos.

As he made his dramatic announcement, it was not immediately clear how much the day's events would damage his campaign. All week, ironically enough, his people had been feeding wild speculation about his running-mate, in a calculated (and successful) attempt to maintain interest in an otherwise foregone conclusion of a convention. Now he was the victim of his own stratagem.

By next day's fevered dawn, it was apparent that Reagan had got away with it. It was, as he said, 'unique' to have had such dealings with a former president, which soon defused the mockery that Bush was his second-best choice. He had, in retrospect, shown decisiveness in personally coming out to end the tumult of speculation.

A few of those close to the day's events maintained that Ford, given more time, would have accepted – a claim which paled when set beside the two months of negotiations already behind them. Those of this persuasion were mainly, naturally enough, Ford men – principally Mr Kissinger, who looked much like George Bush had the night before as he insisted: 'Given another twenty-four hours, it would have worked out. Ford would have liked a night to sleep on it.'

Ford himself looked mightily relieved as he repledged his devotion to Reagan next day. For now, he would go off and 'campaign my heart out' – and come November, either way, he could return to California and dust off his golf clubs. He was confident that Reagan-Bush would be a winning ticket.

Conservative Republicans had waited since 1964 to reclaim control of their party. When Barry Goldwater, their disastrous candidate against Lyndon Johnson that year, took the stand on Tuesday night, he was hailed as 'a prophet in his own time'. As the TV screens reminded us, it was a nationally networked campaign speech for Goldwater that launched Ronald Reagan's political career.

The traditional party split between its right wing and its 'moderates' was only briefly exercised over the vice-presidential choice. George Bush's presence on the ticket ultimately satisfies both camps, as it broadens Reagan's electoral appeal. Twenty-four hours after Wednesday's chaos, united in their obsessive opposition to Jimmy Carter, Republicans left Detroit buoyed up for the battles ahead.

No matter that, six months ago, Bush was the most persuasive critic of Reagan's across-the-board 30 per cent tax cut proposal. No matter that the two men can't stand each other, as witnessed that famous February night in Nashua, New Hampshire, when Reagan seized the microphone at a Republican debate and embarrassed Bush out of contention.

Bush is not too proud to swallow his individuality, and surrender it to a Reagan victory. The Ford débâcle, indeed, promises him a substantial vice-presidential role in the event of electoral success. As a former congressman, party chairman, UN ambassador and CIA director, he knows the value to the ticket of his Washington experience. His time as envoy to Peking is likely to be played down, in light of Reagan's professed desire to re-establish diplomatic relations with Taiwan.

Moments before the two men met the press together on Thursday morning, Reagan received a phone call from President Carter. It was a statutory procedure, offering congratulations on his nomination and promising a good, clean fight. But it heightened the atmosphere that night in the Joe Louis arena. As Reagan and Bush delivered their acceptance speeches to crowd scenes worthy of Cecil B. De Mille, there was a general and justified consensus that Carter is already on the defensive.

Given the tenacity of the incumbent President, and his proneness to political deviancy, the autumn campaign is far from likely to be the good, clean fight he promised. Reagan will benefit from his imperturbable, mild-mannered approach to the fray, in deliberate contrast to the picture of a trigger-happy Neanderthal man which the Carter camp will paint of him.

Taking their cue from the candidate, conservative Republicans were for once almost sociable. At previous conventions, they have been known to leave elevators when a press badge walked in, to go for the collective jugular of the moderate group which has held sway in the party since its eclipse under Goldwater.

Now, they believe, the nation has at last come round to their way of thinking. Goldwater's sinister 1964 slogan – 'In your heart, you know he's right' – was not only on conservative lips last week. Reagan's mission is seen as the reversal of almost fifty years of misguided American liberalism, social and economic.

'Main Street Republicanism', as Reagan likes to call it, was the mood of the hour. After Donny Osmond had urged 'America, arise again', and Ginger Rogers had declared 'Go, Ronnie, Go', Jimmy Stewart claimed the moment by adding 'Family, Neighbourhood, Work, Peace and Freedom' to the familiar American litany of Liberty, Equality and Justice for All.

In apocalyptic mood, the party's 40,000-word manifesto, the longest in US political history, declared the nation on the edge of an abyss. 'History could record, if we let the drift go on,' it declared, 'that the American experiment, so marvellously successful for 200 years, came strangely, needlessly, tragically to a dismal end early in our third century.'

If Reagan wins in November, history could also record that last week's convention marked a turning-point in the American way of life. Detroit would be remembered not for its aborted treaty between a would-be president and a sorely tempted, rather muddled predecessor. It would be the starting-point of a crusade in which an actor-turned-politician uprooted the liberal foundations of a modern America laid by its (and his) sometime hero, Franklin D. Roosevelt.

Observer, 20 July 1980

Kennedy's Convention

New York

It wasn't 1968, when riots spilled from the streets of Chicago on to the floor of the Democratic convention. It wasn't 1972, when prime-time procedural squabbles again squared off party liberals versus the rest. But nor was it 1976, when united acclaim for a fresh-faced candidate-from-nowhere lifted the roof off Madison Square Garden.

Four years on, with that same candidate beneath it, there were times when that same roof seemed more likely to fall in. All last week, with the old familiar factions back at each other's throats, the 1980 Democratic convention was painfully slow to swallow the 'patent unity medicine' of its keynote speaker, Mo Udall: 'Take one tablespoon, close your eyes and repeat: President Ronald Reagan.'

It ended, as it began, more Edward Kennedy's week than Jimmy Carter's. The party has a remarkable capacity to love Kennedy at all times, except when he's a candidate. His perfunctory 'unity' appearance at the convention's close, with its conspicuous coolness towards the President, raised a far greater cheer than had the nominee's acceptance speech.

The same had been true the night before, when the party seemed merely to be fulfilling a reluctant obligation by renominating its incumbent president. Only the spectre of the most conservative opponent since Goldwater in 1964 coaxed them into any semblance of unity. As the state of Texas put Carter 'over the top', the ritual brouhaha reeked of stage-management, compared with the spontaneous emotion that had earlier greeted Kennedy's eloquence.

His speech was an inspirational restatement of liberal Democratic ideals. At its end, it seemed the Senator had come to bury Carter, not to praise him. Twenty-four hours after he had withdrawn from the lists, the convention floor was awash with blue Kennedy placards and chants of 'We want Ted.' For forty minutes, as his major economic planks were hastily cobbled into the platform, there was not a green Carter emblem to be seen.

By eschewing even faint praise, Kennedy had damned Carter as surely as he had Reagan. Suddenly, it was on the Senator's say-so that an incumbent president was winning renomination – and on his terms.

For the next forty-eight hours, Kennedy was careful to endorse the party, rather than its candidate, for a continued lease on power. Like a rejected suitor at a wedding, he was making the bride have second thoughts. As the po-faced groom looked on uneasily, Kennedy did at last part with a reluctant blessing – having first rewritten the major clauses of the marriage contract.

Throughout Wednesday and Thursday, Kennedy's dictat was dominant. Carter confessed that he could not win without him and made concession after concession. As the loser dictated the terms of the winner's mandate, the winner was desperate for the loser to hold his hand on national TV.

What would Kennedy do? It was the talk of New York. When he finally reached the rostrum late on Thursday night he offered even less than the gesture recommended by one of his delegates: 'Hold Carter with one hand and your nose with the other.' He shook the President's hand unsmilingly, gave a victory salute to his supporters and left.

TV viewers around the nation saw the President of the United States look after him in dismay, peering round the corner of the podium in the hope he would return. And so Kennedy did, to acknowledge the cheers of the crowd and as quickly leave again, giving the President a seigneurial pat on the back. 'He looked', said Theodore White, historian of the presidency, 'like a man tipping his chauffeur.'

Out in the streets, the party over, even Carter delegates declared their leader's address lacklustre. He had again proved himself a decent man, a president of piety, high ideals and some moral courage. But in seeking to sound visionary, he had offered merely a string of party platitudes. His delivery was so poor that he even paid tribute to 'Hubert Horatio Hornblower' instead of the late Senator Humphrey.

He touched base with all factions of the party, but not in such a way as to inspire them to zealous work this autumn. The speech suffered by comparison with Reagan's crusading tirade in Detroit – as did the ensuing scenes of celebration, described by a veteran of sixteen conventions as the briefest he had ever seen.

Poor Carter-Mondale. Even the mechanism to release the red, white and blue balloons failed. 'If they can't organize that,' moaned one dismayed delegate, 'how in hell are they going to get the hostages home?'

Nothing in Kennedy's campaign became him like the leaving of it. On Monday morning, at a star-studded fund-raiser in Manhattan's trendy 21 Club, he was promising family and friends he would 'invite you all to the White House in January'. That same evening, after defeat on the crucial rules vote binding the majority to nominate Carter, he promptly withdrew with grace.

In the Starlight Room of the Waldorf Astoria Hotel, flanked by the Camelot clan, Kennedy surprised his own staff and supporters by withdrawing his name from nomination. Not for the first time this year, tears filled the wide eyes of young, idealistic campaign workers. Though defeat had long seemed inevitable, they still could not quite believe it.

But he continued to carry the banner he had promised to bring to the convention. The next forty-eight hours saw continuous, largely successful backstage efforts to win policy concessions from the Carter camp. Hamilton Jordan, the President's Chief of Staff (and temporarily his campaign manager), spent most of Wednesday negotiating in Kennedy's hotel suite.

The effect of the Senator's Tuesday night oratory was to box the President into a corner. Party platforms traditionally lose their meaning after election victories; Carter, in office, has felt free to ignore much of the 1976 platform on which he campaigned. This year, for the first time, the Democrats have institutionalized a degree of accountability.

Within an hour of the final platform vote on Wednesday, Carter was obliged to respond in writing to the minority reports adopted. It took him two hours, which to most seemed fair enough. While skilfully sidestepping detail – notably the $12,000 million demanded by Kennedy for a job-creation programme – he was forced to endorse the spirit of several liberal economic programmes he had sought to fend off.

Kennedy's central achievement was to create an irresistible

'jobs first' mood on the convention floor. Carter, having arrived in New York with different priorities, was forced to put the reduction of unemployment above the fight against inflation. Big city bosses and labour leaders might otherwise, as they say on these occasions, have 'taken a walk'.

Campaigners for the Equal Rights Amendment also scored several platform gains, in stark contrast to the Republicans' abandonment of ERA last month. Democratic candidates who refuse active support for the amendment will now be denied party funds and other organizational support – to the President's chagrin.

The MX missile programme survived intact, to the Administration's palpable relief, despite concerted opposition. But by the close of the platform debate, Carter's victory was looking decidedly Pyrrhic. He had locked up the nomination, but he had lost control of party policy.

The depths of Carter's political trouble were clear in the presidential roll call, when Kennedy's 1,200 votes made American political history. Never had such a total been reached by a candidate not entered in nomination. Immediately beforehand, Kennedy had released his delegates to 'vote their conscience', which only drove the point home. Fewer than 100 had plumped for party unity by endorsing Carter.

For a candidate whose hopes really ended nine months ago, with the seizure of the Tehran hostages and the Soviet invasion of Afghanistan, it was a remarkable feat. As Carter cunningly rallied the nation to his side, deeming the campaign too demeaning to lure him away from the White House, Kennedy was deserted by those who had urged him into the race. Through a string of humiliating defeats, the first experienced by any member of his family, he doggedly soldiered on.

Looking back over the campaign last week, it seemed remarkable that Kennedy's candidacy had failed even before the first primary. His January foreign policy speech at Georgetown University, a month before New Hampshire, is now acknowledged as a watershed – the turning-point at which he gave up realistic hopes of victory and began to fight for traditional Democratic principles.

Until then, it is true, his campaign had been a disaster. In a series of bumbling, inarticulate interviews, he was unable to explain why he wanted to be president. He inadvertently fed resentment around the nation that he was simply out to assume an office he considered his by dynastic right. The lingering memory of Chappaquiddick, underestimated by pollsters and pundits of all persuasions, clinched a string of early defeats.

In adversity, however, Kennedy found inspiration. As the hostages remained in Tehran and the Soviets in Afghanistan, the electorate meanwhile began to wonder what was keeping Carter so busy in the rose garden. By then the President had won too many primaries, and there was no overtaking him. But Kennedy began to score a series of telling home-straight victories.

He beat the President in a string of nine states, including four of the five most populous in the nation. He carried, in the process, the north-east liberal establishment and the woebegotten big cities indispensable to a Democratic victory in November. From Pennsylvania to California, the traditionally Democratic industrial states rejected Jimmy Carter.

No wonder John Anderson was in New York last week, seeking to capitalize on the President's lukewarm support. The Empire State's influential Liberal Party seems likely to endorse the independent candidate, and New York's powerful Jewish lobby has not forgotten Carter's UN vote against Israel.

Here, as elsewhere, Anderson's presence in the race could spell victory for Reagan. Jimmy Carter's aspiration is a come-from-behind victory like that of his political hero, Harry Truman, in 1948. There is no underestimating his campaign skills and his shrewd mastery of the incumbency. Reagan's current lead over Carter in the polls will inevitably diminish as swiftly as did Carter's over Ford at this same stage four years ago.

But Truman's campaign was built on a buoyant economy, while Carter's is overshadowed by the worst slump since the 1930s. He is the first Democratic president in history to seek re-election during a recession, let alone one he has helped to create.

What has happened since Carter's election four years ago is that Roosevelt's New Deal coalition has come unstuck. Southern blacks, without whom he has no chance of re-election, are disenchanted. The Jewish community is dismayed by his inconsistency towards Israel. Hispanics throughout the South and West, America's fastest-growing ethnic minority, are alarmed by his rejection of Kennedy liberalism. Blue-collar workers in the depressed big-city states, from the Midwest to the great industrial belt of the North-East, are defecting to Reagan in droves.

The man who has just twelve weeks to win them all back is not the President himself, but his 'image adviser', Gerald Rafshoon. Carter's curly-haired Georgian crony has already contributed a word to the American language: his boss's return from the political dead these past nine months is put down to 'the rafshooning of the President'.

A Rafshoon-inspired film that introduced Carter to the podium here deftly identified the President with Jefferson, Woodrow Wilson, even John F. Kennedy. The strategy will clearly be to play down Carter's record by focusing on the prospect of Reagan. The President himself will be seen getting on with his job, while televisual appeals are made to the Democrats, America's natural ruling party, to fend off the Republican menace.

Reagan, in turn, will be making hay of the Carter presidency. It was unwise of Carter on Thursday, not to say unpresidential, to quote George Bush adversely on his running-mate. It is not so long since Ted Kennedy likened Jimmy Carter to Herbert Hoover, adding his opinion that Carter was 'Reagan's clone'. Republicans are more than capable of throwing back such sticks and stones.

The winner this autumn seems likely to be the man who most effectively makes his opponent the issue. But the decisive factor for the President may lie within his own camp – in the degree of public support, or the lack of it, he receives from Edward M. Kennedy. On this front, as on so many others, New York has not seen Candidate Carter off to a particularly auspicious start.

Observer, 17 August 1980

Aboard Carter's Campaign Plane

At 30,000 ft over northern California, chasing Air Force One towards Portland, Oregon, the presidential press plane has become Ops HQ for White House wars on two fronts.

It is Tuesday morning. Before take-off, on the tarmac at San Jose, the President has pledged American neutrality in what he calls the 'altercation' between Iraq and Iran. He has refused to elaborate on his earlier remark, repeated three times in Los Angeles, that the choice between Reagan and himself is a choice between war and peace.

'The Tolstoy issue', as it is instantly known, is on everyone's minds as typewriters are settled on knees. The Straits of Hormuz are running a poor second, though we are curious to know how far the President is prepared to go in 'upholding the principle of free passage in international waters'.

The two issues are becoming intertwined, which is the undisguised aspiration of the last man aboard, Jody Powell, the President's press secretary. He grabs the aircraft's public address system, apparently to inform us that the principal customers for Iraqi oil are, in order of importance, Brazil, Japan, France and Italy. Anything else?

Question: 'War and Peace?'

Answer: 'Tolstoy' (laughter).

Q: (from Sam Donaldson of ABC TV): 'Will the President apologize to Reagan for calling him a warmonger? It's unforgivable what he said about Reagan. Have him apologize.'

A: 'Wash your face, Sam, and we'll be glad to deal with you.' (Exit Sam.)

Q: 'Are you going to use those naval units there to keep those straits open?'

A: 'The President doesn't believe it would be productive to make comments about what steps we might take with regard to hypothetical situations . . . ', etc., etc.

Powell goes on long enough to give everyone a few 'positive' paragraphs about presidential restraints in the crisis, monitoring the situation closely, open lines from Air Force One to

Brzezinski, hostages not forgotten, White House calmly on top of things, and so on. Then:

Q: 'Does the President feel that Reagan . . . '

A: 'I guess . . . all these questions are getting at the same point, aren't they? Why don't we wait until Donaldson gets back? I'll just have to go over the whole damned thing again.'

Q: (from the lavatory): 'I can hear every word, and I want to know about the policy on Reagan.' (More laughter).

A: 'Somebody put a chain on that door, will you? Now I suppose . . . did anybody . . . what did Reagan actually say? Does anybody know?'

'That it was unforgiveable that he's being called a man who'd start a war.'

'Let me make a couple of comments on the whole situation.'

Those couple of comments take about half an hour. Seemingly forced into it, though fooling no one, Powell concedes the President's phrasing may have amounted to 'an overstatement', then proceeds to detail eight specific Reagan quotes – dating back to 1968 – urging the sending of gunboats everywhere from Angola to Cuba, Lebanon to Pakistan.

'Just so we don't miss a continent . . . dealing with Africa, June fourth 1976, Governor Reagan suggested that we either be prepared to supply troops to Rhodesia, that is provide supplies for troops in Rhodesia . . . or that we go in with American troops to ensure an orderly transition. AND there's another great one here too. Ah, yes Cyprus, in June of 1976 . . .'

Powell is reading from the *Oops Book*, an official White House document cataloguing outlandish Reaganisms right back to his Hollywood days: President and his campaign staff, for the use of. He's got the lads hungry for more. They're eating out of his hand. Even the photographers are listening.

'You said you had *eight* of them? . . . Give us Ecuador again . . . what's the citation on that? . . . *St Louis Globe-Democrat*? . . . when? . . . a military presence in the *Sinai*? . . . when'd he say *that*? Look, Jody, why don't you just give us a copy of that thing?'

'Because it's got some other things on here I don't want to hand out.'

'Well, just get Carolyn or Connie to type it up, would you?'

Carolyn and Connie are at present trailing up and down the

aisle dishing out 'background stuff', transcripts of speeches, presidential statements and other goodies. All are headed: 'For immediate release. From the Office of the White House Press Secretary.' Ten minutes later, after another furious burst of the airborne photocopier, they are back with another, this one without the heading. It lists all those Reagan 'declarations of war', with dates and sources duly footnoted.

As the typewriters clatter, Powell wanders up and down the aisle, pausing for brief words, exchanging smiles of recognition, looking over people's shoulders as they work, like a fond invigilator helping his pupils through an exam. He's fixed an hour's break in Portland, so that Reagan's murky past may be comprehensively transmitted to the world's great newspapers.

A good day's work well done. The President will be pleased.

Back aloft, amid the home-bound poker games, a consensus has been reached. No one ever thought Carter was going to win Washington anyway. Or Oregon. And he doesn't seem likely to win California – which is where, along with five other big-city states, notably Texas and New York, the election will be decided. Without the Reagan stuff, despite the war, there'd have been no story.

Even the presence of Senator Edward Kennedy, giving Carter a lukewarm endorsement in a Beverly Hills hotel, had injected little excitement. After some good one-liners from Governor Jerry Brown, who had then turned his back on the President, Kennedy shifted from foot to foot as he tried to sound enthusiastic. Afterwards, in private, he was much keener to talk about sailing than his next campaign appearance for Carter.

Andrews Air Force Base, Maryland: wheels down at 3.10 am. With 5,629 miles and almost as many speeches, it seems, logged in just forty hours, it's back to the White House for a council of war. But which war? The one in the Gulf, which America may yet have to police? Or the one supposedly fermenting in the mind of Ronald Reagan?

The President has been out to meet the people. He has again told them little of himself, much of his opponent. It's his only hope of winning the war.

Observer, 28 September 1980

117

The Panicky President

The President, before our very eyes, is panicking. Like a man drowning in front of 200 million people, few of whom seem inclined to throw him a lifebelt, he is thrashing around desperately for something, anything, to cling to.

He knows, with four weeks to go, that he is losing this election. His attacks on Ronald Reagan have produced merely counter-attacks, from all sides, even his own. He does not understand why. He is a man visibly baffled, bruised, angry. In a talk to party workers in Chicago last Monday, the frustration was showing through.

'This is my last campaign, the last policical race I will ever run.' He has departed from his text. He is growing rather emotional. 'I do not intend for it to end by turning over the government of the United States to people whose political philosophies and views about this country are directly contrary to everything in which I believe with all my heart and soul.'

Stirring stuff, but the applause is somewhat embarrassed. Clearly, he's not finished yet. White House aides shoot each other nervous glances. 'You will determine', he tells the TV cameras rather than the audience, 'whether or not this America will be unified – or, if I lose the election, whether Americans might be separated, black from white, Jew from Christian, North from South, rural and urban . . . '

He has gone too far. This is distinctly unpresidential behaviour. Please – you can hear the silent prayers of the President's men – please don't let him say 'war and peace' again.

' . . . whether this nation will be guided from a sense of long-range commitment to peace . . . whether our adversaries will be tempted to end the peace for which we all pray.'

Oh, no! Reagan's going to make hay with this one.

For days, weeks now, Carter's most intimate advisers – primarily Vice-President Walter Mondale, Hamilton Jordan and Robert Strauss – have been pleading with him to stop all this. He is chipping away at his major remaining political asset: the popular perception that, whatever kind of president he has been, he remains a decent and moral man. Jimmy Who has become Jimmy Mean. It's not the way to win.

Next morning, sure enough, Reagan handles it like the old trouper he is. Ambling over with apparent reluctance, he smiles sadly and shakes his head. 'No, I can't be angry. I'm just saddened that anyone, particularly someone who has held that position, could intimate such a thing.'

Another shake of the head, this one on behalf of his fellow Americans, a weary sigh and a slight Hollywood choke in the voice: 'No, I'm not asking for an apology from him. I know who I have to account to for my actions. But I think he owes the country an apology.' That's all he wants to say. He must be off, every inch a president-in-waiting, to talk about the issues.

Carter's attacks on Reagan – simpleton, racist, warmonger – were intended to sting his opponent into angry, unguarded, over-the-top reply. The strategy has not worked. Cumulatively, it has rebounded on the President. He has put himself, rather than his opponent, on the defensive.

The trouble is that Jimmy Carter knows no other way to campaign. In his races for the state senate and the governorship of Georgia, he relied on beneath-the-belt attacks on his opponents – notably the overtly racist ploy of distributing photographs of his liberal Democratic rival with his arm around a black athlete.

By taking what the American news magazines love to call 'the low road', Carter merely gives Reagan daily opportunities to turn the other cheek, and thus to avoid defending his less defensible positions. The irony is that the President still stands every chance of defeating his opponent on 4 November, if only he would use the remaining month to stress – with appropriate dignity – the vast ideological gulf between them.

The two men, at root, have classically opposed views of America, which draw on different strains in the national character. Theodore H. White, the historian of the presidency, sums up the 1980 contest as 'the sheriff versus the preacher'. His neat formula, for all its complex corollaries, can be expounded in one sentence per candidate.

Ronald Reagan, champion of the 'or else' approach to US foreign policy, believes in rebuilding and flexing American muscle in aggressive pursuit of its national interests around the world. Jimmy Carter, by contrast, sees the United States as a moral exemplar, dependent on its military and economic might for a conspicuous display of global restraint.

It thus ill behoves Carter to abandon all morality on the campaign trail. Last Wednesday, at last, he seemed to realize this, and poured his heart out to Barbara Walters on ABC TV. Conceding that he had got 'carried away on a couple of occasions', that some of his remarks were 'probably ill-advised', he had decided, he told Barbara, to put his campaign 'back on track' by eschewing personal attacks on Reagan.

So next day he took the high road to Nashville, Tennessee, where he promptly accused 'my opponent' of wanting to start a nuclear arms race. He got out his *Oops Book* of Reagan gaffes and began reciting old, hoary Reagan chestnuts about gunboat diplomacy and welfare scroungers.

Raising the level of his campaign, it seems, meant continuing the personal abuse without actually mentioning Reagan by name.

Back in Washington, the President's staff hit new lows of despair. 'Accentuate the positive' – the White House prayer mats are out again – 'eliminate the negative'. But no, Carter seems psychologically incapable of containing his pent-up bile, his deep personal hurt that the nation could think of deserting him for a California cowboy.

Observer, 12 October 1980

Aboard Reagan's Campaign Plane

The President has accused me of being irresponsible. Well, I'll confess to being irresponsible if he'll admit to being responsible . . .

He says I don't know the difference between a recession and a depression. Well, I'll tell you. A recession is when your neighbour loses his job. A depression is when you lose your job. And recovery will begin when Jimmy Carter loses his job.

We are in Reagan country with the man himself. In Idaho Falls, Idaho, a packed audience of the faithful is soaking up every syllable of its master's voice, raising the high-school rafters at every full stop. Suddenly, from nowhere, a dark-coated stranger is running towards the podium, shouting: 'Reagan! Hey, Reagan! I've got something for you here!'

The hall freezes, as does the would-be president. There is an uncertain, appalled moment before the secret service heavies fall on the intruder like hounds on a hare. He is swept, feet off the ground, through the nearest exit, his voice still ringing around the hushed hall: 'No, no. You've got me wrong. I've got a letter for him. I've got a letter for Governor Reagan.'

The crowd looks back to the podium, as if for reassurance. Reagan smiles. 'Well,' he says, 'despite all that I'll bet his letter gets to me quicker than it would through the post office.'

The hall erupts; even the remaining secret service men, who model their smiles on those of the guards outside Buckingham Palace, register a visible flicker of amusement. The travelling press corps, long weary of Reagan's standard one-liners, stand to applaud a rare moment of spontaneity. The candidate wears his most modest, aw-shucks grin.

From the outside, on the surface, the Ronald Reagan election machine is ticking along on schedule, exuding good-humoured

121

self-confidence in the face of the worst the White House can throw at it.

Reagan's easy manner on the campaign trail helps; he has come to be perceived as Mr Nice Guy, the warmest, most human of the three candidates. He also knows he is the most adept at manipulating his audience, whether on television or in the flesh.

But inside his travelling circus, as it hopped its way eastwards through eight states last week, there arose a note of anxiety. They have wrapped their man in mothballs all this time, persuaded him to play it safe, avoid specifics, protect his slender lead. Now there are two weeks to go, and Carter – as is the way of incumbents – is closing on them.

The President's politics of abuse may have backfired on him, but they have worked their murky magic. The charges of 'racism' have registered in the black community, crucial to Carter's re-election. The charges of 'warmonger' have registered strongly, it seems, among women voters, who constitute 51 per cent of the electorate. Timely federal hand-outs to the depressed industrial states are improving the President's standing in his private polls.

Off-stage, Reagan concedes that he has two danger zones, which Carter is effectively exploiting. He has to work hard to assuage an ill-defined but pervasive fear of a Reagan presidency skilfully planted by the White House.

Hence his proclamation on Monday, in his first press conference for more than a month, that 'I would consider war the last – the *last* – resort, and that our mission in the world is to protect the peace.'

And he has to woo women voters, angered by the Republican manifesto's abandonment of the Equal Rights Amendment. Reagan's week therefore began with the announcement, plucked like a rabbit from a hat, that he intends to be the first American president to appoint a woman to the Supreme Court.

As John Anderson's support ebbs – from 16 to 9 per cent in two weeks – so Carter's grows. Above all, from Reagan's point of view, the huge number of undecided voters – perhaps even a third of the electorate, unusually high at this late stage of a campaign – must tell against him. People tend, at the last moment, to vote for the devil they know.

Aboard Reagan's Campaign Plane

Each time Reagan's campaign plane – dubbed Leadership 80 – takes off, the indefatigable Nancy Reagan struggles cheerfully from her seat and grabs hold of an orange. As the aircraft climbs steeply, she takes a professional tenpin bowler's run-up and despatches the long-suffering fruit down the aisle of the 727 – the object being to hit the rear door without veering off course beneath the press seats. Nine times out of ten, she succeeds.

Nancy's orange-roll has become a ritual. To at least one of her husband's staff, it has also become a metaphor for the campaign. 'We're sticking, day after day, to the tricks we know. We're pleasing our own people, not winning enough converts. Maybe it's time to take some risks. Go out on a limb, not cling all the time to that centre aisle.'

It was metaphysical stuff, late at night, in yet another Holiday Inn – this one somewhere in South Dakota. But he had a point. 'What the hell are we doing in South Dakota, trying to help some guy unseat George McGovern? We've long since sewn up South Dakota. It's no use unseating McGovern without beating Carter.'

Reagan's lead is slender, and delicately poised. The nation waits, say newspapers wherever one goes, upon the dramatic last-minute surprise the President will surely spring. The numbers game, in which commentators delight, will be fought 'right down to the wire'.

Yet the evidence, as I begin an election-eve Odyssey around these key states, is that the electorate is not quite so excited. Political meetings are poorly attended, people yawn when you pop the question around Main Street, bumper stickers – the traditional index of voter interest – are very few and far between.

The American people may yet make their point on 4 November by registering a less than 50 per cent turnout – thus withdrawing, in effect, their consent to be governed by any of the presidential candidates offering their services for the 1980s.

Observer, 19 October 1980

123

Dazed Washington Packs its Bags

The morning after the night before, President Carter invited journalists into the Oval Office for a long, rambling, melancholy meditation. The White House was like a tomb, its red-eyed mourners reluctant to show their faces, but the outgoing President remained defiant to the last.

He did not, he insisted, feel personally rejected by the electorate. 'History will show that I never flinched in dealing with the issues . . . . I don't know of anything that could have been done better or differently. . . . Whether anybody could do more in the future, I can't say.' And so to Camp David.

It may not prove Jimmy Carter's last disagreement with the American people – he still has ten more weeks in office – but it must surely rank among his most fundamental. Tuesday's historic Republican landslide was a wholesale repudiation not just of Carter, but of the post-war Democratic tradition entrusted to his care. Ronald Reagan comes to power with one of the most dramatic conservative mandates in American history.

Like Carter in 1976, Reagan was elected by barely 26 per cent of the potential electorate. Unlike 1976, however, the victor's support was as broad as it was deep. He carried forty-four of the fifty states, giving him an Electoral College majority of ten to one.

Twenty-five per cent of Democrats and 52 per cent of independents voted for Reagan. He carried organized labour, other blue-collar workers, Catholics and Protestants, his native West, Carter's native South, the rural Midwest, the industrial North-East, most of the traditionally liberal East Coast establishment.

By next afternoon even Massachusetts, home of the Kennedys, the only state in the union never before to have voted for a Republican presidential candidate, had fallen to Reagan.

He brings with him to Washington, on his presidential coat-tails, the first Republican-controlled Senate for a generation.

The nation's capital is still reeling this weekend. Some 2,700 presidential appointees are packing their bags – but so, to their astonishment, are several thousand more Capitol Hill staff. Many have survived recent White House handovers, but nothing like this. Even the Eisenhower landslide of 1952, say the veterans, pales by comparison.

Pollsters, pundits, even the candidates themselves all under-estimated the nation's readiness to desert an incumbent president so overwhelmingly. But it was only in the last seventy-two hours of the campaign, it seems, that Americans finally summoned the courage to do so. As last weekend began, both camps agree, Reagan had a clear but undramatic edge.

Then came Sunday morning's news from Iran, the President's dawn flight back to Washington, his eleventh-hour broadcast to the nation that evening. He waxed cautious but hopeful. Next morning, as if he had never left it, he was back on the campaign trail.

If voters needed a final excuse to desert Jimmy Carter, he himself had provided it. It was not so much another frustration of hopes about the hostages as another demonstration of American impotence overseas. It set the Carter years in stark and damaging focus. Twenty-four hours later the President's own soothsayer, Patrick Caddell, knew he was going to lose by 8 percentage points.

The news was broken, aboard Air Force One, by Jody Powell. Carter broke down and wept. Later that morning he wept again, in front of his own kith and kin, in Plains. That night, at 9.50 pm Eastern time, he became the first president in American history to concede defeat before the polls had even closed.

This last, heedless act was symbolic of Carter's distance from his own party, the Democratic coalition which had elected him in 1976, and to which he had done such grievous electoral harm. By yielding to Reagan while the West Coast was still voting, Carter probably cost the Congress such Democratic stalwarts as Al Ullman of Washington state, chairman of the powerful House Ways and Means Committee.

The history books were quickly out, confirming the feeling

that an epoch-making sea-change had taken place. No elected incumbent has been deposed since Herbert Hoover's humiliation at the hands of Franklin D. Roosevelt in 1932. The last Democratic president to be denied re-election was Grover Cleveland in 1888 – and even he won a majority of the popular vote.

It is Roosevelt's legacy, ironically enough, which Reagan believes he has a clear mandate to demolish. This sometime New Deal Democrat, whose father was saved from bankruptcy by Roosevelt's work programme, who has quoted FDR extensively even in the 1980 campaign, will now set earnestly about 'getting the Government off the backs of the American people, and setting you loose to do what you've done so well for 200 years'.

He will enjoy, moreover, a degree of congressional support which surprised no one so much as the President-elect. Tuesday's Senate and House results were, if possible, even more striking than the presidential rout. A quarter of a century of liberal American democracy was killed stone dead overnight.

There were anomalies, special local circumstances, and some of those who fell were more post-Vietnam neo-liberals than warmed-up New Dealers. But the roll-call of ousted senators includes nearly all the liberal standard-bearers: McGovern, Culver, Bayh, Church, Durkin, Magnuson, Nelson. Edward Kennedy, who loses his Judiciary Committee chairmanship to a pillar of right-wing Republicanism, Strom Thurmond, is going to be a very lonely man in the ninety-seventh Congress.

'Not a landslide, an earthquake' was the verdict of Senator Howard Baker, once Reagan's opponent for the Republican nomination, now a wide-eyed Senate majority leader-in-waiting. A net gain of thirty-five seats in the House of Representatives – the biggest advance by a party out of power for more than fifty years – will also boost President Reagan's legislative clout.

The initial effects should be felt very quickly. As of 20 January, when he will be sworn in as the fortieth president, Reagan will impose an immediate freeze on federal hiring, and introduce his first 10 per cent across-the-board tax cut (due to be the first of three amounting to 30 per cent over three years).

His transition team, already established in smart offices on Washington's M Street, will be looking at the practicality of abolishing two federal bureaucracies: the Departments of Energy and Education, established as separate entities by Carter. Government waste is to be ruthlessly pruned. Phased reductions in federal spending will be one of the first tests of the new President's support from the new Congress.

All eyes in Washington are turned apprehensively towards M Street. The capital has taken the election result very personally, amounting as it does to a national indictment of the federal bureaucracy. The new Senate chairmen are already murmuring darkly about drastic staff reductions. Social life in Washington is expected to be much brighter under the Reagans, but fewer are going to be around here to enjoy it.

Nationally, the most apprehensive Americans are the ethnic minorities: blacks, Hispanics and other low-income, high-unemployment groups who were the only voters to stay solidly with Carter. It seems likely that recent British experience will now be repeated here on a larger scale. Unemployment will be allowed to rise, federal aid to business will be curtailed. Keynesian economics, US-style, were also pronounced dead on Tuesday night. Among those rejoicing was Reagan's fellow Californian, Milton Friedman.

The magnitude of the economic problems facing the new Administration became even more apparent after the election, with Thursday's new rise in the prime interest rate, and Friday's gloomy unemployment and wholesale price figures. Wednesday's record-breaking response on the New York stock exchange, however, reflected the universal enthusiasm for Reagan among captains of industry and big business.

At his first post-election press conference on Thursday, Reagan said he would make the economy – 'the major issue of the campaign' – his top priority. Foreign policy, the area of his least experience and expertise, will be slower to realign.

The most immediate prospects are a sharp increase in defence spending and the formal shelving of SALT II. Some hapless Reagan emissary will soon be en route to Moscow, to talk renegotiation, and no doubt to receive the same cursory rebuff accorded the new Secretary of State, Cyrus Vance, in March 1977.

Both during and since the campaign, Reagan has managed to escape specifics, beyond his reluctance to sell arms to China and his apparent willingness to base US troops in Israel. His quest for the presidency, however, forced him to moderate many of his once hard-line views.

It seems clear that the United States will return broadly to its immediate post-war philosophy: containment of Soviet expansion as the dominant goal, all other foreign policy issues to be seen through the prism of US-USSR relations. In saying on Thursday 'I believe in linkage', Reagan was espousing the Kissinger doctrine of relating arms negotiations to the current state of Soviet adventurism.

Against this backdrop, as yet undefined 'pressures' are to be brought on Cuba, and on Marxist-leaning regimes in South America and the Third World. Israel, it is thought, will be given pre-eminence in continuing Middle East negotiations, again as an anti-Soviet bastion.

The role of human rights in foreign policy-making will diminish. In all other respects, however, Reagan will wish to be seen to have learnt from Carter's mistakes. He promises above all 'consistency and consultation' in re-strengthening the Western alliance, and is determined to avoid conflict between his Secretary of State and his National Security Adviser.

Reagan's Cabinet appointments, due in three to four weeks, will thus be his first major test. On the domestic front, he is keen to draw talent from business and industry – 'men', as he has long put it, 'who have nothing personal to gain indeed plenty to lose financially, by entering public service'.

As the guessing game begins, and the struggle for power develops, a certain friction has already become apparent between the survivors of the Nixon-Ford era and Reagan's 'California Mafia'. The Governor, as his staff still call him (they are busy practising 'President-elect'), is said to consider this healthy. If so, it is an encouraging sign that Reagan will attempt to be responsive to the remarkable diversity of political groupings which elected him.

The great asset of Reagan's electoral landslide is that no one single-interest group – notably the anti-abortion lobby or the fundamentalist evangelicals – can claim responsibility. He was none too reassuring about his freedom from such influences at his Thursday press conference, but perhaps honeymoon indulgence may attribute this to post-electoral shock. When he said he would consult the 'moral majority' on his Cabinet appointments, Reagan evidently thought he was still campaigning.

One-term president or not, Reagan knows that he has a chance to seize the nation's conservative mood, perhaps win the rest of Congress for his party in the mid-term elections, and transform the minority Republican Party into the dominant force in the American Electoral College.

To achieve that, he must spurn the advances of his party's extremists and chart a careful, compromising course. That, from all we know of him, is in his nature. And that, given all we don't know, must remain an interim reassurance to the waiting world.

Observer, 9 November 1980

God Save America

Elizabeth Taylor is in, Dolly Parton is out. Frank Sinatra is in, Kirk Douglas is out. Steak barbecues are in, chicken barbecues out. Black ties are back, blue jeans . . . well, I never owned a pair myself. So *hick*, you know. Yessir, Mr President.

The reason for all these abrupt, Mitfordesque changes of loyalty is, of course, that Ronald Reagan is in and Jimmy Carter is out. We're going through what's known as a transition here in Washington – otherwise known as an *inter-reaganum* – and the smart set are scrambling to realign four years of accumulated tastes, attitudes and wardrobes overnight.

If you want to make your mark in Reagan's Washington – and *hurry, hurry,* there's only two months till the inaugural ball – commit to heart the following precepts . . .

1. Old is beautiful. If you're under fifty, tear up those transatlantic tickets and head East. This town has had it with young things, throwing their Georgian weight about. If you can't afford the plastic surgery, just be polite to your elders. They know best.

2. Rich is beautiful. Prime beneficiaries of the election results were Washington's realtors: the California Mafia aren't interested in anything under $4,000 a month. Private means are in, *nouveaux riches* out. If you can't afford the heat, stay out of the kitchen.

3. Elegance is back. The days of studied nonchalance are over. Sell shares in corduroy, cardigans, sneakers, T-shirts and baseball caps. Buy a white tie, dust off your top hat and tails. No more loosening of ties or top buttons. Cuff-links are in. For the ladies: pink is in (but be careful, it's Nancy's favourite colour). Black velvet or wool flannel in winter – anything by Chanel is fine, but all jewellery *must* be genuine, please.

4. Booze is back (well, Dean Martin's going to be a White

130

House regular). If you must stick to wine, make sure it's Californian.

5.   Food. The President-elect's favourite, if he's just popping round informally, is macaroni cheese. Otherwise stick to veal, not too fancy, followed by chocolate mousse. Genuine silver-ware and crystal glasses, please. Nancy will take careful note of the floral arrangements. Candlelight *va sans dire*.

Chockies are in, calorie-lovers. Nancy loves them. All kinds of sweets, éclairs, ice-cream and candy . . .'though she never', says a friend, 'gains a pound. Disgusting.'

The second time they drop by, vary the macaroni with a little Knackwurst, corned beef and cabbage, steak pizzaiola, fresh fruit and plenty of salad – though not all at once. Small portions are in.

If the President drops off, leave him be. He's earned his nap. Keep a bag of Jellybeans handy – he likes to play with them while he's talking, and apparently reaches for them even in his sleep.

6.   Jogging is out. Get a horse.

7.   Get a Virginia estate to keep it on.

8.   Join a hunt (apply for details at your country club).

9.   Always read your horoscope, and check it against Aquarius (Reagan's sign). He studies his every morning, and bears it in mind when confronted with a spot of decision-making. Watch out, therefore, for KGB moles in the astrological community. No more scoffing/yawning/groaning when asked your star sign at Georgetown parties. Mug up on Lady Luck. Pollsters are out, crystal balls in. Study palmistry, dust off the ouija board and hope for the best.

10.   Religion is in, but you must be born again. Born-again nostalgia won't do you any harm either. Memorize the words of 'Star-Spangled Banner' and Lincoln's Gettysburg Address. Use the phrase 'a shining city on a hill' whenever discussing your vision for the country. Practise generalizations.

11.   Capital punishment is in, abortion out. Sorry about this, but Ted Kennedy's not going to be too much in evidence for a while. Practise saying 'Strom Thurmond' after three martinis.

12.   People. Well, I need hardly say that the Sinatra-Martin-Davis Jr axis is right back. You always loved 'em, eh,

with their cute little backslapping triple-act, their Beverly Sisters innocence, their untrumpeted work for charity, their generosity with autographs. They might even play the White House for free.

William Holden is in. He was Ron and Nancy's best man. Anyone changing his surname by deed poll will be hearing from my lawyers.

John 'Dook' Wayne. A minute's silence, please, at any mention of his name.

Of the old Hollywood gang – all of whom are just swell – particular favourites are Jimmy Stewart (attend all revivals of *Mr Smith goes to Washington*) and Bob Hope. Charlton Heston – 'Chuck' to you and me – campaigned for Ron. So did Roy Rogers (though wear cowboy hats sparingly).

President Ford is in, Nixon on his way back. The Plains retiree is never mentioned by name. Quote FDR and 'Jack' Kennedy, the only okay Democrats. Henry Kissinger is in, but be careful.

Never, never, never mention Oscar-winning actress Jane Wyman, especially to Nancy. If you don't know why, then stay away until you can find someone who'll tell you.

13.   A few tips on talking to the President: address his left ear (the right one's been deaf for some time. And you do, without any smirking, believe his explanation that someone let loose a Colt 45 right next to it in his Hollywood days. *Without smirking*, I said).

Never say he didn't get the girl. He *always* got the girl. Try to catch *Hellcats of the Navy*, so you can compliment him on the scene with Nancy. Say you think *King's Row* was his finest role, a film sorely underrated by history. Moan about the old studio moguls, and the way they type-cast B-movies' romantic leads. Don't make any comparison between pre-war Hollywood and contemporary politics.

Don't be caught peering at the roots of his hair.

Tell him you weep each week over *Little House on the Prairie*. (He does.) Don't go on about how hard you work (you should always be home with your family by six, even if in government). Don't boast about getting up early. Tell him how much you agree that a quick kip or two is essential for getting through a heavy day.

If you're a foreign leader, don't invite him to pay a return visit. Say you'd rather come back to America. Your country's pretty dull anyway – they're all the same, really, aren't they? – and you know how much he hates flying. You, too, hanker for the days when the President of the United States never left its shores.

Don't inquire too closely after his children (they won't be much in evidence). If you went to the ballet in New York, don't say so. Try not to mention the words *divorce* or *Oscar*.

And keep it short. He's a busy man. He's got a country to get others to run.

Punch, 19 November 1980

The Remaking of the Presidency

Twenty-eight years ago this weekend, President Harry Truman sat in the Oval Office and pondered the fate of the man about to succeed him, Dwight Eisenhower. 'He'll sit here in this office,' said Truman, 'and he'll say "do this, do that". And nothing will happen.'

Jimmy Carter seemed to echo that remark on Wednesday, in his dispirited farewell address, when he spoke of the presidency as 'at once the most powerful office in the world, and among the most severely constrained by law and custom'. Of all recent presidents, Carter can testify with most feeling to saying 'do this, do that' and then watching nothing happen.

Ronald Reagan, throughout his campaign, was careful to acknowledge 'the limits of the presidency'. Since his election, moreover, he has avoided making grandiose promises on which he might not be able to deliver. He has avoided saying very much at all, preferring to be seen out of focus, from a distance, as an ill-defined beacon of hope.

But Reagan has now, with evident reluctance, been compelled at last to quit the balmy California sun for arctic Washington, where he will find the political climate quite as nippy. After the ringing phrases of his inaugural address on Tuesday, he will be looked to for specifics. We are unlikely to hear any until an early problem – the domestic economy, perhaps, or El Salvador, or Namibia – boxes him into a corner.

All this week Reagan will be the centre-piece of a massive celebration in the nation's capital; no less than a coronation – at $12 million, the most lavish inaugural in history. He will see his face in fireworks, surmounting the Stars and Stripes. He will see it on inaugural medals, on postage stamps, on lapel buttons, posters and biscuit tins. He may develop delusions of grandeur.

But the parades, banquets, balls and galas will be celebrating a sea-change in American politics as much as the deification, Roman emperor-style, of one particular mortal. This week's junketings – more is to be spent on fireworks alone than was for the 1976 bicentennial celebrations – are being stage-managed by the Republican high command, to mark its return to power on Capitol Hill after a generation in the wilderness.

Reagan has not demurred, because he is anxious to return to the presidency the loftiness and prestige it has surrendered to Watergate and Carter populism. The President-elect is well aware that he is to be head of state as much as chief executive – and the Carter years have shown that Americans no more want to see their president carrying his own suitcase than would most Britons the Queen.

There is a fashionable view in Washington that Reagan intends to act *more* as a head of state than chief executive, attending to the ritual functions of his office while leaving the dirty work to his lieutenants. He will, the theory goes, make 'Silent' Cal Coolidge look like a chatterbox, Eisenhower like a tireless workaholic.

There are also those who think this would be no bad thing. 'The more time Reagan spends asleep,' said one last week, 'the happier I will be.' He was not entirely joking. He was making the same point, approvingly, as does Zbigniew Brzezinski in his interview with the *Observer* today: that Reagan will be one of the 'more passive presidents, who dispose and preside', in the tradition of Eisenhower and Ford.

The United States has voted for respite from what Brzezinski calls 'the activist style' of presidency, the tradition of Roosevelt, Kennedy, Nixon and Carter. The clearest Republican mandate to emerge from their electoral landslide was for less government, less state interference in the nation's public and private lives.

On the evidence so far, his leisurely selection of his Cabinet, Reagan certainly seems to aspire to the style of minimal, remote-control government he practised in California. The ten weeks since the election have underlined three familiar Reagan hallmarks, as summarized by one of his biographers, Lou Cannon: 'His seeming detachment from the daily business of government, his proclivity for balancing conflicting constituencies, and a somewhat contradictory tendency to cling stubbornly to a pet notion or appointment.'

The overwhelmingly male, white, middle-aged, prosperous Cabinet nominees do indeed augur a period of 'passive' (not to say boring) government. The 'Reaganauts' are otherwise a judicious mix of loyalists, cronies, Nixon-Ford 'retreads' and token gestures to minority special interests. But their confirmation hearings demonstrated a loyal capacity to speak as one, and to articulate their master's voice in rather more detail than perhaps he himself could muster.

Reagan's pragmatism has also been conspicuous, and has come as a surprise – often a pleasant one – to those who cast him as an inflexible ideologue. The list of campaign promises on which he has retreated or reneged grows more comprehensive by the day: an immediate tax cut, a balanced budget by 1982, a quantum increase in defence spending, the non-bailing-out of lame ducks, the dismantling of the Department of Energy and Education.

On the domestic front, Reagan has asserted his authority by squelching all talk from his Budget Director, thirty-four-year-old fiscal whizz-kid Dave Stockman, of declaring a state of economic emergency on taking office. 'The keynote', as one staffer put it, 'will be firm but not frantic steps forward.'

In foreign affairs, the Carter-Reagan transition is starkly symbolized by an anxious public debate on human rights, whose very own State Department bureau the new President seems inclined to close down. Alexander Haig, in his appearances before the Senate, made it clear that his State Department will be severely downgrading such considerations in foreign policy-making.

A small group of us thrashed the matter out over dinner last week with Professor Jeanne Kirkpatrick, Reagan's choice for UN ambassador, the only woman and the only Democrat in the new Cabinet. Of many historical, topical or hypothetical instances raised, from Cambodia via South Africa to Latin America, there was not one in which she thought moral values should be allowed to interfere with 'prudential judgements'.

This dire prospect apart, there is scant evidence to suggest what stamp, if any, Ronald Reagan will leave on his nation and the world. If he does, as his many supporters devoutly expect, prove one of those presidents who lends his name to an epoch, it will probably be less through political action or ideology than through his managerial and communicating skills.

Reagan has divined that the contemporary American presidency is as much a matter of style as political substance. (Poor Jimmy Carter, he of the lounge suit and the walk home to the White House, will have to struggle into a morning coat for his political funeral on Tuesday; like everyone else, he has his instructions.) The outward show – be it the silver trumpets at state banquets, or a square jaw on the nation's TV screens – can often transcend the difficulties of the moment.

Nothing has demonstrated the potential of this approach so emphatically as Reagan's own presidential campaign, in which a swaggering gait and a vague ideology masked the need for any substantive thought. Now the new President wants to help the nation follow his example, and walk tall.

Reagan is given less chance to repair the economy or restore the strategic balance than he is to rekindle the spirit of a nation jaded with itself, its government and its faltering role in the world. His inaugural address could well quote Samuel Johnson: 'Where there is no hope, there is no endeavour.' Replenish that hope, he seems to think, and the rest will follow.

That is the kind of new epoch to which Reagan would like to lend his name. For the rest, he will be only too happy if Harry Truman is proved right, and nothing much happens.

Observer, 18 January 1981

Invasion of the Reaganauts

The great and good Mr Henry Fairlie, regarded hereabouts as one of Britain's better-quality exports, has a fond memory of a walk through London some years ago with his friend Gerard Fay, the then London editor of the *Manchester Guardian*. They were about to cross the street when a large Rolls-Royce purred to a halt directly across their path. Mr Fay, who carried a cane as the result of a war wound, raised this handy weapon on high and without hesitation smote the offending vehicle across its bonnet not once but twice, and then a third time.

There have been many occasions just lately, during the inaugural binge for Ronald Reagan, when one coveted both Mr Fay's cane and his guts. The streets of Washington are choked with long, sleek black limousines carrying chic Californians from ball to gala to banquet and back to ball, ever heedless of the attempts at forward movement of the merely indigenous population.

The whole town smelt of money and still does. On 21 January, the day after Mr Reagan took up residence in the White House, the air shuttle from New York got stuck an hour behind schedule, so great was the number of private and corporate jets taking off from Washington's National Airport. Mrs Reagan's inaugural gowns cost her $25,000.

The whole bonanza totted up to $12 million – the most expensive, needless to say, in history – which will be recouped through the sale of inaugural souvenirs, available until 31 March. For a mere $1,050, you can obtain Tiffany's sterling silver bowl, fully six inches in diameter, embossed with the official presidential seal in God-knows-how-many-carat gold. If that sounds a bit tacky, try the nine-inch-high, 'hand-crafted' porcelain American bald eagle, specially created for the occasion by Edward Marshall Boehm Studios Inc.–a snip at $1,200.

Or there's the cut-crystal inaugural paperweight, all three prismatic inches of it, for $950. It is assumed, natch, that you've already snapped up an inaugural medal – every home should have one – bearing Reagan's craggy features in solid gold for $975. Add $12 for delivery.

At first, I confess, I got rather caught up in the spirit of the thing. Well, the kids were enjoying the parade and the fireworks, and I thought the wife might like an inaugural scarf, an inaugural umbrella, a set of inaugural coasters complete with ice bucket, perhaps even an exact replica of the First Lady's inaugural pendant – quiet at the back, of course it's gold – for a little over a month's salary. No thank you, said the wife, I don't want Reagan's ugly mug plastered all over the house.

Not even an inaugural mug? My spirits were a trifle dashed. It was history in the making. The *New York·Times* thought its inaugural front page so memorable that it offered framed, silver-plated versions of it to hand down to your grandchildren. I considered suggesting to the *Observer* that it market my inaugural Reagan profile in a fetching tin-foil scroll, tied with yellow ribbon to mark the contemporaneous release of the hostages. The wife and Mr Fairlie, cruel only to be kind, stayed my hand.

Ever since, all over town, I've seen camels walking through the eyes of needles. Restaurants forced near closure by the Carter years now require lunch reservations a week in advance. Motorcades scud this way and that, some of the back-up cars apparently crammed with dollar bills. The President meal-hops from swanky club to swankier club, his entourage trailing sandalwood perfume in their wake. If this isn't Heaven, they must think, it comes pretty damn close.

The British Embassy is all a-quiver, because Reagan is going to dinner there with Mrs Thatcher on 26 February. (At the end of this piece, there will be a whip-round for my top hat, white tie and tails.) It is some years since a president of the United States went to dinner at the British Embassy. But Reagan is intent on having a good time – and he's perhaps heard that Lady (Mary) Henderson's cuisine is the best in town.

It can't last, of course (Reagan's good time, not Lady Henderson's cuisine). The pomp and circumstance of his first few hours in office are designed to impress upon a new president that it's quite a job he's got himself there, and that the nation is right behind him for a good twenty-four hours.

Reagan saw his face in fireworks, rode in triumph through a

packed and cheering throng, and attended ten balls and ump-teen parties in his honour. At the end of the day, he is said to have sat down behind his desk in the Oval Office and declared: 'Well, I really enjoyed that. Now can I go back to California?'

Alas not, Mr President. Your honeymoon has been unusu-ally extended by the jubilant return home of the Tehran host-ages, but the coming weeks will see the enactment of certain other traditional rituals, designed to wipe away the heady memories of inaugural week, and to deter any Julius Caesar-like thoughts about coronations in the Capitol. Nor does the Constitution provide, as you may currently be assuming, for the deification of presidents.

Before you know it, sir, the Congress will have rejected your very first budget. House Democrats have already been rather rude to most of your Cabinet appointees; soon they'll be trying to interfere with their efficient execution of your orders. By April, and cherry-blossom time, the opinion polls may reflect a new public consensus that maybe Jimmy Carter wasn't such a bad thing after all.

It's up to you, Mr President, to prove otherwise. A good start might be to caution your Californian cronies, ever so gently, that they are endearing themselves to Washington just about as much as did Carter's Georgian Mafia four years ago. If any-thing, the tiaras, Halston gowns and Gucci shoes are even less welcome than the beer cans, flat-bed trucks and good ol' boys' deleted expletives.

This just ain't a town that welcomes strangers. No, siree, especially when those strangers seem to think that excessive amounts of money can purchase the right to talk drivel at dinner parties, let alone a seat in the councils of government.

They're not doing you any good, Mr President. They're get-ting on the backs of people who have lived in this town all their lives, and who have *earned* the right to voice an opinion on the future course of the free world. Even Liz Taylor had the grace to marry a senator. If I were you, sir, I'd say to these people what you said all those years ago to Errol Flynn, somewhere along the Santa Fe Trail: 'There ain't room for the both of us in this town. One of us has gotta go. And it ain't gonna be me.'

Punch, 11 February 1981

Mrs T Goes to Washington

She choked on a jellybean in the Oval Office, but Mrs Thatcher's tête-à-tête with President Reagan was otherwise all sweetness and light. It was after she left the White House – with two hours of talks behind her, and two days of socializing ahead – that things began to go wrong.

Off went the Prime Minister to a private lunch at the British Embassy with senior economic officials from the Administration, led by the Treasury Secretary, Donald Regan. Little did she know that Mr Regan, even while she had been behind closed doors with his leader, had been denouncing her on Capitol Hill.

'Mrs Thatcher's tax cuts', he had told the Senate Appropriations Committee that morning, 'were not as great as they should have been . . . she failed to control the foreign exchange market, and the pound is so high that it ruined Britain's export trade. . . . ' Her policies, in short, had led to 'an explosive inflationary surge'.

The Prime Minister's heavyweight entourage – including Lord Carrington and three Whitehall permanent under-secretaries – were appalled. Was this to be her reward for repeated, unstinted praise, on all available American TV talk shows, for President Reagan's 'brave' economic initiatives? The White House, instead of backtracking, spent the afternoon rubbing salt in her wounds.

A White Paper would be produced, they announced, listing 'differences' between the British and American economic positions. When that was deemed a bad idea – a bit crude, perhaps – they instead wheeled on the new chairman of the Council of Economic Advisers, Murray Weidenbaum, for an 'explanatory' briefing. He proceeded to repeat everything Regan had said, only more so.

It was a case of stiff upper lips all round that evening, as Mrs Thatcher's husband and daughter accompanied her to the first full-scale White House state banquet of the Reagan years.

'Wow, that lady's something else,' trilled Bob Hope, jostling with Charlton Heston for a chance to meet the Iron Maiden. The next US ambassador to London, a Johnson's Wax heir by the name of John Louis Jr, looked on in transparent disbelief at his luck as the President of the United States said how much he looked forward to the Prince of Wales's wedding.

Mrs Thatcher's toast was something of a party political broadcast, echoing the President's extensive quotations from Churchill – but adding, ominously to American ears, 'our problems are your problems'. That is precisely what the Administration had been hoping she would not say.

It had been an extraordinary first day, with the Prime Minister's hosts going to embarrassing lengths to distance themselves from 'Thatcherism', now a synonym here for the failure of her brand of fiscal conservatism. Mrs Thatcher had spent only forty minutes alone with the President that morning, each acutely aware of the other's inexperience of foreign affairs, before advisers were called in to the rescue. What, the British party wondered, as it went to bed dazed and dispirited, would the morrow bring?

The Foreign Secretary breakfasted with his opposite number, Alexander Haig, as the Prime Minister went off to look round a space centre. Here, officials on both sides advised journalists, would be the 'red meat' of the visit. There was a mutual recognition that Carrington and Haig were each the true Svengali to their leader's Trilby.

'You name it, we've talked about it,' Haig told the British press after a long session with Carrington. What, inquired the *Observer,* had been said about foreign aid reductions? Well, they weren't actually discussed, said Haig. And increases in NATO defence spending? He referred us to a speech he had made five years ago: 'None of us is doing enough.'

Nor did Haig have much to say about Namibia, which had been billed as Carrington's most urgent priority. Fully two-thirds of his time was spent talking about El Salvador. 'I'm not', he said, 'trying to turn your knuckles white', but such 'Soviet-Cuban intervention on America's doorstep' was 'no longer tolerable, no longer acceptable', and there was a 'a host of vehicles available to us' to deal with it.

Our knuckles turned white. How had Lord Carrington

responded? Well, the process of 'drawing this problem to our partner's attention has been begun, but there is still a . . . lag of communication'. He was, however, 'in general extremely pleased' with what amounted to 'verbal support from the allies'.

Even for Lord Carrington, it appeared, the visit had been only a partial success. His desire to reaffirm the so-called European initiative on the Middle East, enhancing the role of the PLO, had fallen on stony ground. Haig said he disliked the term 'European initiative', and hoped the allies would 'make no further moves that would result in complicating this process'.

The Prime Minister's party arrived in Washington hoping to distract attention from her domestic woes, news of her humiliation at the hands of the mineworkers having preceded her across the Atlantic. Thatcher's miners, in a way, were portrayed as Reagan's Cuba. She had failed to stand firm in her hour of crisis; she had reneged on her mandate.

She had come, we were told, to offer a European version of 'linkage': support for Reagan's coolness towards the Russians, even for an early confrontation in Latin America, in return for some resumption of arms control efforts and an attempt to address the Palestinian problem. She appeared, at the end of a fraught forty-eight hours, to have delivered her side of the bargain but won little in return.

'These are early days yet,' muttered crestfallen British officials in mitigation, declaring it 'priceless' to have been granted two whole hours of Reagan's time so early in his Administration. The Prime Minister, they began to say, had come with 'no great expectations' for the visit. She felt a genuine personal admiration for Reagan (whom she described during the welcoming ceremonies as 'my deeply trusted friend') but recognized that the true power-centre of his Administration lay 'elsewhere'.

Lord Carrington, for his part, clearly sees Haig as the dominant force in US foreign policy-making for the foreseeable future. The two men know and respect each other from Haig's days as Supreme Commander of NATO, but there is a suspicion in British Foreign Office circles that the Secretary of State's own ill-disguised presidential ambitions may ultimately complicate his relations with Reagan.

Mrs Thatcher, as always, worked herself to the bone –

almost, in the eyes of an expatriate observer, to a needless extent. Her public performances, as a result, were somewhat lacklustre, the much-vaunted Georgetown macro-economic speech earning a Gamma-minus from its audience. There was much familiar talk of 'standing firm' and 'staying on course', but interviewers and dinner guests alike were left feeling hectored rather than cajoled, and less convinced this time round by the bully-pulpit Iron Maiden rhetoric.

That Mrs Thatcher leaves no broader impression behind her was confirmed in New York last night, when veterans of the OSS presented her with the 'Wild Bill Donovan' award, traditionally reserved for those with distinguished wartime or intelligence records. On inquiring how the Prime Minister qualified, I was told : 'For showing balls in the face of communism.'

Observer, 1 March 1981

Reagan's First 100 Days

'We have every right to dream heroic dreams,' said Ronald Reagan last January, on taking the oath of office as the fortieth president of the United States. 'Those who say we're in a time when there are no heroes, they just don't know where to look.'

They do now. In the ensuing 100 days – for reasons he cannot have envisaged, let alone hoped for, on that heady inaugural day – Reagan himself has become an authentic American hero. His brush with death a month ago, still re-enacted most days on the nation's TV screens, has left him the most popular president in the history of the Union.

Eighty per cent of Americans, many of them disagreeing with his economic policies in the same breath, tell pollsters they approve of the job Reagan is doing. What they really mean is that it's hard to knock the guy right now, regardless of what he's about to do to the country – and perhaps the world. The 'second honeymoon', it seems, will be lasting a while yet.

Even his most diehard political opponents joined with a will in the several standing ovations the President received last Tuesday evening at his first public reappearance, an address to a joint session of Congress. Those few who didn't will now be receiving bulging mailbags of complaints from constituents. Ronald Reagan appears to be making rapid progress towards immortality.

All in 100 days. The milestone is, of course, among the most arbitrary, not to say premature, available for the judging of political leadership. It has been in common practice in this country since the dynamic first 100 days of Franklin Delano Roosevelt, whose furious spate of liberal legislation Reagan is now busy trying to erase from the record.

American presidents get scarcely anything done in their first three months in office (though John Kennedy did manage to tuck in the Bay of Pigs, and Jimmy Carter a humiliating rebuff from Moscow on arms control). It's really a time for putting selected campaign promises on display in the congressional shop window.

More to the point, as Reagan himself observed to the Congress on Tuesday, is the fact that it is now six months since the American people gave him a convincing mandate to set up a siege economy. No such legislation has yet been signed. Half a year of American history, and nothing at all has been done.

The would-be assassin's bullet has, it seems, now ensured passage of Reagan's proposed budget cuts – if not, perhaps, of the tax cuts he would like to accompany them. Speaker Thomas 'Tip' O'Neill disappointed his fellow Democrats the other day by conceding defeat to the President in the great Capitol Hill numbers game.

Foreign policy, however, is a very different story. The real reason Al Haig has been in such trouble is that his tantrums have been distracting public attention from Reagan's assault on the domestic economy. Every foreign policy bungle of the last three months, it is now clear, has been caused at root by presidential dithering, followed by a presidential decision made entirely for domestic political advantage.

Secretary of State Haig, in his notorious confirmation hearings, promised a diplomacy of 'consistency, reliability and balance'. He has not been able to deliver. The ensuing three months have seen chaos and disarray worthy of the worst of the Carter years – the villain of the piece again being an American president's craven desire to please domestic special interest groups.

Both Haig and the Defence Secretary, Caspar Weinberger, have toured Europe and beyond to explain that arms control talks must be shelved because of the Soviet Union's 'threats of violence or intimidation' against Poland. They returned to Washington to find that the President was lifting the Soviet grain embargo – ostensibly because of Russia's 'restraint' in Poland, but in truth to line up America's farmers behind the grand economic strategy.

AWACS surveillance planes are now to be sold to the Saudis, over Israel's vociferous protests. Nobody in the White House will take much notice of Israel's feelings about anything until 30 June, when they will find out who is to lead that country for the next few years. In the meantime the interests of the

Pentagon and the Energy Department have been allowed, once again, to override those of state.

Europe's concerns about Reagan's belligerence towards Moscow might have suffered a similar fate. But Europe has a trump card in the 1979 NATO agreement on deployment of US nuclear missiles. The Administration has been forcefully reminded of late that that agreement was dependent upon progress towards arms limitation.

So Reagan will drift slowly and reluctantly towards a summit with Brezhnev, once his economic programme is in place. Dust storms like El Salvador will meanwhile come and go, and will continue to be handled in a gung-ho way which will rightly cause the Western allies considerable concern. Secretary Haig's days in office may well be numbered, but even his departure would be unlikely to ease Reagan's alarming penchant for macho, muscle-flexing brinkmanship.

The solemn truth is that the Reagan Administration does not yet have a foreign policy, beyond the President's apparent determination to answer Soviet adventurism with a renewed and immensely costly arms race. If his economic programme falters – as all manner of think-tanks, including the congressional budget office itself, believe it will – defence spending alone will ensure a deficit approaching \$100 million by 1984, the target year for a balanced budget.

Whatever dark days lie ahead, at home or abroad, Reagan himself seems set to remain immensely popular. He has already restored to his office much of the dignity and prestige Jimmy Carter squandered with his sordid, panic-stricken two-year campaign for re-election. He has in three months established better relations with Congress than were dreamt of in Carter's philosophy.

Reagan has also restored the grandeur Americans look for in their leadership. When you enter the west wing of the White House now, a razor-sharp marine presents arms with great ceremony. As a right royal head of state, Reagan is turning in an Oscar-winning performance; as a decisive chief executive, he has yet to prove himself better than B-grade.

The first real test is still to come: perhaps Poland, perhaps El Salvador, perhaps Namibia. Wherever the emergency occurs it will, for Reagan, be in uncharted waters. His first three months have provided a surfeit of evidence that he is a well-intentioned, courageous and disarmingly pleasant man. They have not proved reassuring about his ability to keep an unsteady world on an even keel.

The end of Reagan's first 100 days coincides with the end of my own two years as the *Observer*'s Washington correspondent. The process of growing disillusioned with the American political system has proved both riveting and enjoyable, as enjoyable as the opportunity to broaden my knowledge and love of this country. But I leave with a sinking feeling that Reagan will soon be well on his way towards proving Goldman's law, a modest but telling aphorism coined by Guido Goldman, director of Harvard's Center for European Studies. 'The primary purpose of any Administration', it states, 'is to make the last one look good.'

Observer, 3 May 1981

Reporting Britain

The Poisoner Trapped by Pride

At just twenty-four Graham Young has, it seems, achieved his well-documented life's ambition to go down in criminal history as Britain's most notorious poisoner. His, one hopes, final tally of three dead and at least seven other known victims far outstrips the single murder of his early hero, Crippen, though falling short of the thirteen of his other idol, Dr William Palmer. But it is Young's scientific expertise from childhood, his drawings, poems, diaries and above all his panache – quite apart from the circumstances of his release – which will win him the place he covets in Madame Tussaud's.

It was characteristic of Young that he himself stage-managed the trial which brought him renown. Irritated by his mistake in 1962, when he pleaded guilty on all counts and the trial was over in ten minutes, he doggedly resisted defence pressure to make the same plea this time round, and lost several distinguished QCs in the process. He knew the trial would be a long and much publicized one (seventy-five potential witnesses were named at the committal proceedings) and he knew that the only defence witness – with at least two days on the stand – would be Graham Young.

'He was not unimpressive, was he?' Sir Arthur Irvine QC, former Solicitor-General, asked the St Albans jury about his client's performance. Sir Arthur showed an increasing mastery of understatement during the trial, but this capped the lot. Young's performance was superb. It was born of the arrogance he has always shown, and which was to be his undoing, but it was an arrogance securely based on confidence in his own powers and resignation about his prospects. He corrected police accounts of interviews by pointing out that chemical formulae he was said to have trotted out were 'meaningless'. He provided details of the physical nature and effects of various poisons which had stumped doctors, pathologists and forensic scientists. (He had smiled in the dock the previous day when Professor Hugh Molesworth-Johnson, senior lecturer in forensic medicine at St Thomas's Hospital, had confessed ignorance of whether thallium had any taste: 'I contemplated making experiments personally, but decided against.' Laughter in court.) When it was put to him that he carried a phial of thallium in his top pocket as an 'exit dose' in case of emergency, Young explained that thallium – with which he had poisoned four men, two fatally – caused a particularly slow and painful death, and he had many more palatable 'agents' available for suicide.

Young's only stage weakness during the trial was his verbosity; he never used a monosyllable when a lumpy officialese compound would do. He admitted as much about his diary, whose style he described as 'stilted' and 'melodramatic' while confessing that he had submitted short stories to the *Reader's Digest*. This foible was seized on by prosecution counsel John Leonard QC, clearly irritated by Young's self-assurance. He taunted Young for saying 'homicidal administrator' for murderer; but it led to the trial's finest exchange, in which Leonard came off decidedly second-best. He was quoting a diary entry in which Young wryly rebuked the 'Bovingdon bug', a local virus to which doctors had attributed the illnesses and deaths at Hadlands photographic laboratory. 'Is someone setting up in competition to me' Young had written, with a question mark and three exclamation marks. 'Isn't that, Mr Young, a rather flippant remark in what is purported to be the serious journal of a fictitious poisoner?' Leonard asked.

Young: 'Since when, Mr Leonard, have poisoners been noted for their absence of humour?'

Leonard: 'I don't know, Mr Young. I've never met any.'

Young (very quick on it, and with a courteous bow): 'Thank you, Mr Leonard.'

Leonard (flustered and clumsy): 'You appreciate, Mr Young, that this trial is not yet concluded.'

Young would have been delighted by the mayhem in perpetual reign at the smart new courthouse, never designed for trials of this scale. Two telephones for upward of thirty journalists. Poison victims giving exclusive interviews to each newspaper in turn, and then both television channels. An unholy row when the *Sun* published a picture of Young released (at his own request) to all papers well in advance for use at the end of the trial; defence lawyers and police broke off diplomatic relations with the press, and a round-robin was dispatched by the press corps to the NUJ complaining of 'gross professional misconduct'. The queues for the public gallery (when plane wreck spotters were being chastised as ghouls) stretching right down the stairs, and starting on the final day at 6.15 am, with Young's own family and the widows of his victims having to hang about and be jostled among the *tricoteuses*.

It seemed, furthermore, that the jury were about the only people in the building who – one assumes, anyway – did not know about Young's past. This caused problems. When one went to the gents or to the tea-room (scene of many a nasty joke) there they were. The temptation to tell all was, for some reason, enormous, and overcome only by the thought of instant incarceration. There was also the Monday morning on which the man from one of the posh nationals (he'd better remain nameless) rushed breathlessly into the canteen to say he hadn't been to Istanbul on the Davey case that weekend, he'd been down to Broadmoor and talked to some blokes and there wasn't anything in that line about the belladonna plant in the kitchen garden. As it happens, there were no jurors there; but there had been seconds before and he didn't look first. I kept thinking of the Manson jury, sealed up in seclusion Howard Hughes would have envied throughout the months of the trial.

Back in court, meanwhile, Young's ego-trip was meeting all his expectations. Generally completely impassive as the evidence against him mounted, he swelled with pride on two occasions: on the first day, when Mr Leonard read the entire diary, a document of astonishing calculation, expertise and eloquence; and on the second, when the hapless chemist who had sold him the thallium said he'd been convinced the customer was a 'university student, engaged on complex medical research'. Young's *coup de grâce* came after the verdict (which he took quite without expression) when Sir Arthur told Mr Justice Eveleigh: 'Young himself thinks that a prison sentence would be better for his condition than a return to Broadmoor.' He had even sentenced himself.

Young had also planned a final act, precluded in fact by his own compulsive boasting. Waiting in the cells below, during

the ninety minutes the jury were out, Young told guards that
when sentence was passed he would commit public suicide by
smashing the back of his head down on the dock rail, thus
breaking his neck. And so it was that he faced verdict and
sentence with his usual guard of two doubled to four,
forewarned and so forestrongarmed. Victim of his own vanity,
Young – like the sporting batsman who doesn't wait for the
umpire's finger – was the first to turn, leading his warders
down the stairs.

It is reassuring, if rather sinister, to note that had the jury,
by some quirk of fate, acquitted him, Young would not have
left the court a free man. A warrant for his arrest was issued
and ready on a charge of obtaining poisons by deception – he
gave a false name and address – while on licence.

Young's arrogance, as much a constituent of his psychopathy
as his indifference to human life, dominated the trial. It was
evident in his bland rebuttal of overwhelming evidence, in his
chill indifference to the sufferings of which the court heard.
And without it, of course, a trial of these dimensions would
have been prevented. It is manifest throughout his life: in his
condescension to his less clever schoolfriends, for which they
called him The Mad Professor; in his aspiration to a Hitlerian
omnipotence; in his programme of ruthless pogroms to solve
the Ulster problem; in his not being able to resist, while
denying a poison charge, telling the police to pass on to doctors
the cure for his dying victim – dimercaprol and potassium
chloride – and smiling when a senior detective asked him to
spell it. He went so far as to deny feelings of remorse implied
by concessionary police quotations.

But the most frightening thing about Young's arrogance –
and here a-chance-in-a-thousand blushing shrugs from those
in authority are rather less than adequate – is that without it
he would have got away with at least triple murder. His
murder victims would have been certified as dead from natural
causes, those he poisoned would have been treated for mi-
graine, fibrositis, an assortment of viruses, or at best accidental industrial poisoning. And Young would still be at large,
and about his business.

It was only because of his arrogance that police caught up

with Young in November 1971, just after the death of his second victim at Hadlands. A local GP, Dr Iain Anderson, went to the firm to give the worried staff a morale-boosting talk, in which he eliminated fears about radioactivity (caused by recent work on the adjacent airfield) and contamination of the water supply – and assured them it was just the Bovingdon bug. At the end he asked for questions, whereupon one staff member at the meeting – Graham Young – engaged him in lengthy and complex discussion of the similarities and differences in the symptoms of those who had died and those who had not. Among the points he put to the doctor was 'Are you suggesting that alopecia [loss of hair] can be psychosomatic?' – a vexed medical question well above the lay head. Dr Anderson candidly admits that Young had left him far behind. Then Young's urge to show off in front of his colleagues got the better of him and he asked if the symptoms were consistent with thallium poisoning, the first time anyone had mentioned it. His persistent and expert questioning aroused the suspicions of both the doctor and the managing director; that night, as Dr Anderson wrestled with his Hippocratic conscience, the boss went to the police, who in turn went to Young's bed-sitter in Hemel Hempstead, unvisited by his probation officer, and found his arsenal of poisons, his drawings and his diary. The order immediately went out to arrest Young at his father's home in Sheerness; at that moment there was only circumstantial evidence against him, the medical and police authorities in question did not know of his past, and there was no proof that anyone had been poisoned.

The following Monday a post-mortem was held at St Pancras mortuary on the second man at Hadlands to die, Mr Frederick Biggs. Professor Molesworth-Johnson, the pathologist, could find no thallium at all, despite having been told to look for it, and despite a police delegation peering over his shoulder. It was only when the organs were sent away for analysis by a police forensic scientist, Mr Nigel Fuller, that traces were found.

Professor Molesworth-Johnson had been 'unable to establish the cause of death'. Had the law not been on to Young, it seems probable that Mr Biggs would have met the same fate as the first victim, Mr Robert Egle – certified dead from natural causes (bronchopneumonia following Guillain-Barré polyneuritis), cremated and buried. Mr Egle had died in agony the previous July in St Albans City Hospital; Young had, at his own request, attended the cremation and – as he thought – watched all evidence of his crime destroyed by fire. But when police charged Young with Biggs's murder, they decided to exhume Mr Egle's ashes – buried four months earlier – and an analysis by Mr Fuller again revealed traces of thallium. Had Young not used a heavy metal poison, the only type which partially survives fire, the charge against him could never have been proved. As it was, it became the first murder charge in criminal history to follow the exhumation of cremated ashes.

The same could have been true of Young's now self-confessed murder of his stepmother in 1962. She had been cremated – at fourteen-year-old Graham's insistence – and her ashes scattered, before police were on to him. A post-mortem had decreed that death was due to collapse of the spinal cord, attributed to a bus crash in which Mrs Young had been involved a year before. One effect of antimony is to crumble the bone-matter in this way. Detective Chief Superintendent Ronald Harvey, head of Hertfordshire CID, wanted to press this, a third murder charge, against Young at the St Albans trial, but was prevented by the inadmissibility of evidence relating to his earlier crimes.

The Brodrick Report on Death Certification and Coroners, published earlier this year, concluded that the undetected homicide rate in this country is 'not significant'. The Young case throws some doubt on this; and a major revelation, quite separate from those to be investigated by the Home Secretary's commissions of inquiry, is the pervasive ignorance of the medical profession about poisons, and about forensic medicine in general. The point was made in the first major speech about the case (at a forensic conference at Porton Down) by Professor Francis Camps, now legendary in the annals of criminal pathology; he has always complained of the profession's tendency to dismiss forensic science as 'just bullet-holes' and is a campaigner for wider forensic instruction. His criticism is dismissed by the GP in the case, Dr Anderson, as 'unrealistic'; yet Dr Anderson admitted at the trial that 'I, as a medical practitioner, do not know all that much about poison.'

It was neither medical expertise nor enlightened detection

which removed Graham Young from society at large; it was his own vaulting ambition. Only his family knew both of his past and of the progressive illnesses at Hadlands (of which he was telling them himself); which should perhaps prick their consciences as they disavow their fledgling in the popular press. If Graham Young were not his own worst enemy, he would by now have committed at least three undetected murders, and many more perfect crimes.

New Statesman, 7 July 1972

Enoch Campaigns in Northern Ireland

Craigavon, Co. Down

'I am like Saint Paul,' Enoch Powell tells Ulster Loyalists. 'I was born elsewhere, but I have come here to say what needs to be said.' His progress through their heartland last week, however, was more like a motorcade Messiah's – with his own tape-recorded voice, heralding his arrival from the loudspeaker car, a stirring John the Baptist.

The mantles of Carson, Brookeborough and other Unionist heroes seem almost too small for Powell. To the rapt Loyalist audiences of South Down he is a saviour, come from across the water to lead them to victory at Westminster. After a campaign speech on Thursday – his tenth that day, and his third that evening – a Dromore housewife leapt to her feet: 'I had the temerity', she said, 'to ask the chairman before the meeting whether Mr Powell had a grasp of Irish affairs. Now I know better.'

She was drowned by applause. For Powell's great asset is that Ulster Unionists are used to hectoring politicians who tell them only what they already know. Powell puts their case as they have never heard it put before. The contradictions and anomalies of Irish politics are perfect meat for his own brand of ruthless partisan logic.

Power sharing, to Powell, is 'the absurd and insolent insistence that those who have won an election shall only exercise authority if they divide it with those who have lost the election'. A Council of Ireland would force 'those who uphold the existence of the state to admit to their counsels those who deny that the state has a right to exist – and who wish to abolish it, if necessary by force'.

His great emotional trick is to compare Ulster with other 'far-flung regions' of the United Kingdom. On border polls: 'Imagine the humiliation of any other part of the UK if it was regularly asked if it still wanted to be part of its fatherland.'

Audiences share his histrionic anger at 'the arrogant assumption that this part of the UK has kindly been lent someone else's army, which they can have back on demand'.

In moments of the highest emotion, Ulster becomes 'this jewel, a kind of miniature Britain, a place that might have been invented to prosper'. It is 'the test of Britain's national will to live'. And there are two enemies. One is the gunman – who, if the Unionist voice is heard at Westminster, 'will not of course surrender at once, but in a long low drawn-out growl of defeat will slink away'. The other, for the past five years, has been the British Government.

Now, both major British parties, he reassures them, are 'beginning to understand that the majority in Northern Ireland want to remain part of the UK' – perhaps Labour more than the Conservatives. So the Labour Government responds to Loyalist calls for the return of the 'B' Specials by increasing the police reserve. 'Very good. Much obliged. One out of ten. But the pupil will have to try harder.'

Who is to be the headmaster? Powell knows well he will have to fight hard for acceptance by Unionists wary of carpetbaggers. Part of the time he modestly cast himself as a visitor: 'However often I land in Northern Ireland, I never fail to shudder with the feeling that something is fundamentally wrong when one sees a soldier – and I am a soldier – playing at being the policeman.'

For the rest, he is campaigning as if his undoubtedly safe seat were a tight marginal. 'I've never seen anything quite like it,' said one retiring MP, in Ulster as an interested observer, as Powell scuttled up and down council house paths. 'He's wearing me out, and I can give him thirty years,' said Powell's armed bodyguard, forlornly watching his charge stride off round the corner.

Powell himself has decided against carrying a gun, as do many Ulster politicians, although he has yet to venture into hostile territory. He is determined, he says, to canvass Newry and other IRA strongholds on the border, but so far he has only been led in triumph through inland Orange towns.

His only real difficulty there is understanding what people say to him. Voters with thick Irish brogues sometimes have to repeat themselves three or four times before he gets their name. 'Listen to that chap over there,' he tells them, pointing at the loudspeaker pouring forth his disembodied voice. 'He talks a lost of sense. I'll have to do something about his Black Country accent, though.'

The hustings also see Powell in some unlikely company, as local party leaders tout him round. In the village of Magheralin on Thursday he was escorted by seventy-three-year-old Colonel Peter Brush, chief of a 3,000-strong paramilitary Down Orange welfare group, and a member in May of the Loyalist strike co-ordinating committee. 'If you want a grave in Ulster, this is the man to see,' said Brush darkly, introducing him to the local sexton. 'Not yet, thanks,' replied Powell quickly.

Apart from familiar anti-Common Market noises, wooing the farming vote, Powell has yet to discuss anything but Ulster in this campaign. Even on that subject, he refuses to take awkward questions from journalists privately. 'Wait', he says, 'until you can ask me that in public.'

This week, however, brings him back to England for two speeches on anti-Market platforms, which may offer new answers about his future. Meanwhile, he unconsciously put the question to himself, when talking to fancy-dressed school children on a campaign stop. 'What are we dressed up as?' he asked. 'What are we pretending to be?'

Sunday Times, 29 September 1974

PEN Friends

The Egyptians wanted to expel the Israelis. The French tried to force the Russians to go home. The Dutch called on the South Africans to explain themselves. The East Germans protested about anti-Communist bias. Nobody wanted to admit the Chileans.

Thus nation spoke peace unto nation in London last week at the forty-first international congress of PEN, which calls itself a 'non-political' world-wide organization of writers. This year's chosen theme for discussion came from Keats: 'What the Imagination seizes as Beauty must be Truth.' PEN's non-political debates, among some 500 delegates from fifty-five world centres, appeared to reach a remarkable reinterpretation of Keats as a cold warrior.

It all started last Tuesday, when the conference's 'keynote speech' (on Beauty, Truth, etc.) was delivered in the Queen Elizabeth Hall by Arthur Koestler, the Hungarian writer living in exile in this country. It is twenty years since Koestler published any political writings, but he was promptly denounced by the East German chief delegate, Dr Heinz Kamnitzer, as 'blatantly anti-Communist'. Dr Kamnitzer was reminded of the PEN charter, which promotes – among other things – 'the unhampered transmission of thought between all nations'. His reply was blunt: 'Unfortunately, such sentiments and such relationships are not embodied in Arthur Koestler.'

Everybody had forgotten about it all by next morning, when Koestler's speech, reprinted in *The Times*, did appear after all to deal with Truth, Beauty, etc. Delegates went off on a non-political coach tour of literary London, while a few remained to hear an impassioned plea on behalf of an imprisoned Soviet writer, Vladimir Bukovsky.

The plea was delivered by Victor Fainberg, a Soviet writer exiled in this country. He was supported by Stephen Spender, president of the British branch of PEN, who stressed he was there in his personal capacity. Such moving speeches were made about Bukovsky's plight that a West German delegate leapt up to suggest a PEN demonstration outside the Russian Embassy.

Alarm set in. There were three Russian observers at the conference, and nobody wanted to upset them. Fainberg, not a member of PEN, loudly denounced them as KGB agents. Spender took the situation in hand:

> There is nothing to stop individual PEN members protesting outside the Russian Embassy, but it cannot be an official PEN protest. We are a non-political group. We do not believe that writers from a country with a dictatorial government represent that government.
>
> But then perhaps I'm a sucker. My record shows that I've done a good deal of being a sucker in my lifetime.

That afternoon, Iris Murdoch and others lectured on Truth, Imagination, etc., in the novel. At the close of the meeting the chief Russian observer, Nikolai Federenko, publicly presented Miss Murdoch with a Russian translation of one of her novels. When she accepted it there was non-political pandemonium.

'How can you accept that from the imprisoners of Bukovsky, especially when they steal your royalties?' demanded one angry delegate.

Miss Murdoch looked confused and upset. 'I didn't wish to be impolite,' she murmured.

'It is a gift from the KGB,' quipped Federenko, who as Russia's Ambassador to the UN in 1968 is famous for defending the invasion of Czechoslovakia as being 'in the interests of Czech writers'.

Next morning, Federenko put it about that any motion of protest about Bukovsky would be regarded as 'provocation'. Bukovsky, he told people, was not a writer, because he did not belong to the Writers' Union. (He was never allowed to join it.) His aides went so far as to suggest Bukovsky didn't exist.

Nevertheless, the French persisted with just such a motion, and Fainberg was busy lobbying people everywhere. The climax came when he invaded the closed session of the PEN executive and started an impassioned appeal. He was promptly ejected, to cries of 'Who is that man?'

Behind-the-scenes complaints led to the arrival of the hotel bouncer, who was guiding Fainberg towards the door when Spender intervened. 'This man is very upset about a friend of his who is in prison in Russia,' Spender patiently explained to the strong-arm man. 'I will take personal responsiblity for his behaviour whilst he is in the building.'

The bouncer reluctantly handed over his charge.

News then arrived that an American amendment toning down the French motion had been passed – largely because delegates were anxious to get away to lunch. A telegram of protest about Bukovsky was dispatched from PEN to the Kremlin.

As Susan Sontag and others expounded the need for Truth, Imagination, etc., in films and TV, news of other non-political developments emerged. The Egyptians had sent a telegram saying they intended to move the expulsion of Israel, but their delegate – who had checked into the hotel – appeared to have vanished. The South African delegates had successfully argued, in reply to their Dutch critics, that they were working against apartheid. PEN pals happily went off to the National Theatre.

Next morning, Tom Stoppard and others orated on Beauty, Imagination, etc. in the drama – in total calm. Penguin Books held a party to celebrate the award of the first George Orwell Memorial Prize to a Czech writer, Ludvik Vaculik, who was refused a visa to attend. Federenko was seen leaving the hotel as the party began.

At the closing ceremony that afternoon, Stephen Spender quoted the remark of one delegate to a *New Statesman* correspondent: 'All we come here for is a good screw.' Said Spender: 'We trust you've all had that. I myself have enjoyed some remarkable intercourse – er – interchange – er – of ideas.'

Sunday Times, 5 September 1976

Private Eye v. Goldsmith

For the past several weeks, a food millionaire called Sir James Goldsmith has been trying to buy one newspaper and jail the editor of another. To him the two ends were not contradictory. To those whose newspapers he is trying to buy, they were. Beaverbrook executives kept trying to drive this into his skull, desperate to convert their knight (Wilson vintage) into one in shining armour before being seen to be bought by him. Would you have let your newspaper marry this man?

Given the choice, Goldsmith would rather face the future as boss of Beaverbrook than as Grim Reaper of *Private Eye*. Ideally, he'd like to have been both. But a week ago, he at last capitulated to the insistence of Charles Wintour – ironically enough, one of the *Eye*'s favourite and most resentful Aunt Sallies – that he must unload his octopoid litigation against the magazine if he wished ever to occupy the Aitken upholstery. So Simon Jenkins, the editor of the *Evening Standard*, became the last in a long line of Goldsmith emissaries, lunching, telephoning, meeting and negotiating with Richard Ingrams. Last weekend, the settlement hurdles were already behind, and the home straight in view. By Monday afternoon, the agreement of Goldsmith's QC, Lewis Hawser, had been secured and the champagne began to flow in Greek Street.

So on Monday morning, Hawser will stand up at the Old Bailey and announce that his client wishes to offer no evidence. A long-awaited trial, which would have thrown badly needed light on an ancient law, will end in a whimper – embarrassing to one side and merciful to the other. The losers, apart from Goldsmith's pride, will be the press; it will not get its clarification of the criminal libel law, it will have to labour under a disastrous ruling on distributors, and it will lose one of the richest, longest-running stories of recent years.

Through it all, Richard Ingrams and James Goldsmith have never met. They have eyed each other – Goldsmith with hostility, Ingrams with bafflement – across many courtrooms.

Their paths – and swords – crossed, because of one of Goldsmith's friends, Lord Lucan. On 12 December 1975, *Private Eye* published an article entitled 'All's Well That Ends Elwes', which discussed the recent suicide of Dominic Elwes, the painter, a close friend of Lucan and Goldsmith. The piece, written by Patrick Marnham, who was to join Ingrams in the dock on Monday, mentioned a lunch held by some of Lucan's friends the day after his disappearance, when he was suspected of – but not yet charged with – the murder of his children's nanny. It went on to say that Goldsmith was present at the lunch – among 'the circle of gamblers and boneheads' with whom Lucan had associated – and to suggest that those present were conspiring to obstruct the course of justice.

Goldsmith was not at the lunch. He was, as it happens, addressing a meeting of accountants in Ireland. An error, of some consequence, by *Private Eye*. But an error which had already been made by two other newspapers, the *Sunday Times*, and – now a delightful irony – the *Daily Express*. Both papers had said Goldsmith was at the lunch, without going on to make that highly libellous suggestion about its purpose. So Goldsmith was not as miffed with them as he was with *Private Eye*. He made his peace, privately, with each. Now he has made a separate peace with the *Eye*.

And so we will have no answer to the central question which the action posed: when does a libel become a criminal libel? When is a man defamed so seriously that civil remedy is deemed insufficient? Journalistic swots, remembering their over-simplified handbooks, will tell you it is when that libel is 'likely to cause a breach of the peace'. That's what everyone had always thought. But this was radically contested at the committal proceedings; and now we won't know until the next time.

With the Lucan matter rumbling, over eighteen months, towards the Old Bailey, the antagonists were hard at it elsewhere. 'Slicker' of the *Eye* published several articles about Goldsmith's financial affairs, notably his connections with Slater Walker, and Goldsmith sued, sued and sued again. Ingrams lost count of the writs after they passed 100 last summer. Goldsmith meanwhile tried very hard, without success, to have Ingrams jailed for contempt of the criminal libel trial. But the most tortuous litigation, and the worst legacy of the whole débâcle, was Goldsmith's assault on *Private Eye*'s distributors.

Between 15 January and 2 February last year, Goldsmith issued eighty civil libel writs against forty of *Private Eye*'s local distributors, retailers and wholesalers. Four actions were dropped – in his over-enthusiasm, he had sued people who didn't handle the magazine – and nineteen were settled when the firms apologized and agreed to stop distributing. *Private Eye*'s circulation of over 100,000 dropped to about 80,000 – a substantial loss of income.

Seventeen firms, however, resisted, and appeal followed counter-appeal all the way to the Master of the Rolls, the last stop before the House of Lords. Denning delivered a masterly judgement, ludicrously underplayed by most national newspapers, stressing the dangers and absurdities of holding a newspaper seller responsible for the contents of the newspaper he sells. His colleagues, Bridge and Scarman, then proceeded to adopt the straitjacket position, and overruled him. James Comyn QC aptly referred to their banalities as 'the two minority reports', but *Private Eye* was refused leave to appeal further.

Goldsmith's settlement this week has released those distributors from their undertakings, so *Private Eye*'s normal circulation should soon be restored. But that appalling recent decision will, of course, stand. It will be interesting to see the response of Goldsmith, as newspaper baron, when someone tries to do it to him.

Indeed the attitude of Goldsmith, prospective press Lord, has been revealing throughout. He has resisted all accusations that he was out to close *Private Eye* – even on the evidence that he was sealing off its distribution, trying to jail more than one of its staff, and involving it in litigation it could afford less easily than he. His answer was that he had offered settlement – true, but on the understanding that the paper would cease writing about himself or his solicitor, Eric Levine. Ingrams quite rightly refused such a settlement. What other newspaper editor would accept it?

What other publication, on the other hand, would have received some £40,000 from its readers to fight a case like this?

(All of which and more will be swallowed by the settlement.) Goldsmith's answer would be that it is all a sinister plot by extremists of every kind. He has accused *Private Eye* – and let us not forget he is a friend of Harold Wilson – of retaining a tightly knit group of politically motivated friends in the media. In one American interview, he referred to them as 'the pus seeping through the system'; or perhaps I should say *us*, as he has accused me of belonging to this gang. ('You're against me,' he once told me, pacing up and down his suite at the Ritz like a caged tiger, complaining that I had described him as pacing up and down the witness box at Bow Street like a caged tiger.)

No one has sued him for such remarks. But two other journalists – Michael Gillard and Phillip Knightley – have sued him for other remarks he has made at various stages of the affair. A lot of slate-wiping and face-saving has gone on this week, but those two actions apparently emerged unscathed. They could both prove the most revealing yet.

Ingrams has said that the affair might make *Private Eye* 'a little more careful in future', though he has every intention of continuing to write about Goldsmith and Levine. Goldsmith, meanwhile, may or may not become boss of Beaverbrook Newspapers. If he does, he will have to prove that *he*, not Charles Wintour or Simon Jenkins, wants Jimmy Goldsmith to be thought an enlightened Crusader.

Spectator, 14 May 1977

A Letter to Peter Jay
(on his Appointment as Ambassador to Washington)

Dear Peter,

I've just been reading Geoffrey Moorhouse's new book on the Foreign Office* and you were constantly in my thoughts. There's a lot of stuff about ambassadors, and what Extraordinary and Plenipotential people they are – and having read, and indeed written, so many adjectives about you these past few weeks, it struck me no one found two quite so appropriate! Anyway, knowing how busy you've been lately, what with the Ramsbotham business and *Weekend World*, I thought I'd just pass on a few tips I've gleaned. (Oh, by the way, in case you'd thought of skimming the book during the in-flight movie to Washington, don't bother. It's mostly anecdotes and colour stuff, quite apart from being insufferably sycophantic, and I know how you hate anything but the most scrupulously cerebral approach.)

First things first. There's quite a bit about Washington, which seems to be the job they're all after. You'll be the only ambassador, for instance, with *two* Rolls-Royces. And *sixteen* servants. Moorhouse says some people cut down their household staff – 'partly because they don't believe the taxpayers' money should be spent on more than necessities, partly because they don't really feel comfortable with lackeys anyway' – but apparently you haven't *got* to. You get heaps of money for throwing parties and dinners, but you sometimes have to invite people you don't like. And you get lots of people coming to stay – Cabinet ministers, MPs, captains of industry, even the royals – but you have to have breakfast with them, which can be boring. Moorhouse also says it makes it more difficult to have rows with your wife.

Before you go, you have to put on a beaver cocked hat (the ostrich feathers are nylon) and a sword, and go and kiss the

*The Diplomats: The Foreign Office Today

Queen's hand. I think she kisses yours too, but it's not quite clear. She'll give you a letter to take to the President, saying what a terrific chap you are, and that he's got to believe everything you say comes from her. When you get there, you take it straight round to Carter; but you can take off the gear, and there's no need to kiss him. Take a good look, while you're waiting, who else is there. When Ramsbotham arrived, Nixon apparently gave him only three minutes between the blokes from Haiti and Rwanda. That's the kind of thing these diplomats attach a lot of importance to.

When you've been there six weeks, you have to send back a report saying what's going on. Then you do it every three or four months. Most people seem to get their assistants to do it for them; but I'm sure you'll want to do this yourself, and you may find one problem here. Moorhouse says you ought to keep it short, and I know how difficult you'll find that. But if you write too much, you see, David Owen won't have time to read it. And there's no point, I suppose, in warning you to keep it as *simple* as possible. It seems Ernie Bevin once told some diplomats: 'I sympathize with you; you have to encipher your ambassador's telegrams. I have to read them.' But then, I should think David and Jim will be keeping a special eye out for yours. Jim will probably take them home for Audrey to read too.

Then there's the diplomacy itself. Moorhouse doesn't seem quite sure what that is. Lots of people have tried to define it, and finished up coining clever aphorisms which I'm sure you can improve on. For instance, Sir Henry Wotton said that an ambassador was 'an honest man who is sent to lie abroad for the good of his country'. (I never realized that was a pun, did you?) Somebody else said it was the art of letting the other side have your own way. Moorhouse, poor dear, finishes up saying, 'Diplomacy can be seen as a contraceptive, whose function is not so much to seek solutions as to prevent the worst happening.' I think Harold Nicolson (a diplomat who became a journalist, I trust you've realized!) is probably better on this area. It seems to me the whole business is pretty simple, more demanding on the liver than the brain. Sort of glorified travelling salesman, really. The only problem is you can't say what you *really* think of the product. You've *got* to stick to the

Head Office line. So do be careful about Concorde and Europe – you know how keen Carter is on the Common Market – and for heaven's sake none of that stuff about Britain going down the drain.

You *must* tell Margaret that Moorhouse says an ambassador's wife is as crucial to a mission's success as her husband. She's got to keep an eye on morale in the embassy without getting *too* friendly. Don't forget everybody's going to be calling you 'Sir'. So it's probably better, if you ever have any of your staff to dinner, for Margaret to take a tip from another ambassador's wife and not allow second helpings. She's also got to make sure the other embassy wives don't misbehave, and then she should have a wonderful time. Lady Tonks even got to open the Paris branch of Marks and Spencer's.

That seems to be about it. Oh, one last thing. It's a bit sticky, actually. It seems you're bound to be offered a knighthood. Now I know how much you deserve one, but I do say you ought to think of Jim. He's had enough trouble over this already, I'd have thought, without Dennis Skinner dragging up Lady Forkbender and all that. Anyway, I'm sure Maggie will give you one when she calls you back.

Lots of love and luck to you both, then. I'll hope to come and have breakfast before the Think Tank abolishes you. Put in a good word for me!

Bon Voyage, Tony.

PS:Moorhouse says there was a chap who had to take 'sex' out of his recreations in *Who's Who* when he became an ambassador. So it might be as well to take 'balls' out of yours.

Spectator, 28 May 1977

Day Trip to Blackpool . . .

Wednesday: to Blackpool, for the Tory Party conference, to renew the friendship I forged with Margaret Thatcher in China last March. My appetite is whetted before I have even left Euston; in the adjacent sleeper I hear: 'No, I'm with Ted on this, Dickie. Willie's let Margaret go too far. Not even Keith or Francis can stop her.'

Still trying to work this out next morning, I enter the Winter Gardens betimes and bump into our next prime minister but, oooh, five?, the Hon. William Waldegrave. Erstwhile grey cell of Edward Heath, Willy now has himself a safe seat in Bristol and eagerly awaits the starter's gun. Meantime, he's doing the first-hand industrial bit at GEC and is reluctant to be seen talking to the likes of me.

So I move on to the Central Office bookstall, heaped high with The Leader's newly published collection of speeches, *Let Our Children Grow Tall*, a slim-volume snip at £4.95. While resisting the furious sales patter, I learn that Mrs Thatcher does not like the picture on the book's cover. 'It makes me look sixty,' she tells confidantes, who know she is fifty-two next day. The party faithful do not share her concern. Later in the day, she signs sixty-five copies in ten minutes.

Across the conference hall I stride to greet her, but she turns away to move among her people. Nicholas Scott MP, recently embattled in Chelsea, passes by to nudges and many an admiring female glance. Sir Keith Joseph, his hair making him look somehow as if he'd been grilled on toast, goes almost unnoticed in Scott's wake. This is no longer Sir Keith's hour. Today is the day of the conference favourite, Michael Heseltine.

Or so it seemed until young William Hague takes the stand. After the sixteen-year-old's triumph, Peter Walker goes around saying *he* made his first party conference speech at the age of fourteen. Mr Walker is not a happy man. The next day sees publication of a rude book about Slater-Walker; what's more, Reg Prentice was his parliamentary 'pair', so he's going to have to turn up to all votes until he can find another. For now, he takes solace in a long, intense conversation with Denis Thatcher. Across the central lobby, Patrick Cormack stands alone, as he has done most of the day, waiting for his attention to be attracted.

I am examining the large, new, heavily touched-up colour portrait of Mrs Thatcher, coy enough to be a study of Miss Blackpool, when I turn to confront the lady herself. Her eyes look much more tired than of yore, and are certainly more heavily mascaraed, in a tasteful green to match her dress. I am granted a rather curt 'Hello'.

As Michael Heseltine gets into his stride, I join most notables in repairing to the Imperial Hotel for a party to mark Sir Ian Gilmour's new book. There is much hilarity that Heseltine's speech again overran, forcing TV to cut his standing ovation and get on with their lunchtime programmes. Everyone is wondering what Ted Heath is going to say tonight, which is slightly odd as I've already been given a copy of his speech in book form.

Then in he sweeps, bullishly, with a flotilla of aides, including his doctor and friend, Sir Brian Warren. Mr Heath has precisely fifteen minutes to spend among us. He retires into a conspiratorial corner with Lord Carrington. He then emerges to address a few unattributable, off-the-record remarks to me. It is a pity I cannot repeat them, as they are rather amusing; suffice it to say they prove him an avid Atticus reader.

Throughout the afternoon, I meet people who want to talk about Reg Prentice. He won't get a seat, you know, they say; Tories don't like turncoats. Truro is his only chance. I discover that Prentice discussed his move with *Weekend World*, on which he finally made it, as long as two months ago. But it was only early last week that he let Mrs Thatcher know. There was a very nasty moment when Croydon Conservatives nearly decided not to have him. In the end, they got his wife and daughter, both sometime fiery socialists, as part of the package.

The evening draws on, and 2,500 people are heading for Ted Heath's speech. Back at the Imperial, Peter Walker is still pacing the corridors. John Davies mistakes me for someone else, but disappointingly doesn't say whom. Evening-gowned Young Conservatives are everywhere in full bray, beside themselves with excitement about their ball. I am offered a £6 ticket, but alas I have no evening dress, and I must return to my sleeper to ask Dickie if Keith or Francis got Willie to stop Maggie upsetting Ted.

. . . Where Media Child Is Born

'When did you first enter politics?' asked Sir Geoffrey Howe politely, his interest in the answer apparently dimmed by thoughts of his imminent television interview.

'Three years ago, during the 1974 elections,' replied the Boy Wonder politely, not appearing particularly interested in anything, least of all *his* imminent television interview.

'Ah, so you would have been, um, thirteen at the time?' ventured the Shadow Chancellor, as the two were ushered into the adjacent studio. 'That's correct,' said the BW, setting down his Britvic orange beside Sir Geoffrey's gin and tonic.

'Good heavens,' said Lady Howe, left alone with her thoughts and myself. 'Three years. To us that's, three years. To him it's, it's . . .'

'Quarter of a lifetime?' I suggested. 'Yes . . . *yes.*' Together we settled down to watch her husband do battle with the infant, before the eyes of one quarter of the electorate.

Eight hours earlier, the Boy Wonder had been sixteen-year-old William Hague of Rother Valley, Yorkshire. Then he had ascended the rostrum of the Tory party conference for three minutes, and offered a few home truths with a self-confidence rare in one so young. I would have missed it, being in the press room at the time, had not the extraordinary cheering drawn me back into the stadium. I was just in time to see David English, editor of the *Daily Mail*, station himself beside the rostrum to sweep the sudden hero away.

'Churchillian,' said one senior lobby man. 'Bionic,' said another, into a telephone. I set off in search of the phenomenon, to become inextricably caught in a mass of my colleagues, recording for posterity Mrs Thatcher's drawing of a raffle ticket. I had scarcely cursed my luck when there, suddenly, somehow, in the middle was Mr English, thrusting young William into Mrs Thatcher's arms, and making urgent gestures towards a photographer. The moment passed, he hustled the youth away, seemingly wishing to put him in his pocket. Wherever I went for the next couple of hours, there was Mr English producing William as from beneath his coat, to be patted on the head by a photogenic Shadow Minister.

During the afternoon, after he'd done *The World At One*, fixed the evening interviews, posed for the pictures on five national front pages next morning, and telephoned his mum like Mrs T had told him to, I managed to corner William with Mr English nowhere in sight. He told me, as he'd already told everyone else, that he'd got As in eight of his nine O levels and had been Yorkshire TV's public speaking champion last year. Mr English, he told me, had commissioned him to write some articles. I didn't ask him if he intended to be prime minister; if I had, people kept telling me, he would have said, 'Perhaps'.

By now it was 6 pm, and I was sitting with Professor Robert McKenzie, he of the LSE and the swingometer, awaiting William's arrival in the *Nationwide* studio. The BBC's excited plan was 'to get the kid on toast'. McKenzie quoted Hugh Dalton: 'The vilest of all emotions is the envy of the old for the young.' Then he quoted Andy Warhol : 'Everyone should be a celebrity for fifteen minutes of their life.' Then he said he was going to get the kid to tell the next Chancellor of the Exchequer how to run the country. Then the kid arrived and said he'd been Yorkshire TV's public speaking champion last year. 'You can't say that on the BBC,' said McKenzie.

As Lady Howe and I watched, the kid did indeed tell Sir Geoffrey how to run the country. Professor McKenzie then asked Sir Geoffrey how he intended to run the country. As Sir Geoffrey took three of the remaining four minutes to tell him, in somewhat soporific vein, the urgent message came down the line from London into McKenzie's earpiece: 'Get the kid back in.'

The kid got in one more word – it was 'Yes' – and then all three bounced back into our presence. McKenzie was excited, Sir Geoffrey still blinking sleepily, the kid intent on getting a good seat at Ted Heath's imminent meeting. Before leaving, he reopened his evening paper for another quick look at the large front-page picture of himself and Mrs Thatcher.

Oh yes, he came back to say he'd agreed to pose for pictures for the *Sunday Times* next morning, and he hoped he'd see me in Brighton next year.

I thanked him politely.

'Atticus', *Sunday Times*, 16 October 1977

Oxford's Quinquennial Poetry Punch-Up

The most difficult phone call I have ever had to make was to Stephen Spender, five summers ago, bearing across the Atlantic the unwelcome news that John Wain had pipped him to the Oxford Professorship of Poetry. A veil should be decently drawn over his response; I well remember an emotional, mumbled '*Sic transit gloria.*' In that unhappy moment Spender had suddenly sensed, like so many before him, the dire consequences of putting his poetic reputation on the line in this most irrational, unpredictable and often unworthy of all such contests.

Among the opposition had been Muhammad Ali, the head caretaker of Oxford County Hall, and a clutch of minor poets sponsored by friends. Ladbroke's had taken heavy investment on Spender as 4-6 favourite, leaving Wain out in the cold at 4-1 against. When Wain sneaked home by a mere 18 out of 763 votes, Spender rued the day he had decided to stay at his teaching post in Chicago, leaving W. H. Auden in Oxford as his campaign manager. He had tried to do the dignified thing.

Robert Graves had proved luckier, twelve years before, by entering much more into the spirit of it all. He and Sir Isaiah Berlin conspired together to help out two anthropologist friends, who had long sought a Western equivalent to the convoluted system used to elect tribal headsmen in New Guinea. The search was on for a successor to Auden, professor from 1956 to 1961, and Graves agreed to stand.

The Oxford election process was, and remains, appropriately bizarre. Just two of the university's 35,000-odd MAs can nominate anyone they like – not even needing, until recently, their victim's permission. (In 1968 John Wells and friends put up Mary Wilson, then Britain's First Lady; she remained in the lists until she found out about it and withdrew, since when the authorities have demanded the candidate's agreement in writing). On the two polling days all 35,000, known collectively as Convocation, have a vote, but they must travel to Oxford to cast it in person.

Graves was particularly well suited by the unwritten rule (now largely ignored, but crucial to the anthropologists) forbidding personal canvassing. Whilst expatiating upon 'the serious purpose behind this project', he realized he need not disturb his Majorcan tranquillity. The whole experiment nearly foundered when an ingenuous Graves relative descended on Oxford to canvass at street corners – 'at least', moaned the senior anthropologist, head in hands, 'a hundred votes lost'.

The next hurdle arose when the Oxford establishment, desperate for a torpedo, dug up a statute requiring nominees to be of MA status; Graves, it transpired, had never bothered to go through the formalities of a degree ceremony. Oxford's legislature, Hebdomadal Council, obligingly responded by abolishing the statute – 'throwing the post open', as Professor Nevill Coghill passionately declared, 'to the whole world'.

But the establishment wasn't beaten yet. Its attempts to woo a substantial enough figure to oppose Graves at first came to nothing; T. S. Eliot, aware of the perverse support last time round for Harold Nicolson against Auden, declined, as did John Betjeman: 'I have nothing to say about poetry.' Two women dons, Helen Gardner and Enid Starkie, attempted to pick up the gauntlet, but the Graves camp smartly unearthed another statute excluding nominees who already held Oxford lectureships. This too was helpfully thrown out. There was only one solution, only one man, equal to the task of splitting Oxford down the middle: F. R. Leavis, the turbulent guru of Cambridge English studies. The fight was on.

For an apparent two-hander, the contest was unusually acrimonious. Partisan posters appeared, illegally, all over town – among them, in the classic Oxford manner, elegiac couplets in Latin punning on the resemblance of Graves's name to *gravis*, serious, and Leavis's to *levis*, slight. When the voting figures were announced – again, of course, in Latin – Robertus Graves romped home with 329, exactly half the poll. Oxford bookie Jim Bailey, who had quoted Graves as 2-5 favourite, declared he had 'caught a cold'. Gardner (8-1) was second with 117 votes, Leavis (2-1) third with 116, while

Starkie (100-8) brought up the rear with 96.

Said Leavis, without a trace of resentment: 'It is well known that Oxford and Cambridge differ a great deal in the Humanities – that Oxford, for instance, can honour a man like P. G. Wodehouse.' Said Graves, to the triumphant war-dance of anthropologists: 'My function, as I understand it, is merely provocative.'

In fact, the sole duty of Oxford's poetry professor is to deliver three lectures a year for five years. For Auden and Graves, both of whom lived abroad while in office, the statutes were again bent to allow them to deliver all three in one term. Graves, who is registered as a company in Liechtenstein, had to insist on this for tax reasons. Auden, by contrast, is fondly remembered as the professor who made himself available to students each morning, during the few weeks he spent in Oxford, in the unlikely setting of the Cadena café; the scene, as aspirant poets approached the great man – they clutching their sheafs of vellum, he a cup of coffee – reminded one observer of 'a huge craggy-faced Socrates among the tidy women shoppers'.

I visited Auden in Oxford on the occasion of the last election, shortly before his death, and he remembered valuing equally the professor's other duties – judging university verse prizes and (his special favourite) delivering the Creweian Oration in Latin every other year at the Oxford festival of Encaenia. He admitted to some assistance from the University Orator (whose job it is to deliver all Latin speeches), and to 'getting tanked up on champagne beforehand'. But he was strongly resentful that the then professor, Roy Fuller, had 'funked it' by resorting to mere English. It is little more than a century since Matthew Arnold, in 1857, broke the 150-year-old tradition of delivering *all* the poetry professor's lectures in Latin. 'Punk,' rapped Auden, his eye a-glint, his fondness for Latin perhaps exceeding his command.

The world of letters has never been quite the same since the death in 1696 of Henry Birkhead, born the son of a London innkeeper, later a Fellow of All Souls, Oxford, elected on the recommendation of Archbishop Laud. Birkhead, author of some undistinguished Latin verse, was known to hold a low opinion of Oxford lecturing standards, but he surprised everyone with the contents of his will. To his wife, 'though I was never married to her or betrothed to her', he left just one shilling 'because she has been extream false and many ways exceeding injurious to me'. After other derisory bequests he left his estates in Monkwearmouth, County Durham, 'with all the rest of my goods and chattels in trust to maintain as far as it can for ever a Publick Professor of Poetry in the University of Oxford'.

Ominously enough, storm clouds gathered right away. The minister who held the living on Birkhead's land, understandably piqued, refused to recognize the will, appealing for help to the Dean and Chapter of Durham. The stalemate lasted eleven years, until the Dean and Chapter called it a day and handed the land over to the University – who promptly sold it. 'Had they not done so,' sighed J. W. Mackail, elected professor in 1906, 'it is possible that the endowment of the Chair would be much bigger than it is.' The first incumbent, Joseph Trapp, was elected unopposed in 1708 because 'others did not stir for it on account of the smallness of the salary' – £25 a year. It has been noted, however, that Trapp received for the copyright of his first series of lectures twice as much as Milton was paid for the copyright of *Paradise Lost*. Professors of poetry have published lucratively ever since.

The centuries have boosted the professor's stipend to £1,079 a year, recently increased from £717, and the notoriety of the elections to a favourite place in every Fleet Street news editor's five-year diary. The tremors leading to the 1968 débâcle, in which Mrs Wilson's opponents included an unemployed Newcastle gardener and a computer, can be traced back to 1951, when the post-war term of the unopposed Sir Maurice Bowra came to an end. A succession of respected literary critics – A.C. Bradley, J. W. Mackail, W. P. Ker, H. W. Garrod, Ernest de Selincourt – had occupied the chair in the first thirty years of this century, and an angry movement now gathered around the slogan: 'A poet, not a critic.' It appeared, as ever illegally, on long-suffering Oxford walls, in support of Cecil Day Lewis (later to become Poet Laureate). The poets' candidate was fielded in a straight fight against the obvious critics' candidate, his namesake C.S. Lewis of *Screwtape Letters* fame. The

179

contest set all standards for subsequent savagery.

Enid Starkie, just emerging as the doyenne of campaign managers, pulled out so many stops for the poet that even the science faculty rallied to his support; Helen Gardner, for the critic, had to resort to rounding up clergymen in coffee-houses. The poet-critic rivalry, which was to characterize most subsequent elections, was mercifully short. Day Lewis won the day narrowly, and a Chair of Medieval Studies was especially created at Cambridge for the loser, who never quite recovered from the whole hurtful business.

Next time round, in 1956, Auden was declared the 'Popular Front' candidate, while the Shakespearean scholar G. Wilson Knight represented the forces of criticism and Harold Nicolson, it can only be assumed, those of anarchy. *Isis*, the undergraduate magazine, expressed the student fervour for Auden: 'not just a Bohemian with an output of imagery corresponding to his intake of liquor'. Nicolson, scarcely renowned for his interest in poetry, was billed as 'one of the more versatile ornaments of the academic dinner table', proposed on the principle that 'a classical education fits a gentleman for any career'.

'Auden for Pope' became the latest embellishment to college walls. To his dying day, the poet kept a photograph of a misspelt slogan adorning the hallowed stone of All Souls: 'Auden for Proff.' At the time, he rested content with the straightforward manifesto: 'A poet will talk nonsense, but it will probably be interesting nonsense.' The outgoing Day Lewis lent his support, with former incumbents Garrod and Bowra inexplicably backing Nicolson. Enid Starkie returned to the epicentre, all vigour renewed, cycling round Oxford in her *matelot* outfit and beret, showering pigeon-holes with pro-Auden leaflets. He couldn't, he said, have had a better agent: 'You know how good the Irish are at local politics.'

The result, as it turned out, was much closer than expected: Auden 216, Nicolson 182. Wilson Knight 91. Auden delighted students at his inaugural lecture with the revelation that he 'began writing poetry one Sunday afternoon in March 1922, when a friend suggested I should. Until then the thought had never occurred to me.'

Much of Auden's major criticism in his late collection *The*

Dyer's Hand began life as these Oxford lectures – a cautionary reminder to all aspirant professors. In the Chair's long history, the only major critical works it has fathered have been Arnold's *Culture and Anarchy* and Bradley's *Shakespearean Tragedy*. 'I didn't vote for Auden as I thought he'd make fun of it,' Bowra told me years later. 'But he turned out to be the best ever.'

The election of 1955 drew a contemptuous sniff from the *TLS*: 'Would it be wicked to feel that none of the four candidates [Graves, Leavis, Gardner, Starkie] is likely to tell us anything we do not know already?' The net, it declared, should be thrown wider. Young provincial poets should be nominated, or distinguished poets from overseas. The battle lines for 1968 were drawn in remarkably prophetic terms.

Between the two, however, came the struggle to succeed Graves in 1966, when feathers again began to fly. Bowra had nominated the American poet Robert Lowell, who was heading for a not undeserved walkover, when Starkie, with the admitted purpose of 'mischief-making', put up the British war poet Edmund Blunden. Not one critic or academic was fielded as the confrontation between the contemporary and traditional schools of poetry grew ever more agonized.

As Starkie re-oiled her bicycle, poor Blunden was subjected to patronizing abuse, not least because he kept wicket for Hong Kong University until he was well into his sixties. The poet himself, then seventy and not in the best of health, came to Oxford a reluctant candidate, only to be forced to hold the first press conference in the professorship's history.

Ladbroke's, at it again, quoted Lowell as 4-6 favourite, Blunden the 5-4 long shot. But Oxford's mysterious ways produced yet another shock result: Blunden 477, Lowell 241 – a record poll, leaving Lowell muttering about 'the Wallis Simpson syndrome'. Students and modernists alike were disgusted. Day Lewis pronounced the whole business out of date: 'Students should be allowed a vote.'

Lowell retained a dignified silence. Blunden, for his part, sadly described the whole affair as 'a bullfight' as he watched his wife and daughter dance for joy in the Bodleian quadrangle. Then off he went, somewhat wearily, for a celebration drink with Richard Burton and Elizabeth Taylor, who happened to be in town for a forthcoming production of *Dr Faustus*. Most of the evening, however, he spent in the corner of the pub, talking to local farmworkers. When the poetry hordes tried to claim him for their own, the locals pleaded 'Don't take him away. He speaks our language.' Blunden's subsequent lectures were generally accounted undistinguished; ill-health forced him to retire after only three of his five years, setting the scene for the greatest bunfight of them all.

The 1968 lists were declared open by Barry MacSweeney, a twenty-one-year-old Newcastle corporation gardener, at the time 'a poet on the dole', who was vigorously promoted by his publishers with posters and glossy paperbacks. Next, briefly, came Mrs Wilson. Then Richard Cobb, the then Balliol historian, got 'yes, perhaps a little drunk' at a Merton wedding reception, and sent off a telegram to Christopher Hill, Master of Balliol: SUPPORT NOMINATION OF YEVTUSHENKO. All very well, except that he signed it ANDRE MALRAUX. A student ballot, thanks to an undergraduette Godiva riding through the city streets in his support, endorsed the Russian, and called on *Times* readers to exercise their votes. But would he be allowed to come? A student journalist's phone call direct to Brezhnev at the Kremlin raised only an office cleaner, who thought he 'probably would'. The more pressing problem was that he couldn't speak English.

Isis, then edited by one Anthony Holden, threw its utterly ineffectual weight behind another of the legitimate candidates, A. Alvarez, who thought he had 'about as much chance as Governor Wallace' in the simultaneous US presidency race. Roy Fuller had the support of many famous literary names; Kathleen Raine was adjudged 'an outsider to watch'. Less easily identified names like Joseph Braddock and Paul Rosenberg, who respectively declared all twentieth-century poetry 'jazzy, hoodlum stuff' and 'crap', weighed in.

Welsh Eisteddfod bard Caradog Pritchard had the support of the *Daily Telegraph*, where he worked as a sub-editor, and the Argentine poet Jorge Luis Borges was put up by the modern languages faculty. Alan Bold, a socialist Scot, thundered down from Edinburgh 'to add a little sanity to the proceedings'. A BBC-TV confrontation between Bold and MacSweeney was never shown because it ended in blows. The inevitable Starkie came in again at a late stage, this time as a candidate, with the support of ex-Professor Graves – 'her brother William procured an honorary doctorate at Trinity College, Dublin, for my father, Alfred Perceval Graves, who had long desired one'. Bernard Levin put himself forward on the strength of 'an improper limerick I once wrote about Tariq Ali'. Plans to nominate a computer, there being nothing in the statutes to say the professor must be human, finally broke down; it could be programmed to write poetry, but not to give lectures.

The victory, announced in English for the benefit of the TV cameras, was another surprise. Roy Fuller, recent winner of the Duff Cooper prize for a book his publishers had scattered liberally around Oxford common rooms, won 'a victory for common sense' despite odds of 3-1 against. His 385 votes put him 104 ahead of Starkie, who had come in to 4-5 favourite. Third at 5-1 was the still *incommunicado* Yevtushenko, fourth at 10-1 Raine with 99, and fifth at 4-1 Alvarez with 58. Pritchard's twenty-nine votes exactly corresponded to the number of Fleet Street MAs he had brought to Oxford in a charabanc equipped with bar and TV; his daughter Mari had enchanted voters with the sweetness of her singing to the Welsh harp outside the polling station. Borges received sixteen votes, Braddock five, MacSweeney four, Rosenberg three and the hapless Bold none – no, not even those of his nominators. When Yevtushenko and Borges supporters demanded an honorary degree for their men in recompense, the *TLS* put Bold up for an honorary O level.

The only serious attempt at electoral reform, proposed in 1967 by the Franks Commission, was thwarted after yet another nationwide rumpus. Convocation, once denounced by Curzon as 'the worst of all methods of electing a professor', was to yield its powers to Congregation – those senior members actually working in the university. Enid Starkie, for once, spoke for the majority: 'This would deprive a Wilde, an Auden, a Day Lewis and so forth of a vote, while leaving it to the most junior chemist and soil expert who happen to teach in Oxford.'

Experience of previous years has prompted a gentle defusing of the 1978 election. The authorities put it back to November, ensuring a long summer calm before what may or may not be the storm; as a result, furious activity marked the end of the summer term last month, leaving the critic John Jones out in front of the poet Peter Levi, and all other runners nowhere. There is, for those with any energy left, the prospect of E. J. Thribb's collected verse in October, which has his Greek Street employers intent on nominating this mysterious figure. Pam Ayres, against all the odds, remains unnominated.

In 1973, Dame Helen Gardner, then Merton Professor of English Literature (now, like her successor John Carey, a John Jones supporter), called for 'a poet on the campus, elected by an editorial board such as that which elects the Slade Professor of Fine Art'. It was unrestricted nomination, she believed, which led to 'the indignities of recent years, more suited to the Miss World contest'. She was, and remains, one of the many respected figures who supported the unheeded call for student franchise. 'After all,' as Auden rightly pointed out, 'they're the ones who have to listen to the bloody lectures.'

Sunday Times, 16 July 1978

Muddling Through

The obituary column of *The Times* of London always speaks in the authentic upstairs tones of the British establishment. But that august paper tends to excel itself on the death of what it likes to call 'a socially significant performer of the popular music of his day'. I well remember Elvis Presley being sniffed off to eternity as 'a totally uninteresting person'.

John Lennon was accorded a rather warmer farewell last month, his forty-five posthumous inches rivalling the space accorded many a senior civil servant or retired army officer. Well, he was British born (even if he chose exile in Babylon), and he did do a lot for exports. I had not previously realized, however, that his elevation by Her Majesty in 1966 to Membership of the Order of the British Empire 'echoed a general feeling that the Beatles had been at the spearhead of the formation of a new role for Britain in the world'.

So it was John who finally exorcised Suez, Paul who helped us over devaluation, George who blew raspberries back at de Gaulle, Ringo who symbolized Harold Wilson's white-hot technological revolution. The Fab Four were our consolation for loss of empire. And all these years I'd thought they were just paying off the national debt.

The Times obituarist, his pen dipped in the same concrete, could well have been ghosting a chapter of this, his colleague Geoffrey Smith's book.* In the 1960s apparently, the Beatles

> appeared to advertise abroad an English way of life – dynamic, creative, progressive, forward-looking – that was pleasantly at odds with the received image of a country suffering economic, political and foreign policy problems, with only a past to find pleasure in.

So say Smith and Polsby. They don't mention 'the greatest songwriters since Schubert' (*The Times* again) or even Carnaby Street by name, but there does seem to be a lofty consensus

British Government and Its Discontents by Geoffrey Smith and Nelson W. Polsby

that the swinging Sixties were Britain's finest post-war hours.

It is no wonder American Anglophiles grow confused. One minute we're a nation of sex-crazed Cabinet ministers, pricing defence secrets at our mistress's eyebrow, the next we're a lovable, mop-haired bunch of cockeyed optimists. To make matters worse, Americans were told in 1977 by R. Emmett Tyrrell Jr (and others) of *The Future That Doesn't Work: Social Democracy's Failure in Britain.* The following year Bernard Nossiter, then the *Washington Post's* London correspondent, hit back with *Britain: A Future That Works*, arguing that it is the mark of a mature and civilized society to prefer leisure to toil. Now along come Smith and Polsby, the latter also an American, to tell us that the present may seem a bit grim, but they too have seen the future – and it works. Maybe.

That is not a widely held view, even in official British circles. Our present ambassador here and his immediate predecessor were both unlucky enough to be caught issuing prophecies of doom, just before receiving their unexpected assignments to Massachusetts Avenue. In an Institute of Economic Affairs lecture in 1976, when still a mere journalist, Peter Jay argued that Britain's four contemporary objectives are fundamentally incompatible, namely: full employment, stable prices, free collective bargaining, and a parliamentary system of democratic government. His proposition was applied to all modern democracies, but above all to Britain because of the unparalleled political strength of its trade unions. And in what he thought his farewell dispatch, on his retirement as ambassador to France in March 1979, Sir Nicholas Henderson wrote:

> Income per head in Britain is now, for the first time in over 300 years, below that in France. We are scarcely in the same economic league as the Germans or French. We talk of ourselves without shame as being one of the less prosperous countries of Europe. The prognosis for the foreseeable future is discouraging. If present trends continue, we shall be overtaken in GDP per head by Italy and Spain well before the end of the century.

Now, less than two years later, even *The Times* itself is up for sale (the *Observer* already being, greatly to its benefit, American owned). With the Dorchester Hotel in Arab hands, what else can befall? How long before Buckingham Palace follows the *Queen Mary* and London Bridge, brick by brick, across the Atlantic?

Europe's Organization for Economic Co-operation and Development predicts a much worse future for Britain than for its European co-Marketeers, thus nailing any political evasions about inexorable world market forces, etc. By mid-1982, said the OECD last month, unemployment in the United Kingdom will have reached three million (12 per cent of the work force), the worst since the 1930s. But there is worse.

Despite the blessings of North Sea oil, predicts OECD, Britain will be the Western country worst hit by recession over the next eighteen months. The balance of payments deficit will continue to deteriorate; there will be further reductions in industrial output, investment, and international competitiveness. The gross domestic product will shrink by 2 per cent, just as Sir Nicholas Henderson predicted.

The immediate causes of this dismal decline should be of great interest to the new Reagan administration. Mrs Thatcher's election promises in 1978-9 were very similar to those of the Republican candidate in 1979-80: reduce government spending, eliminate waste, cut back the bureaucracy, tighten control of the money supply. For all Thatcher's patient sincerity in applying what she thought appropriate, if painful, remedies, none of them has worked.

Mrs Thatcher's few American critics – be they supply-siders, Laffer curvers, welfare-cutters, or the purest of pure monetarists – offer different explanations of what has gone wrong. The great guru Milton Friedman himself has been in and out of Downing Street, offering to run the Bank of England as he would the Federal Reserve, but monetarism plainly has failed as yet to find an exit from Peter Jay's cul-de-sac. Reagan, Regan, Stockman, and others should note that the application of strict monetary controls in a society with wage-push inflation (and without a free market in labour) just deepens recession.

Mrs Thatcher has cut back to 12 per cent the 22 per cent inflation rate she created – a year before her election, it was in single digits – but only by offering sugar lumps rather than jobs to the despairing, and still growing, unemployed. She now has been reduced to calling home an expatriate British economist, Dr Alan Walters of Johns Hopkins and the World Bank, to apply his even more stringent brand of fiscal conservatism for a salary exactly twice her own.

Economics may dominate the state of a nation's morale (as I believe it dominated the thoughts of American voters last November). But in Britain's case there are historical reasons for its shrinkage from a colussus bestriding the world to an embryonic banana republic with a monarchy but no bananas. The authors construct their book around such symptoms of the British malaise as declining productivity, regional in-fighting, a shrinking role on the world stage, and the need for reform of the major political and social institutions. They profess themselves optimists, but offer no specific solutions, concluding rather vaguely (and in a direct echo of *The Times* obituarist): 'The question for Britain is whether it will recover its readiness to hope and to renew constructive endeavour, or whether the pride that it retains will come only from contemplation of the past.'

'I have not become the King's first minister', said Winston Churchill in 1942, 'in order to preside over the liquidation of the British Empire.' But that, of course, is precisely what he did. The process was already irreversible, and altogether healthy. The remark is a direct historical precursor of Dean Acheson's equally famous statement, twenty years later, that Britain had 'lost an empire and not yet found a role'.

It was, as the authors say, in looking to Europe in the early 1960s that Britain sought to find that role. Suez had put a disastrous lid on the era of empire, proving that even the United States thought such British belligerence mere *folie de grandeur*. No longer invited to superpower summits – our presence at Yalta and Potsdam had been much more a reflection of Britain's war record than of our economic or military might – we now were spurned even by the Common Market. De Gaulle understandably thought Britain's entry would render Europe a mere adjunct to the US. And even as the 'special relationship' was providing our European undoing, the US itself went all coy. Britain without Europe was too weak a partner to share a bilateral Atlantic alliance. 'Britain was forced to conclude', as Smith and Polsby put it in their swift historical résumé, 'that the United States was prepared to live in a commune with her, but not to marry her.'

Britain has been a member of the European Economic Community for eight of the past twenty years, and a decidedly mixed blessing it has proved. Mrs Thatcher has renegotiated our budgetary contribution, but it is still far too high to make economic sense. Our productive farmers are properly resentful of subsidizing their less efficient French counterparts. Continued trade with the Commonwealth would have left such staples as meat and dairy products much less expensive. Surplus butter is sold off cheap to the Russians while many Britons can afford only margarine (a pure example of Marie Antoinette economics). If another referendum were held today, Britons, for all their love of the status quo, would vote overwhelmingly for withdrawal from Europe. In the last six months withdrawal has become official policy of the opposition Labour Party, which has elected as its leader a lifelong anti-Marketeer. Both Party and Leader, it should be noted, also favour unilateral disarmament, which would inevitably mean withdrawal from NATO. This despite the fact that Britain's role as a world power depends on its membership of Europe (quite apart from NATO). The Common Market was founded as a specifically economic entity, but it is metamorphosing into a homogeneous political unit – each separate democracy now has surrendered sovereignty on many issues to a European Parliament in Strasbourg – which is gingerly beginning to proffer its own communal foreign policy.

Thus President Kennedy's vision of the Atlantic alliance, with Europe a united bulwark against the Soviet advance westwards, and Britain's expertise supplying Europe a global view, has not quite come to pass.

As Britain goes deeper into recession, Mrs Thatcher also will be unable to meet NATO's commitment to a 3 per cent real increase in defence spending, however much she may want to, and whatever skilful fudging of the figures she may use to disguise the truth. The Prime Minister will have some explaining to do when she meets President Reagan, and NATO's favourite son, Secretary Haig, in Washington on 25 February.

Britain's unique problems, even within Europe, stem from historical causes rarely mentioned in current debate. All blame is placed on the 'suicidal' greediness of trade unions, yet it is more the constant *threats* of strikes than strikes themselves which have so bruised British industry. The British strike record, as the authors point out, is no worse than in many other countries; in terms of working days lost, it is in fact better than that of the United States. Little is heard of the strains imposed on the 'United' Kingdom by regional interests, notably those of Scotland and Wales, yet it was a vote on devolution that brought down the Callaghan Government.

Britons are much prouder of their regional identity than Americans, and thus less mobile in their pursuit of happiness. This in turn means, as a rule, that economic hardship is the price of social stability. By contrast, the black immigrant community, now numbering about one million, is much less integrated and thus more restive. Whereas black Americans have lived in the United States since before the adoption of the Constitution, nearly all black Britons have arrived only since the war.

Members of the British Parliament, moreover, are much less subject to pressures from their home base than are members of the United States Congress. The obligation to vote the party line, at the peril of losing political advancement, leaves their constituents even more cynical about Westminster than the middle American voter is about Washington. British parliamentary democracy, to put it bluntly, reflects – and is in large part responsible for – the country's state of decay. A system perfected by a nation at the height of its powers ill serves that same nation now it is all but on its knees.

Smith and Polsby devote the major – and most original – section of their book to an analysis of British political institutions, suggesting that they may be 'less unchangeable' than is generally acknowledged. They rightly conclude that the system, described by the Lord Chancellor, Lord Hailsham, as 'an elective dictatorship', is in dire need of reform. Parliament, as they argue, is powerless to guide or scrutinize the policies of government. A half-baked version of the US committee system is now being tried out, but Mrs Thatcher's parliamentary majority affords her despotic powers. The electorate, both sides of industry, and half the Cabinet – once known as pragmatists, now dubbed 'wets' – may have deserted her, but not until her backbenchers flex what pass for their muscles will she fall.

Parliament's growing ineffectiveness is compounded by the power of the Civil Service, a self-appointing, self-perpetuating secret society that ensures more continuity of policy than either the electorate or successive governments have in mind. Americans would be horrified by the examples quoted in this book of senior civil servants withholding from their ministers information that would rock the boat, or conspiring together to outflank their political 'masters'. The power and unaccountability of the Civil Service has ensured, since the war, that there has been a broader consensus, a greater continuity, than might be expected of a series of governments elected on drastically differing mandates.

It was not his rudeness about Edward Heath or his evident crush on Mrs Thatcher that drew gasps from an American Enterprise Institute lunch addressed by Dr Walters, the new economic czar, shortly before he left Washington. It was his revelation that his new job made him one of fewer than ten political appointees in the British Government, even as, around the corner, the Reagan transition team was struggling to select several thousand.

Each of these important areas merits more extended study than space permits here, or than the authors allow themselves. The plain fact is that it is difficult to feel optimistic about Britain's future. But it is not enough to pin the rap, as do Smith and Polsby and so many in Britain today, on an ill-defined attitude of defeatism, the notion that a tired old sometime superstar is quietly giving up the unequal struggle.

Perhaps history will see the decline of Britain as the hallmark of a uniquely munificent, even-handed welfare state, funded by cripplingly high personal taxation. A Briton living in the United States may be forgiven a particular outrage at doctors' bills, prescription charges, the lack of legal aid, the cost of higher education. This one, at any rate, misses little else about home but his friends' sense of humour, good television, Test cricket, and certain culinary delights. By way of recompense there is fresh adrenalin to be derived each day from the sense that this is a country mature enough to acknowledge its comparative youth, brash and resourceful enough to look to a better future, for all its current problems. I've gotten to be quite a bore at Washington dinner tables, droning on about self-evident truths and last, best hopes.

For Mrs Thatcher, despite the best intentions, is steadily eroding Britain's major remaining virtue: that it is an extremely pleasant place to live. Americans may still delight in the charms of London – how many venture farther north? – but the natives themselves rarely have had it so bad. Emigration figures have never been higher. Bernard Nossiter may be right that civilization goes hand in hand with increased leisure, but he is surely wrong to expect the British economic desert to bloom as a result. The British traits behind it all have been caught best by – *sic transit gloria* – yet another American, one who chooses to live in the place, Paul Theroux:

> The British do not say 'You're welcome' and they seldom shake hands. What they do best is empty trash, deliver mail and milk at dawn, run schools, provide dental and medical care and eye-glasses for a pittance, broadcast intelligent radio programmes, plant pretty gardens, produce articulate debate, maintain the character of villages and parks, brew real beer, finance a spectacularly good library service, stand politely in line, avoid talking to strangers, and make amateurism and uncompetitiveness the goals of nearly every endeavour. There is no money in this.

Well, quite. The best that can be hoped is that Mrs Thatcher will not also undermine the one British quality which may yet save the day: an eternal capacity for muddling through.

New Republic, 24 January 1981

Back to Blighty

This final, forlorn, farewell transatlantic cable is addressed primarily to my wife, who has remained transatlantic some weeks after I have not. When I snuck back into this country a month ago, it was with every certitude that she and the Holden brood would be following hard upon; with each day that passes, I grow less sure.

Perhaps it's the phone calls, designed to boost morale, to rekindle her memories of the delights of the British summer. 'Hello, love . . . yes, well, pissing with rain again . . . no, there's been no play at all yet this season . . . ninety, eh? No humidity? Kids frolicking in pool? No, no, don't hurry back . . . *I'll* come and see *you* . . .'

'When are you coming home?' she then asks, confusing my other, hard-won certitude: that I *was* home. After two-and-a-bit years away, without setting foot on British tarmac all that time, and not having missed anything much to speak of – except, I hastily add, my friends – the re-entry symptoms are even harder to handle than those of withdrawal.

The drive in from Heathrow is a hell of a culture shock in itself. Who asked my permission to change the Martini clock into the Fiat clock? OK, they're both Italian, but that particular landmark used to be peculiarly British. Chucking £10 notes like confetti at the taxi driver, my gloom is deep enough to shock me out of my jet-lag.

London looks like Belfast. Corrugated iron everywhere, where there used to be terraced houses. Rubbish everywhere, after the pristine sidewalks of Washington. Long faces crowd the streets. Nobody looks as if they much want to be going wherever they're going. Brace yourself, we're about to circumnavigate the Palace.

I close my eyes; that one I'm not yet ready to handle. A few £10 notes later, we're at the National Gallery. It's a Bank Holiday, and of course it's closed. What kind of a country closes its museums on the one day most people can go to them? I don't think I'm going to be the life-and-soul in the pub any more.

No Sex Please We're British is still playing, I see. Is that the only thing that can make me feel at home? *The Best Little Whorehouse in Texas* is gracing the Theatre Royal, Drury Lane; well, at least if nothing's sacred, it's American unsacred. Centre Point still looks empty; that must be a good sign.

As we approach *The Times*, my new berth, I see a picture of Freddie Laker plugging the *Guardian*. If he's joined the enemy, whose side am I on? It's no good: I just can't face entering the building. Too much to think about. More £10 notes and the cab diverts towards my new residence, a hotel aptly called The President. That should make me feel at home.

One look at the President's Black Hole of Calcutta suite, and I flee across the road to the Russell. It is mid-afternoon, and I am munching the first pork crackling I've tackled in two years, when an American couple enter to reserve a dinner table for 6 pm. Now that's more like it.

I won't trouble you with my diary any further. Suffice it to say that a few evenings later I am to be found in a friend's home, watching another friend on television, plugging his latest book. The conversation is, granted, rather serious, but even so they seem to be speaking in slow-motion. Robert Kee, whom I seem to remember as sort of normal on telly, is being impossibly earnest. I suppose this should be a reminder of the quality of British intellectual life, I should be reassured that prime-time BBC rests content with rambling heads, but I'm afraid I just find it hysterically funny.

I was right all along. The only things worth missing about Britain were Radio Three, Test cricket, pheasant at Rules (out of season; will report back later) and treacle tart at Simpsons (still *sans pareil*). To list the things I miss about the United States would require several of those bound volumes of *Punch* which prop up the ceilings of Pall Mall.

But there are delights of British life I hadn't realized before I left. Talking to complete strangers on the telephone, for instance, after several times attempting to dial old chums. I've lost my British inhibitions, and rather enjoy making random new friends by courtesy of the GPO (now, I understand, called Telecom).

A weekend in the British countryside reassures me that the

Grand Canyon should stay where it is – rather than, as I had hoped, being resettled in the Cotswolds. London's stunted, style-less skyscrapers rather suit it, I gradually realize; the Thames looks at its best when pockmarked by rain. I think it's all going to be all right.

So, if you're listening, dear, I think you *will* feel at home here. The street dogs still foul our front doorstep, that neighbour still spends his weekends chain-sawing, the telly still needs a kick when Angela Rippon comes on. Life's little verities are as they were, a constant source of reassurance.

It'll be such fun fighting your way round the Essex Road shops rather than having it all carried to the station wagon by Giant Supermarket flunkies. Think what good it will do your complexion to escape the constant bruising of the sun. Imagine the fun we'll have exploring all those new motorways, untroubled by road signs helping us towards our destination. And the kids, they need discipline, you know: not good for them to grow up in a country where restaurants are geared around them, local authorities provide vandal-free playgrounds, and people smile at them in the street. They say William Tyndale is the best school in London, now; they do, honest Injun.

Look: the nicest thing happened to me here the other day. I lunched with a foreign correspondent based in London, did all my usual moaning, made a delightful new friend. Next day, lunch at the *Spectator*, just two blocks from the office, got drenched on the sprint back. 'How much', I asked my secretary, 'does a bally umbrella cost these days in this bally country?' 'Go', she said, 'and look on your desk.'

And there, beautifully wrapped, lay a beautiful golf umbrella, with a note from my new friend saying: 'This will help you get over the culture shock.' Now, there's a stylish gesture for you, eh? Makes you feel good to be back. Warms the cockles . . .

What's that? What nationality? Well, since you ask, he is – um – yes, American.

Keep the meatloaf on hold, honey, I'll be back next week.

Punch, 3 June 1981

On the Prince of
Wales's Engagement

'Married, aren't you?' Prince Charles once said to me. 'Fun, is it?'

The second question was by no means rhetorical. It expected the answer Yes. But it was a searching, almost desperate inquiry, addressed to someone his own age who just might, for once, give him a straight answer. The poor chap seemed really in need of one.

Beyond making appropriately reassuring noises, I don't remember much of what I said. Nobody who speaks to royalty ever does, the most ardent republican being reduced to mumbling jelly by the Royal Presence. In my case, as I burbled a few banalities, I was still transfixed by the question.

Here we were at the British Ambassador's reception in Brasilia, with local and Commonwealth dignitaries queueing to press the princely palm, and the guest of honour's thoughts were on domestic bliss.

Had he, I inquired, any specific party in mind? No,no, he said absently, not quite getting the journalist's little joke. No, no, he was just wondering.

It was the beginning of a long trail of evidence laid before me, as I spent two years of my life living his, that HRH was obsessed with the subject of his marriage. So, of course, were the British press and public – a fact he came increasingly to resent, but a fact which just redoubled his own preoccupation. Princes of Wales are not supposed to reach thirty unwed.

Apart from his great-uncle, the late Duke of Windsor, Charles was the only one to do so since James Stuart, the Old Pretender, in the early eighteenth century. 'You'd better hurry up, Charles,' his father would tell him, 'or there won't be anyone left.' He noticed, he told a friend, that 'whenever I invite people to a dinner party these days, they all seem to be married'.

To his small circle of intimates, he has talked these last few years of little else. His mother showed forbearance, trying to jolly him along each time the pop papers married him off again. But he was ever more aware of the public's growing impatience, of the increasingly wild rumours: that he was going the way of the Duke of Windsor, that he was interested only in married women, even that he was homosexual. Something, as the last Prince of Wales once said, had to be done.

So there is perhaps an appearance this weekend, as the genealogists settle over their family trees, that this is a marriage as much of necessity as of true hearts and minds. It may seem unfair to the happy couple, but the notion merits a moment's thought. For in recent years Prince Charles has developed a religious – literally so – sense of duty. And his most pressing duty just lately has been to find Britain its future Queen.

'I know the people of this country. I *know* them. They 'ate 'aving no family life at Court,' said J. H. Thomas, the great trade union leader and Labour politician, to King George V's biographer, Harold Nicolson, at the time of Edward VIII's abdication. 'And now 'ere we 'ave this obstinate little man with 'is Mrs Simpson. Hit won't do, 'arold. Hit just won't do. I tell you that straight.'

Elizabeth II regards herself as a religious figurehead, as titular leader of the Church of England, much more than as a tourist attraction or Commander-in-Chief of the British Armed Forces. The monarchy's primary function, perhaps, in an increasingly secular age, is to be a public symbol of family morality and family life. The Queen is well aware of this – just as she is quite as aware as J. H. Thomas of the public's dire need for royal children to coo over.

And so, through her, is the Prince of Wales, whose hunt for a bride had recently come to haunt him. The historical restrictions on his choice merely grated. He could not, since the 1689 Bill of Rights, marry a Catholic. 'It's just not on. If I do that, I'm dead,' he told a friend when the rumours about Marie-Astrid, the Roman Catholic Princess of Luxembourg, were at their height. 'I'm not going to sacrifice myself on that altar.'

Nor, even forty years after the Abdication, could he marry a divorcee. Constitutional niceties take little note of social change, even though royal mores have altered perceptibly during Elizabeth II's reign. In 1953 the Queen forbade her sister to marry a divorced man; twenty-five years later, she allowed her to divorce the man she married in his stead.

But for the heir to the throne, the future 'Defender of the Faith', there could be no such relaxation of the royal rules. Several potential Queens fell by the wayside when jealous boyfriends informed gossip columnists of their past. One bit the dust when she talked to a women's magazine, another when she was found naked in a men's changing room. At least one other, in this liberated age, decided the life of the Queen of England was not for her.

Another reason Charles dithered so long is that he has always boldly refused to contemplate an arranged marriage. He did his mother's bidding, and slid off secretly to Brussels to check out Marie-Astrid. He endured a mutual sizing-up session, highly unsuccessful to both parties, with Princess Caroline of Monaco. He dutifully did the rounds of those English stately homes boasting eligible, nubile daughters.

But he told the world he was waiting to fall in love, and now he says he has. After all we have put him through, the least we can do is to take him at his word. Now, at last, for both Prince and public, the long ordeal is over. For the Princess-in-waiting, however, it is only just beginning.

The thrill of the chase is dead; long live happily-ever-after. Britain's future Queen is everything the nation's racing heart has hoped for: a demure English rose, to the manor born, blushing sweetly over her engagement ring, giggling happily on the TV news. If the match was made in heaven, it was also heaven-sent for the media.

I hate to compare my future Queen with the Loch Ness Monster: but to Fleet Street, the end of the quest for the Royal Bride is almost as if Nessie had, after all these years, been found. One of the great, long-running stories of our time is no more. Exit the investigative teams, enter the saccharine squad.

Lady Diana Spencer, in the last few months, has more than earned her Princess of Wales's spurs. She has survived ordeal by paparazzi like a seasoned royal trouper, flinching only when a French camera lens came through her bathroom window, closely followed by its owner. Very sensibly, once the question had been popped, she fled to Australia to prepare for the real onslaught ahead. She must be wondering, with some reason, if life is always going to be like this.

At just nineteen, she faces a daunting prospect. Not merely will her every hiccup be chronicled, most probably with artist's impressions of her Adam's apple, but she has irrevocably chosen to surrender much more than her privacy. She will have to surrender a good deal of herself.

'A woman not only marries a man,' Prince Charles once said. 'She marries into a way of life – a job.' That, coming from him, was right royal understatement. A self-proclaimed opponent of women's liberation, the Prince will be expecting his Princess to merge her identity into his own. She is unlikely, being almost half his age, to put up much of a struggle.

Her future security is assured. Her husband, in time, will become one of the richest men outside the Arab world, yet still live largely at public expense. She will never have to wash her own dishes, worry about her mortgage, change her children's nappies or fret about their education. She'll have a choice of seven places to call home.

Her children's job prospects look pretty good, too. But the price she must pay for all this is unenviable. She must make polite conversation to interminable mayors at interminable dinner parties, and take a passionate interest in Girl Guides and Women's Institutes. She must cut ribbons, plant trees, lay foundation stones, declare things open, declare things closed. She must maintain a polite smile at all times, and be very careful what she says. She must never – but never – appear anything other than radiant and gracious.

She must do it all, what's more, for a very long time before she and her husband come into their inheritance. Charles and Diana, like Bertie and Alexandra, will most likely be grand-parents before they are King and Queen. They will have no defined role to play in British society, yet they must ultimately steer the monarchy into the twenty-first century.

In the meantime, as they establish a 'junior' court, London society will glitter. The Queen will retreat imperceptibly into the less visible, more tranquil life of a country lady.

She will not, however, abdicate in Charles's favour, as much as public opinion polls may increasingly wish her to. He will be forty-two when she reaches sixty-five – an ideal age, it may seem, for the dashing Prince to step from the wings to centre-stage. But such a move, they both agree, would be the beginning of the end of the British monarchy.

The question was once discussed in royal circles. The Queen herself raised it, at a dinner party in 1965, when the Prime Minister and the Archbishop of Canterbury were among the galactical guests summoned to discuss Prince Charles's education. 'It might be wise', said Elizabeth II, 'to abdicate at a time when Charles could do better.'

'You may be right,' joked her husband gently. 'The doctors will keep you alive so long.' But, of late, the matter had been declared taboo. If the monarchy became a pensionable job like any other, to be handed on at retirement age, its irrational, almost mystical hold on the British imagination would begin to crumble. Both Queen and Prince agree on this, however much as human beings they may think it a consummation devoutly to be wished.

So Charles is well aware that he is likely to spend many more years as Prince than as King. He is proud, in his way ambitious, and anxious to carve himself a place in history. But how on earth is he to do it?

He now devotes much of his time to unsung social work, and likes to think of himself, when on his travels, as an ambassador for exports. But he has so far shown little willingness to involve himself in British industry, despite developing his father's penchant for 'fingers out'-type speeches.

There is a dispiriting belief in the status quo around Prince Charles. As he chooses 'safe' friends, prone to fawning and flattery, so he appoints cautious staff, intent merely on oiling the wheels of the royal juggernaut. The most prominent example is Edward Adeane, whom he chose two years ago as his private secretary, and who is more of a protector than the innovator Charles needs.

The proof of all this, perhaps, is that this Prince of Wales appeals less to his own age group than any other. For all his consistently high popularity, Charles is out of touch with the values of his own generation – and unashamedly so. 'Proud to be square' was once his slogan. It bodes ill for the future, with his contemporaries approaching the seats of power as remorselessly as he approaches the throne.

In so many other ways, he and his parents have taken so many worthy initiatives. He was the first Prince of Wales to go to school with other children, the first to win himself a university degree. He has since become the first to captain his own ship and lead a national sports team, to have trained as a frogman and a commando, to have braved a parachute jump.

All rather outdoor, hairy-chested stuff of the kind his public has come to expect of him. But he was also, it should not be forgotten, the first English Prince of Wales to learn Welsh. Such symbols are important, and of late they have been less in evidence. From a man of such palpably good intentions, this has been a disappointment.

Perhaps he has been distracted by his long search for a bride. And perhaps Lady Diana, soon to be the intimate of a man with few close friends, will help. She at least brings to his life the freshness of her generation – and, for all her privileged background, some of the values of the outside world, which is often perceived but dimly from behind the windows of Buckingham Palace.

The celebration of his marriage, moreover, provides an apt turning-point. He will lead, in the public mind, a more 'identifiable' life. The national yearning will continue for him to have a more identifiable job, though he has, if truth be told, worked very hard these last few years.

He takes note of such mild criticisms, I know from experience. And he has inherited his mother's keen sense of public relations on matters royal. He knows that July's royal bonanza in London – the first marriage of a Prince of Wales since 1863, and the biggest royal occasion since the Queen's Coronation in 1953 – is a timely opportunity to seize the public imagination.

The darkness of depressed, rationed, post-war Britain was brightened, one rainy Sunday in 1948, by the news of the birth of an heir to the throne. So in a grim way it is appropriate, three decades later, that his wedding should bring some summer cheer to this hard-pressed, long-faced, Thatcherized land.

Observer, 1 March 1981

The Downfall of a Football Manager

The day I checked in at Highbury, spirits were pretty high. Arsenal had just knocked their old London rivals Spurs out of the Milk Cup, to be greeted off the pitch by Eamonn Andrews with one of his big red This is Your Loif books for veteran goalie Pat Jennings. And the previous Saturday, after an erratic home record this season, they had notched up a satisfying win against Everton, leaving them in touch with the league leaders.

Around noon that Friday morning, £5 million worth of footballing flesh frolicked happily in the sunken baths after a sweaty five-a-side training game. In the league's most luxurious dressing-rooms, bumps and bruises were examined amid the ritual signing of autographs – on footballs, photos, programmes, scraps of paper, anything the devoted fans could smuggle in. Dressed in a towel at most, North London's contemporary heroes looked, appropriately enough, like Greek gods – right down to the Apollo hairdos.

The only jarring note came when someone inspected the notice-board, where a formally typed memo from manager Terry Neill announced that there would be no free turkeys this Christmas 'due to severe economic restrictions'. The bird blight was instantly blamed on Scottish striker Charlie Nicholas, who last summer had cost Neill £750,000 – and had yet to score at Highbury. It was not a subject on which Charlie much welcomed jokes.

By the end of the week, Nicholas was to prove strikingly loyal to Neill, publicly offering to step down to the reserves until he found his form. That, alas, was not quite what the manager needed. He needed points, which meant he needed goals. His problem was: how to encourage his team of talented individualists to score them? The next two weeks were to prove how swift and brutal, when his players don't deliver, is a football manager's doom.

That Friday morning, there was nothing in the Highbury air to suggest the dramas ahead. 'Friday?' said England left-back Kenny Sansom, before going home, like his colleagues, for an afternoon off. 'Friday is Friday is Friday. It's not until you wake up on Saturday morning that you try and remember who you're playing.'

So the atmosphere on the luxury coach to Leicester next morning is distinctly relaxed. Only nineteen-year-old John Kay, a schoolboy signing making his league debut this season in place of the injured Talbot, is prepared to confess to a degree of stage fright.

Neill sits up front with his travelling physio, while the team's four superstars – Nicholas, Sansom, Rix and Tony Woodcock – play a big-money card game all the way up the M1. Fellow Irishmen Pat Jennings and David O'Leary, neither the most talkative of men, sit together in thoughtful silence – as do the younger trio of Stewart Robson, Paul Davis and today's substitute, an unhappy £500,000 worth of Lee Chapman.

Alan Sunderland, a prolific goal-scorer for Arsenal in his time, sits alone at the back of the bus, reading a Harold Robbins novel. Old hands like Sunderland admit they don't these days take much in the way of special precautions on Friday nights: 'A couple of jars, and bed around 11.30.' Kay and another young defender, Chris Whyte, tell me they were both tucked up by 10.30.

The coach left Highbury at nine, but Neill and most of his team have boarded it half an hour later at Arsenal's London Colney training ground, near their homes in *nouveau riche* suburbia. Coffee and biscuits are served soon after Hemel Hempstead, and high-decibel Radio One whiles away the motorway miles. The only incident of note comes near Newport Pagnell, when a passing busload of Leeds United fans mouth excited obscenities at the Gunners stars, none of whom takes the slightest notice.

So we are at the Leicester Holiday Inn bang on time at 11.25, and sit straight down to a lunch of corn flakes and poached eggs, ordered in advance by telex. Only Rix varies the diet with a side order of baked beans. The players sit in the same groups as on the bus; when they wander out for ten minutes' free time – 'but don't', orders Neill, 'leave the hotel' – bars of chocolate are left behind, untouched, to be snaffled by eager schoolboys.

Neill and his coach Don Howe remain behind in a corner of the dining-room, chatting conspiratorially. They look like a couple of anxious teachers in charge of a schoolboy outing.

At 12.20, in a private room, we all sit down to watch BBC TV's *Football Focus*. The telly experts' comments bring the odd snort of professional derision, but the atmosphere is otherwise rather heavy. The fact is not mentioned, but present company is pretty conspicuous by its absence from the endlessly re-played goals and dribbles, through passes and floating balls.

Arsenal's reputation for 'dull' football means they don't get on *Match of the Day* much these days, and weren't even invited to join this year's pre-season negotiations over live Sunday games. It was one reason they splashed out on 'exciting' Charlie Nicholas.

At 12.45, when the Beeb moves on to boxing, the pre-game tactics session begins. Neill and Howe secure the doors before passing on a few tips from their colleague George Male on Leicester City's strengths and weaknesses. (Male, one of the stars of Arsenal's glory days in the 1930s, is now employed to spend each Saturday 'spying' on the team they are playing next week.) Leicester are next-to-bottom of the table: they should be easy meat.

An hour later, in optimistic mood, we pick our way through mobs of autograph hunters back to the bus. It's only a ten-minute ride to Filbert Street, but the Fab Four have got the cards out again, and Sunderland's back into Harold Robbins. I express mild concern that he might find himself unable to put it down at 2.55; he asks me to stand on the touchline during the game and read him the next chapter.

Young Leicester fans have arrived early to jeer the opposition, but swoon into wide-eyed sycophancy at the sight of such national heroes as Rix, Woodcock *et al.* in the flesh. There's an hour in the dressing-room for Neill and Howe to hype up the lads – while the rest of us, in the Leicester board-room, take medicinal precautions against the cold outside. On both teams' current form, the Arsenal directors are looking for a useful away win this afternoon, to start a steady climb up the league table.

Forty-five minutes later, back in that same board-room, the chill of the directors' box has followed us back inside. The home team is two goals up – and the visitors, after an overly casual start, don't look like pulling it back. Arsenal's Old Etonian chairman Peter Hill-Wood, whose family has run the club for sixty-five years, puts a brave face on his anxieties. Surely they ought to beat this lot?

But the second half only sees the gloom deepen. For no apparent reason, Arsenal are all over the place. The attack is lacklustre, the defence panicky; in the end, they're lucky the defeat is no worse than 3-0, giving Leicester their second league win of the season. Arsenal leave the field to cries of 'BO-O-O-RING', amid sundry obscene explanations for Nicholas's continuing goal drought.

As the final whistle sounds, a grim-looking Hill-Wood stalks out in a haze of cigar smoke, closely followed by his club secretary and managing director Ken Friar. Heads, one feels, will roll.

Don Howe, beside himself with rage, is touring the Arsenal dressing-room, haranguing them one by one. Neill, with a look of pained disgust, adds the occasional barbed one-liner. As a double-act, they are not unlike the 'hard' and 'soft' interrogators of a thousand cops-and-robbers movies.

Outside, as Friar climbs into his chairman's Rolls-Royce, the conversation has already turned to that new defender they've been thinking of buying.

Back on the bus, the verdict of caterer, kit manager and assorted groupies is unanimous: the boys just seemed to give up. Bob the driver, who also takes Spurs and QPR to their away games, knows all too well what it means to slip behind schedule like this: 'They're getting a right bollocking in there.' Sure enough, when the lads finally climb aboard, they're looking pretty sheepish.

Neill walks straight past them all, without further comment, and joins me at the back. His anger has almost, but not quite, melted into resignation. Before sighing over his soup, he lets off a lot of steam about the way players' contracts and transfers are organized these days. Himself captain of Arsenal in the 1960s, he never had the kind of financial security these guys enjoy. 'What use is a £250 win bonus when they're on

£1,500 a week?'

To my surprise he tells me, one by one, what he *really* thinks of his players. 'They don't know what it is to hunger for goals and glory. On days like today I think they just want to pick up their money and go home.' Neill is not a neurotic man, but his is such a high-risk profession that one bad defeat like this has even him, the most relaxed of football managers, worrying about his future. 'I tell you now: we'll finish in the top six again this season. Whether or not I'll be around to see it is another matter.'

Heat of the moment stuff. He'll feel better, he says, in the morning – and so it proves, despite a withering press. Ten am on the Sabbath sees unwonted activity at Highbury. Downstairs, Rix has come in for treatment on a strained Achilles tendon. Upstairs, Ken Friar is in his office, advancing negotiations with Manchester City for Tommy Caton, the strapping young defender Neill's had his eye on for two years. The need has suddenly become urgent.

Friar joined Arsenal at the age of eleven, when he retrieved a football from beneath a large limo outside Highbury's front door. The car's owner turned out to be the club's then manager George Allison, legendary successor to the even more legendary Herbert Chapman. He offered young Friar a job as messenger boy – and here he still is, thirty year later, as secretary and managing director.

But then Arsenal, which prides itself on its 'family' atmosphere, is that kind of club. Nearly everyone but the players has been here a generation or more. It has had only seven managers since the war, while other clubs have had as many in a season.

Neill joined Arsenal at seventeen, spent eleven years here as a player, and has now enjoyed seven as manager. Don Howe was Neill's room-mate when both were Arsenal players; he has since had seven years at Highbury as coach with Bertie Mee, and now seven more with Neill. Continuity has been Arsenal's creed. The club's motto, '*Victoria concordia crescit*', means 'Victory through harmony' – but most people around here prefer to translate it 'Don't rock the boat'.

Monday morning sees Neill and his lads in the frosts of London Colney, where he and Howe spend much of their time dealing with press inquiries about Saturday's defeat. After training, I ask the players what a result like that does to their weekend. 'Spoils it,' says Pat Jennings, unambiguously. 'Well,' says Stewart Robson, 'it should, but you can't take it all home to your family, can you?' 'No,' says Tony Woodcock, 'you can't let it spoil your weekend. You must take a rest, cheer yourself up, and get on with winning the next one.'

As we chat, they pick the mud out of their studs over an old tin bucket. In my innocence, I express surprise at seeing highly paid superstars cleaning their own boots. Back at Highbury, there's a full-time kit manager and a fleet of apprentices to cater to their every whim. 'If we don't win tomorrow night,' says Alan Sunderland, 'we won't be doing anything but cleaning boots.'

Tomorrow night sees the third round of the Milk Cup, in which the draw has blessed Arsenal with a patsy home tie against third division Walsall. If ever Charlie's going to score at Highbury, this must surely be the night? All over the ground, staff and fans alike are looking for a big win to exorcise Saturday's shame.

The team train in the morning, then lunch on steak at a hotel near King's Cross, where they sleep away the afternoon. As their pre-game session begins below stairs, the board-room is a hive of activity. Before tonight's guests arrive Hill-Wood and Friar are fêting Caton, flown down today from Manchester, and listening to a public relations firm's ideas for advertising their product.

Ever aware of its dignity and traditions, Arsenal has been reluctant to follow Spurs' lead into TV advertising, pre-game entertainments and other such showbiz *folderol*. But gates are consistently below their 30,000 break-even point, and another indifferent season from the players will bring big financial pressures. Among the directors' guests tonight, as £500,000 worth of Tom Caton takes them into the red, is Arsenal's bank manager.

Caton himself, a twenty-one-year-old incredible hunk of defensive muscle, is looking a bit bemused by it all. As a Japanese contingent sweeps in with the boss of JVC, Arsenal's sponsors, he tells me he has had little to do with the negotiations. 'I was just told this morning to get on the 1 o'clock shuttle to London.' Now he'll be an Arsenal player by Saturday – so will he be training with the lads tomorrow? 'No, I'll 'ave to go back to Manchester to get me boots. I left in such an 'urry I forgot 'em.'

Among the gathering crowd of dignitaries is Sir Stanley Rous, grand old man of football and president of Arsenal. Now eighty-eight, Sir Stanley doesn't like to miss a game at Highbury: 'I've been coming here since the ground was opened in 1913.' He shares a general sense of foreboding about tonight's game. 'Against a third division side in a cup tie, we're on a hiding to nothing.'

He knows a thing or two, does Sir Stanley. By half-time Arsenal are a goal up, but Walsall are fighting like dervishes. With a worried look, Friar hands me a slip of paper showing that tonight's gate is 22,406, and the gross receipts £69,963. 'Before you ask, 15 per cent goes in tax, expenses are taken off the top, then 40 per cent to each team and 20 per cent to the League. Work it out for yourself.'

In the second half, extraordinary scenes. I myself have taken the precaution of asking if it is decorous, in the directors' box, to leap up and cheer when Arsenal score. I need not have worried. When Walsall equalize, there is an excited buzz among the visiting directors. When they ram home another, these captains of Midland industry are jumping around like schoolboys.

Friar slumps in his seat: 'A quarter of a million in revenue gone.' Hill-Wood's features remind me of those of my late headmaster on seeing twenty illicit Woodbines fall from my pocket.

Arsenal are again outclassed, and never look like equalizing. It is a defeat echoing one fifty years ago, when third division Walsall shocked the nation by knocking league champions Arsenal out of the FA Cup. On that notorious day, Herbert Chapman fired half his players. Half a century later, it is clear, Arsenal expects a similar gesture of Terry Neill – unless Hill-Wood fires him first.

For now, the chairman is displaying magnanimity in defeat – 'and bloody difficult it is, too' – as he toasts his visitors in double Scotches. Before the game, he told me he understood his manager's problems in motivating today's rich young players –

'but I suppose it's also my job to motivate the manager'. A busy international banker, he says that at times like this Hambros seems light relief compared with Highbury. The trouble is that it's supposed to be the other way round.

Sir Stanley beckons me over. 'Which one', he asks, proverbial twinkle in eye, 'was the third division team?' Beneath the window, a crowd of several thousand is baying for blood – or at least a scapegoat. NEILL MUST GO is their chant, which they know he and the team can hear only too clearly in the dressing-room – as indeed can the directors in the board-room.

Well, Neill *is* going – after a quick glare at his players ('There didn't seem to be much to say'). He's going to face the football press, who at times like this take on the aspect of vultures. 'No, I'm not going to resign' is his defiant, much reiterated theme. 'I've got a job to do, and I'll see it through.'

The crowd below is still in full voice as he then presents himself, with hang-dog expression, in the board-room, which by now resembles a funeral parlour. Even I, intrepid sports-writer though I've become, daren't ask the bank manager what's on his mind.

An hour after the final whistle, it's still impossible for us toffs to leave – 'Not this way, sir,' says the commissionaire on the front door, 'you'll get lynched.' I am shown to a discreet side exit and leave in low spirits. I feel angry with the players and sorry for Neill. Highbury's despondency is catching.

Next morning, its marble halls are so bleak that I half-expect to see the Gunners flag flying at half-mast. As his wife Ethel launders last night's dirty linen, kit manager Tony Donnelly, who's been at Highbury for twenty-two years, waxes nostalgic about the great 'double' team of 1971, which won both Cup and League. Will Highbury ever see their like again?

In the Gunners shop, where 1950s goalkeeper Jack Kelsey sells everything from Arsenal wallpaper to Arsenal knickers, I receive a polite 'no comment' on last night's events. Today's best news, Jack is prepared to reveal, is that this morning's post has brought £350 worth of mail orders.

Next door, beside the Indoor Training School, road managers Chris Davies and Paul Johnson are planning well into next year in booking trains, coaches, hotels, and meals for 4,000 members of the official (and well-behaved) Arsenal Travel

Club – quite apart from the team itself. Last season they saw them all safely through 13,000 miles around Britain and Europe. As of today, however, 'it doesn't look like we'll be booking them through Europe this year'.

Beside them Debbie Wakeford sifts through the mountains of team pictures, scarves, newsletters, pens and autographed photos she must despatch to the nearly 2,000 members of the Junior Gunners Club, the most successful 'future supporters' scheme in the land. This office also serves as an unofficial 'bank' for the players, as is proved when a furtive Woodcock looks in to cash a £100 cheque.

Out on the sacred turf itself, head groundsman Jimmy Hosie is repairing last night's damage – and whistling as he does so. He's the only remotely cheerful person I've met all morning. 'Ah well, you see,' he confides in broad Scots, 'I'm a Glasgow Rangers fan.'

The lads themselves haven't shown their faces, but Neill is digging in for trial by ordeal. Highbury's famous front lobby is full of Fleet Street vultures, noses atwitch, sensing blood. Every single one of this morning's back pages predicts the manager's demise in inch-thick, mile-high headlines.

They sit on his desk in front of him as we talk. For a man under such huge public and private pressure today, Neill is amazingly relaxed. He's certainly known his ups and downs as Arsenal manager: the only trophy they've won under his stewardship is the FA Cup (though they reached three successive finals), and the highest they've finished in the league is third. It's not the first time the fans have rounded on him: there was once a string of seven successive defeats. But this must surely be the low point?

'Last night will be with me till I'm six feet under. I heard the fans, and I don't blame them. We were awful. So they want my head. But last month, when we beat Spurs, they sang a different song. And last night, apart from Rix, I fielded the same team. So why did they go out there and play like pantomime horses? You tell me.'

Now forty-one, Neill has known his chairman, Peter Hill-Wood, since he was seventeen. At times like this, he has thus had more claim than most managers to the benefit of his chairman's doubts. But he knows what Hill-Wood's criterion must be: he can ignore attempts at mob rule outside the stadium, but he can't ignore empty seats within it.

And football managers aren't exactly in there for job security. So why stick to so thankless a task? 'Because I love this club. It's my life.' Would all his players say the same? 'Well, if not, it's my job to make them.' Which, after declining to resign for TV and yet more newspapers, is what he goes off to do.

So 'motivation' remains the bogeyword on everyone's lips. But whose fault is Arsenal's apparent lack of the stuff? You hear differing viewpoints all over Highbury. Down at the Supporters' Club, secretary Barry Baker injects a note of calm on behalf of his 4,000 members. 'We're the official supporters. Our job is just that: to support the club. We don't endorse mob protests. We're 100 per cent behind Terry Neill. If someone else is manager next week, we'll be 100 per cent behind him.'

A mixed blessing, perhaps, for Neill – who swiftly asserts his clout by cancelling the team's three-day golfing break in Spain, scheduled for next week. Then, after the morning's suspense, Hill-Wood makes his position clear by summoning all the players to an unprecedented chairman's wigging on Friday afternoon.

The newspapers go berserk. The chairman has publicly usurped the manager's function. The Prime Minister's problems in Delhi are as nothing compared to NEILL'S much-vaunted AGONY. Before Saturday's home game against West Brom, the photographers laying ambush to the manager's dugout almost outnumber the crowd. His only consolation this chill afternoon is one of Highbury's best-kept secrets: his 'cage' is heated, while the visiting manager's isn't.

Small consolation it proves, however, as 600 dissident fans deliver a petition demanding his sacking, and the team again go to pieces. The demos threatened for half-time don't materialize – but Arsenal lose again, a desultory 0-1, and are booed off the pitch.

The following Saturday, at West Ham, sees another poor performance and another defeat. Hill-Wood tells press and fans alike that he refuses to be rushed into panic measures. He still wants time to think about the team's performance – and Neill's future.

He gives himself just six days. The following Friday, nine

days before Christmas, Terry Neill is fired.

That same week, in that same Milk Cup, mighty Liverpool were held to a second draw by lowly Fulham, and the next week Manchester United were knocked out by third division Oxford. There was the usual press hype about 'giantkillers', but no talk of lynch-mobs.

So why the Highbury hysteria? Maybe history has given Arsenal fans, more than most, a sense of divine right to trophies. Maybe the critics are right – and today's football stars, as personified by Arsenal's front row, are spoilt little rich boys not hungry enough for goals. Maybe Terry Neill was just too nice a guy to make them really frightened of losing.

But why do they care so much more than the players? Is there some deep underlying problem requiring Ken Friar to get out his long-suffering cheque book and sign on a club psychiatrist? Or is it, as Don Howe kept telling me, 'a question more of physical than mental attitudes'?

Perhaps it is simply a question of 'You win some, you lose some' – Terry Neill's last words to me, as he drove off, in his Mercedes, to an unemployed Christmas.

Sunday Express magazine, 22 January 1984

The Falklands Revisited

January on New Island, West Falkland: fifty-mile-an-hour winds, sub-zero temperatures, horizontal rain turning to stinging sleet. I'm wearing an anorak designed by Chay Blyth for rounding Cape Horn, but the weather still manages to join me inside it. My companion, trying to photograph some penguins, is blown clean off his feet into a pile of their filth. So this is the Falklands' summer.

We struggle through the storm to a nearby cottage, home of the island's only residents. 'This', they say, while brewing us some tea, 'is the kind of weather you journalists keep saying we get in the Falklands.' There's no answer to that. I'm still trying to think of one that midsummer evening, as we stay on a farm where forty-two newly shorn sheep die overnight of exposure.

The Falkland Islands have problems enough without surviving a war to face up to its consequences. This is proving a bad summer weather-wise, but that's the least of their worries. Nearly two years after the war the 1,893 islanders are now sharing their bleak and remote fastness, two-thirds the size of Wales, with as many construction workers, development advisers, wily entrepreneurs, and sundry government, commercial and other boffins, not to mention a 4,000-strong British garrison. In less than two years, the number of people around has more than trebled.

In a week-long visit, I get around enough to meet fully a third of the resident population. Their current mood is summed up by Tony Blake, a sheep farmer who is also an elected councillor, and has spoken eloquently on the Falklands' behalf at the United Nations in New York. 'We are', he says, 'an island drowning in a sea of advice.'

The only way to fly to the Falklands, since all travel via South America has become impossible, is via the RAF 'airbridge' from Ascension Island: thirteen hours of unmitigated hell aboard a Hercules, strapped to the throbbing wall amid long-faced squaddies. You can't speak (because of the noise), can't read (because of the dark), can't sleep (because of the crush), let alone drink, smoke, or watch movies. You eat stale pork pies and soggy Bovril crisps out of an army-issue 'white box'. The only diversion, viewed by special permission over the pilot's shoulder, is the mid-air refuelling: a tense, 300-mph airborne ballet.

The airbridge flies five days a week, at around £100,000 a trip. Our travelling companions include the Foreign Office minister with responsibility for the Falklands, Baroness Young, and her three FO staff; the court of inquiry into a fatal helicopter crash; a brigadier going down 'to sort out a few problems'; a contractor heading for the new airfield; some housing workers; some development 'scrutineers'; an official from the new bank – and assorted officers and men from all three services, who glumly face a four-month tour 'down *there*'.

It's not untypical of the daily load disgorged, with bleary eyes and singing ears, at Stanley airport, now rechristened RAF Stanley (without the locals' permission, and somewhat to their annoyance). A fleet of Land-Rovers – the most comfortable ones, power-steering and all, being captured Argentinian Mercedes – disperse us to our billets. The three-mile dirt-track 'road' into town has to be resurfaced almost weekly: like peas on a drum, we bounce over the potholes dug by incessant military traffic.

At first sight, Stanley looks the quaint seaside town now familiar from a thousand wartime photos. Its corrugated metal roofs, painted in bright primary colours, slope down in tidy rows towards the harbour, where a dozen big ships are at anchor. In peace, it all still smacks of war, as Phantoms and Harriers screech overhead, and Chinook choppers chug by bearing cars, containers, even Portakabin 'homes' on the umbilical cords beneath their bellies.

The bulk of the garrison is now leaving Stanley, withdrawing to its new floating 'boatels' near the airfield, but there are still enough around to make it feel like Aldershot-on-sea. There has, Stanley folk complain, been much misreporting of their feelings: the vast majority will be sad to see them go.

'Our boys' have brought the place to life a little. They've lived in people's homes and become 'part of the family'. And the noise? 'We don't mind the noise, so long as it's *British* noise.'

Nearly all Falklanders, especially those in Stanley, have remarkable tales to tell about life with the Argies, during those two traumatic winter months of 1981. Most of their stories ring with stoic British fortitude, some with personal heroism; nearly all have proudly preserved bullet-holes to prove it. The town itself is now pretty much tidied up – the debris of war has gone – but, to be frank, it was a bit of a mess in the first place.

Not in terms of litter and the other dismal dross of British urban life. If a soldier drops a beer can in the street, you can be sure a resident will make him pick it up again. It's more the dank shabbiness of poverty. 'Before the war', says artist and shopkeeper Tony Chater, 'we were going down the drain.'

A few Falklanders are rich, some very rich. They have houses in 'camp' (the collective name for the countryside) and in Stanley; they fly themselves to and fro in private aircraft. They host endless cocktail-parties, where they smoke a lot and get drunk through sheer boredom. For the rest, however, for the taciturn majority, life is rather different.

Stanley's social elite has the twang of a Home Counties golf club gin-and-tonic set. I attend one of their parties on my first evening, my internal organs still firmly aboard the Hercules. Our host is a senior government official, whose home just happens to be one of the fifty-four new Brewster houses, comfy timber-framed villas of Swedish design, built under the British Government's £15 million rehabilitation programme – the overture to the £31 million development scheme based on Lord Shackleton's report.

These houses have cost £130,000 each to build – which seems a bit steep, even allowing for the fact that all the materials, and the labour which built them, have had to be imported from the UK. Even our host can't afford that, so he rents it for a subsidized £145 a month. Either figure is way beyond the pocket of all but a handful of islanders. Through the window, a local dissident points out to me a traditional waterfront home, stone walls, tin roof, which is on the market for £12,000. A year ago, it was £7,000.

It is not only property values which have zoomed, mostly to the benefit of absentee landlords. There is many a quick buck to be made here, and many a quick buccaneer arriving to make it. The idea was that the aid money should stay, for once, in the islands – but things aren't altogether working out that way.

The million pounds a day being spent in 'Fortress Falklands' by the British taxpayer is breeding a get-rich-quick industry which will last, with luck, another couple of years – until the new airport is built and the garrison reduced. By then, however, a fortunate few should already be able to retire on the proceeds.

Take, for instance, food. There are three cafés in Stanley, two of them started on their life-savings by islanders, who for now tentatively serve fish-and-chips two days a week in converted peat sheds. The choice being not exactly worthy of Michelin, the hungry visitor skips full guest-house board at his peril. But the mutton on offer at mine – known as '365', after the number of days per year it is served – is so awful that I opt out in favour of Stanley's latest post-war attraction: the muttonburger.

A few streets away at Kelvin's Café, I order a 'Port-Stanley-burger' from twenty-nine-year-old Simon Powell, an ex-public schoolboy of Wiltshire military stock who fetched up here last August. Though the cheapest thing on his menu, it costs me £1.60, and is really rather good. Despite his high prices, Simon is doing a booming business in takeaway 'Stanley-burgers' and 'Goose-Green-burgers', even the montainous 'Triple K' at a cool £3. Most of his customers, of course, are troops; few locals can afford to eat here.

Simon is a bit coy about figures, but he must be taking a good £500 a day. After selling his London decorating business, he sailed south, bought the Kelvin building, imported his kitchen equipment from the UK and set up shop. He sells everything from postcards to model Harriers, and rents motorbikes for £15 a day. All the raw materials for his 'burgers are home-made. (There is no bakery in Stanley – though he is about, naturally, to start one.)

Open sixteen hours a day, Powell works very hard and is making a fortune. He wanted, he tells me, to flee the British 'rat race' – but why on earth did he choose to come *here*? A knowing grin: 'For adventure.'

Down the road at Everards' brewery, Phil Middleton is the one-man-band brewing, marketing, promoting and delivering Penguin real ale, launched last year amid much sympathetic publicity. The unheated lean-to shed in which Phil mashes and sparges was bought from the Falkland Islands Company (a subsidiary of Coalite, the UK fuels congolmerate) for a staggering £23,000. Everards then invested some £250,000 in importing a mini-brewery from Blighty.

To pay his way, Phil should be brewing three times a week (each brew producing 360 gallons). So far, after a year in business, he is brewing only once every three weeks. So what's gone wrong?

'Ferkin Phil' (as he's locally known) sells his excellent beer for 50p a pint, with a recommended retail price of 60p. His main competitor, Courage special bitter, sells to the NAAFI at 40p a pint, thanks to various freight and excise concessions, even though it is imported from England. Some bureaucrat somewhere, as Phil points out, takes an odd view of encouraging local Falklands industry.

Such anomalies abound all over town. At the Upland Goose, for instance, Stanley's (and the island's) only hotel, proprietor Des King is having trouble getting a development grant to add ten new bedrooms – even though the Goose is now full all year, and Shackleton recommended more hotel rooms.

Falkland islanders have a reputation – also enshrined in Shackleton – for being slow to speak their minds. When the troops first arrived, they christened the islanders 'Bennies' – after the half-witted character at ITV's Crossroads motel. Many Falklanders may be rather retiring characters, as is only to be expected of people who have opted for a solitary way of life. But they're not all dim. They now make jokes about 'us poor Bennies', so the troops have taken to calling them 'Bubs'. It stands for 'Bloody Ungrateful Bastards'.

Most islanders are at pains to avoid appearing ungrateful, and sympathize with the huge burden on the British taxpayer – but they crave some local control over the way all this money is being spent, supposedly on their behalves. 'The Prime Minister', says Councillor John Cheek, 'promised us control over our own destiny. We're not getting it.'

Part of Lady Young's mission was to explain why: 'British Government ministers', she told them, 'have to account for that money to Parliament. HMG must retain control.' The locals did not appear to find this news reassuring.

Walking down Stanley's front one evening, I followed warily behind six very drunk, rather agressive squaddies, who threatened to turn ugly any minute. Nipping safely past as they paused to pee in someone's front garden, I felt for the minority who say they want the troops out. The worst offenders, apparently, are the 'gozomees' – those about to go home, who spend their last week amid the 'Bennies' painting Stanley red.

One important Stanley figure who takes a dim view of post-war life is Dr Alison Bleaney, head of the island's only hospital, where she must now share command with the military (who have no separate facilities of their own). As military personnel change every four months, her life is one of 'constant disruption' – and she's had enough. Dr Bleaney and her husband, a Falkland Islands company manager who came here thirty years ago, are 'getting out'.

Mike Bleaney doesn't trust the Foreign Office – 'they'll sell us out sooner or later' – but his wife has other reasons. Last Guy Fawkes night, she and her two young children were menaced on their way home by drunken and abusive troops. On Christmas Day the army laid on entertainment for the locals: it consisted of a British landing force 'wiping out' defending 'Argentinians'.

The young Bleaneys are already playing war games and asking their parents for guns. It was to escape that side of 'civilized' European life that Dr Bleaney came here in the first place. As a doctor, she must cope with all the new disease imported into the Falklands by the new arrivals; as a mother, she must worry about 'video nasties', and other such previously unknown imports. She'll be very sorry to go, and Stanley will be sorry to lose her.

Others confirm that life in Stanley can never be the same again. At the Upland Goose, Des and Nan King and their three daughters bemoan the new restrictions on their freedom of movement. The family used to be great picnickers; now all the beaches are mined. Des runs the annual island races; now Stanley Common, where horses were stabled and trained, is a no-go area – and probably always will be.

Out in 'camp', where roughly half the islands' population is scattered through thirty-odd settlements, the rugged, yeoman way of Falkland life has altered less. This starkly beautiful countryside, you feel, is the heartland of the Falklands, Stanley the urban aberration en route to it. Out here there are no roads, no telephones; you get around by helicopter – or, at a stretch, Land-Rover – and you keep in touch with the world by radio.

A few 'camp' settlements have troops for company, and enjoy it: they do each other favours. In the Goose Green social hall, where forty islanders were held captive by the 'Argies', I attended a joint military–civilian Sunday morning service; despite a highly militaristic sermon, the event bore witness to the ease with which they've learnt to live together.

Nearby, the spot where Colonel 'H' Jones fell has become a place of pilgrimage on army-conducted tours of the Goose Green battlefield. Though buried in the British cemetery overlooking San Carlos Water, another affecting must on every post-war visitors itinerary, 'H' is immortalized with an impromptu pile of rocks, poignantly surmounted by a china rose. The debris of war has been left scattered around the Darwin and Goose Green hillsides – a deliberate reminder of 2 Para's fierce struggle against huge odds.

In time, the battlefields may well become something of a tourist attraction, along with the wildlife which brought in several hundred visitors a year before the war. But tourism must remain an unknown – and pretty marginal – quantity while there is no air link with South America. Out here in 'camp', the central change overtaking many lives is the sudden opportunity to buy land.

At Packes Port Howard, across Falkland Sound from Goose Green, Tim Miller and Jimmy Foster have between them invested £110,000 in 2,400 acres – and 6,000 sheep – to call their own. Ninety per cent of the money was borrowed from the Government, at a fixed interest rate of 11 per cent. 'A daunting prospect,' they declare, 'but well worth it.'

They are among the first to benefit from the land reform

scheme, adopted from Shackleton's post-war report as one way of keeping Falklands money in the Falklands, rather than enriching the absentee landlords who own 2.4 million acres – or 80 per cent of the entire place. Forty-three per cent of the land, for instance, belongs to Coalite, in the shape of the Falkland Islands Company.

Many young Falklanders are now keen to invest in their own land – though few have the necessary down payment, and most are deeply worried about the 11 per cent. Acreages vary according to their quality, but the ideal equation is reckoned to be 3,000 sheep per man – each fleece being worth an average £5 at shearing time.

After years of seeking some stake in the land they work, Falklanders are now dismayed at the snail's pace of land reform. The applications queue is a long one, the red tape immense, and the procedures very slow. HMG calls it 'gradualism', and takes the kind of paternalistic line the islanders hate. 'This is a huge economic revolution,' I was told by one administrator. 'Some of these people don't quite realize what they're taking on. It's as well to keep the pace slow, and watch how the pioneers get on.'

Many Falklanders themselves admit that their islands cannot live by sheep alone. They clamour for a 200-mile fishing limit to be imposed – but again get evasive answers from visiting London bureaucrats. Apart from the conservation arguments – the waters, say the locals, are being 'fished dry' – it galls them to see the Poles alone taking some £12 million worth of fish a year out of their seas, without paying any licensing fees.

Some estimates have the Poles, Russians, Spanish, Japanese, East Germans and others taking as much as £50 million worth of fish a year between them. But the FO mandarins point out that none of these countries recognize British sovereignty of the islands: so how would such a limit be policed? And the unspoken truth, for which the islanders feel only contempt, is that a fishing limit would be an act of provocation towards Argentina, at a time when Britain is working towards closer relations.

There are other points at issue: a constitutional quibble, for instance, in which London is resisting the islanders' wish to retain a two-tier system of self-government. The arguments are complex, but amount on the Falklanders' side to a suspicion that Whitehall is trying to minimize their autonomy.

But above all, right now, there is much local distress at the way the development money is disappearing. 'Most of it', said Graham Bound, editor of the island's monthly newspaper, *Penguin News*, 'is being spent deciding how to spend it.'

Even establishment figures such as Councillor Bill Luxton, on whose 150,000-acre West Falkland farm, Chartres, I spent a night, blames the Overseas Development Administration for mishandling sundry projects. 'Those houses in Stanley are very nice,' he says, 'but at £130,000 each so they should be. They've eaten up half the rehabilitation fund. And the new roads they're building there: two-lane tracks costing as much as a four-lane motorway in the UK. The fund's all spent – and there's not a lot to show for it.'

Eric Goss, manager of North Arm, the islands' second largest farm, pointed out perhaps the most striking anomaly of all. To prevent the land being over-grazed, Falklanders slaughter 10,000 sheep a year, and have to burn the carcasses – a tragic waste, caused by the sheer expense of exporting them. As this goes on, the 4,000 troops manning Fortress Falklands are eating mutton and lamb imported – via London – from New Zealand. Why? Because Falklands' mutton is not slaughtered to EEC standards.

On the way back to Stanley I visited Mount Pleasant, site of the new £215 million airfield, due to be operational by March of next year, and fully complete by October 1986. Four hundred men are already at work on this vast and impressive project, which is bang on schedule. At the height of the work 1,400 construction workers will be employed – all shipped out (via South Africa) from England. That's almost as many airport-builders as Falklanders – yet not one islander is being employed on the project.

In Britain, there were 14,000 applications for the 1,400 jobs: partly through unemployment, partly because they can expect to earn two to three times UK rates, free of income tax, for a year and more. It is officially denied, but the Foreign Office has privately instructed contractors not to employ local workers. It would deprive the island, especially its overstretched Public

Works Department, of essential labour – there is no unemployment on the Falklands – and the rates of pay would throw the
islands' economy out of kilter.

Again, not surprisingly, there is deep local resentment. 'All
this development', says Patrick Watts, manager of Radio
Stanley, 'is supposed to be enriching the Falkland islanders.
Some of us may be enjoying a little temporary boom, but in the
long run we're the last people being enriched.'

The more wordly, realistic Falklanders, who recognize the
need for a resumption of relations with Argentina, are quickly
turning cynical. 'We're going to give it all to the Argies in ten
years, anyway,' they say. 'That'll drive me out. So why bother?'

The most vociferous dissidents, native islanders point out,
tend to be the 'expats' – people who, for whatever reason, left
the UK for a Falklands way of life which is now immutably
changed. 'Kelpers' – those born and bred in the islands – prefer
on the whole to let their gratitude, and relief at their rescue
from the hated Argies, overcome their reservations. Many
agree that 'Galtieri's folly', for all the waste of human life, has
proved a blessing in disguise. 'But it's a pity', said one kelper
typically, 'that after fifteen years of neglect, it took a war to
remind Britain we were here.'

To preserve their fragile way of life, they're prepared to
accept all its built-in disadvantages – inadequate education,
poor housing, a humble (and monotonous) diet, a bleak climate, a life free of all luxuries except the two necessities seen
in even the humblest homes: video machines and short-wave
radios. But can the self-sufficient life they love ever be the
same again?

To this visitor, it looks unlikely. The remote country
shepherd riding out to tend his flock seems, on the contrary,
lucky to have survived so long – defying economic logic, and
escaping the shadow of modern geopolitics. As for the post-war
plight of the urban Falklander: 'Never mind all this high-
minded stuff about sovereignty and constitutions,' says Phil
Middleton. 'Can somebody tell me how I can sell my beer?'

Sunday Express magazine, 26 February 1984

People

Sir Harold Wilson, Author

Sir Harold Wilson did me his (rather good) Stanley Holloway impersonation, reciting one song about Albert and another about young 'Arold. He is in a very bouncy form. 'It's fun watching Jim cope,' he says of retirement. 'I've had no withdrawal symptoms at all, though I'm working just as long hours as I did at Number Ten. The difference is that when the phone rings, it doesn't mean you've got to deal with another hijacking or some ghastly ministerial indiscretion.'

The fruits of Sir Harold's long hours, *A Prime Minister on Prime Ministers*, will be in your bookshops next week and on your television screens this Saturday. A very wonderful David Frost enterprise – the book's copyright line reads 'David Paradine Histories' – it is regarded by its author as a film of a book rather than a book of a film. Though you could be forgiven a moment's confusion. 'No, the book came first. It's different from my other books – being history, you know – but I think it is, er, significant.'

Its author spent Monday, Tuesday and Friday of last week signing 10,000 copies – at a peak of twenty per minute, with tea breaks – for distribution to book clubs. (He is still finding it difficult to hold a knife as a result.) This week he sets off on a brief promotional tour, 'though nothing on the scale *he* does' – a reference to his rival in the bestseller lists, Mr Edward Heath, of whom, between ourselves, Sir Harold has some surprisingly generous things to say just now.

The book, some 140,000 words in first draft, was written between 9 January and 6 April. It was a period of all-night sittings, which, says Sir Harold, 'helped'. In his room at the House, in his London flat, in his Great Missenden study, weekends and all, writing longhand with 'throwaway pens', he would toil till well after midnight, working from sourcebook notes which in Disraeli's case reached fully sixty pages.

Then: 'Marcia read it. She's a history graduate, you know, and she had a lot of comments to make. I changed a good deal

on her advice. And she'd spot things I had left out. She'd say:
"But why *didn't* Pitt marry so-and-so's daughter? David's
going to ask you about that, I'll bet." And she was right. He
did.'

The adviser on the television series was another history
graduate, Lord Blake. Once, sometimes twice a week throughout the spring and summer, Wilson and Blake would meet for
lunch with Tony Jay, the editor, and Frost if he were in the
country. Blake, says Wilson, was fascinated by his new approach to history. Looking at Pitt, Peel, Disraeli, Gladstone
through a prime minister's eyes, the eyes of a parliamentary
master tactician, produced new judgements. Then off they all
went to the appropriate locations, Caernarvon for Lloyd
George, the war bunker for Churchill, where Frosty would
walk up and down interviewing Wilson and 'most of it would
end up on the cutting-room floor'.

Wilson has made one historical discovery: that Canada
asked the Duke of Grafton to act as mediator during the
American war of independence. He learnt this from the present
Duke of Grafton whilst they were both being installed as
Knights of the Garter at Windsor last year. Apart from that, it
is 'the judgements that are new'. He thinks he has made a
particularly devastating reappraisal of Baldwin.

Far be it for me to judge. I am not a history graduate. But I
thought the recent appraisals (which stop at Macmillan, because his successors 'cannot be adequately assessed until the
miasma of day-to-day parliamentary conflict passes into history') were rather generous. 'Well, Mac and I were always on
good terms. When he was Chancellor and I was Shadow
Chancellor, those were golden days. Then I lost him – he
became PM – and got saddled with Amery and Thorneycroft.
What fun can you have with them?'

Before going to see Sir Harold (armed with questions from
colleagues on matters whose very subject-headings I dare not
print), I received a message saying he would not wish to
answer questions about anything but his book. So I asked him
what he thought about the Thorpe Affair.

'Oh, yes,' he replied, 'I'm very busy just now. There was my
film industry committee yesterday, the D'Oyly Carte today,
the Royal Shakespeare Company annual meeting last week,

and the City inquiry going on all the time.'

Yes, but how did he feel now about the South African connection?

'No, I'm not planning to write any more books just yet.'

Then he took the words out of my mouth. 'Can we go off the record?' We did. I stayed another half-hour and a good time was had by all.

'Atticus', *Sunday Times*, 30 October 1977

I-Spy Spiro

In the beginning there was Spiro T. Agnew, governor of Maryland, who became Vice-President of the United States. Then there was Ted Agnew, business man, roving the world incognito, trying to scratch a living after 'a deeply traumatic experience'. Now there is Spiro T. Agnew, writer, who just happens to have written a novel about a vice-president of the United States.

An inside job? 'It's not a romanaclay,' he insists over lunch at the Dorchester, where he tinkers with a plate of cordon bleu scrambled egg. Just as well, for Vice-President Porter Canfield has a torrid affair with a blonde, buxom thirty-four-year-old Cabinet minister. What's more, Canfield's headlong lunge for the presidency has him sanctioning the murder of, among others, his best friend. Are such desperate remedies, I ask, now endemic in High American Office? 'Well,' says Agnew, 'I want to make it clear I don't endorse Canfield's position on this.'

Agnew himself believes he could now be president. He resigned before he knew Richard Nixon's veep would succeed, but he was already laying plans of his own. 'I had a large and devoted constituency. No one could have stopped me getting the nomination.' He believes, not unnaturally, he would have been a good president. In what mould? Well, he thinks Richard Nixon's 'finest achievement' was the invasion of Cambodia. 'The Cambodian War could by now have been won, quickly and concisely, as the Vietnam War should have been in Johnson's time.' And the man he admires most in the world is Lee Kuan Yew, Prime Minister of Singapore, 'who understands that for freedom to be absolute, it must have limits'.

Relentlessly hard-line and enormously bitter, Agnew has been debarred from voting, from practising as a lawyer, and from membership of the Royal and Ancient Golf Club. When he had to resign – 'When I *chose* to resign, Mr Holden' – he was destitute. Nelson Rockefeller's law foundation refused him finance for a study of the law of immunity. So he borrowed

$200,000 from his pal Frank Sinatra ('What a man'), and he's still paying it back. 'But I'm pleased to have made a success in a wholly new field.'

It is comforting that Agnew himself – and, it must be said, the American bestseller lists – think his novel a success. It is very long, and it is full of very long words. A cumulo-nimbus drifts across the Jersey flats; motorists seek exculpation from causing a traffic jam; the UN Security Council is dysfunctional; the Senate majority leader brushes back his contumacious shock of white hair, and the senator from Wisconsin is noted for his epideictic orations.

But such words fall easily from lips that scarcely move. He tells you he still signs 300 autographs a day. You look surprised. 'Well, would you believe thirty?' Then he tells of a lift ride with a man who says what a tragedy his resignation was, how he would have been a fine president, etc., to trip over him ten minutes later haranguing his wife about that sonofabitch crook. 'I looked him in the eye. He went florid . . . quite rubescent.'

The novelist is now writing a work of non-fiction, an apologia for Spiro T. Agnew, the wronged would-be president. Will it create, er, problems for people still around? 'Yes it will. But they're all people with quite a few, er, problems already.'

Can we take it the book will say Agnew did nothing dishonest, corrupt or illegal?

'Yes, you can. Well, wait a minute. Dishonest, no. Corrupt, no. Illegal . . . mmmm.'

'Atticus', *Sunday Times*, 24 April 1977

Hot Ayer

In his rooms in New College, Oxford, the philosopher and I tackle a large pre-prandial jug of Bloody Mary and an immediate terminological problem. Though best known by his initials, he is properly addressed as Sir Alfred, whilst preferring his friends to call him Freddie. Greatness, in the shape of a knighthood, thrust upon him a forename he had always disliked and eschewed. My initial compromise, as a respectful and relatively recent graduate, is to try a cautious 'Professor'; once the Bloody Marys and an excellent lunch have achieved a satisfactory synthesis, strengthened by some gossip about a number of mutual friends, we are on a firmly 'Freddie' footing.

A. J. – 'Freddie' – Ayer has some of the characteristics the man on the Oxford train expects of a philospher. He talks very fast, his voice trailing away at the most difficult point in his sentence, and displays a certain scattiness when confronted with mundane practical problems, such as the breakdown of a friend's car and the (not unrelated) telephone number of the AA. He can use the words Logical Positivism and Tottenham Hotspur in the same sentence, and finish *The Times* crossword in 'an average of some seventeen or eighteen minutes' even on Saturdays. He has no knowledge of the art of driving a motor car, and crosses the road with some uncertainty.

It may, therefore, come as a surprise to the man on the Oxford train that A.J. Ayer once dated Lauren Bacall. Those who accept that philosophers are also human beings, however, will be more interested to learn that he now describes her as 'a girl whom I should have liked to know better than I did'. The revelation is one of the most trivial to be gleaned in Ayer's partial autobiography, which covers the period from his birth in 1910 to his move from Oxford to London in 1946. He decided to write the volume just over two years ago, when he felt guilty that he was not writing anything, yet also felt he had nothing of philosophical moment to say.

Those familiar with Ayer's philosophical works will be intrigued to learn, among other things, that there is a village in Switzerland called Ayer, from which the family took its name, that he is related by birth to the car-making Citroens, and that his name in Spanish means 'yesterday'. Those less familiar should be interested in a philosopher's clarity of thought, and thus of prose, about Eton, Oxford in the 1920-40s, his service in the Welsh Guards and Special Ops Exec, and a vast range of Glittering Prizewinners from Maurice Bowra and Isaiah Berlin through George Orwell and e.e. cummings to Bertrand Russell. Those closer to the subject will be intrigued to learn that it was Ayer's disappointment with Russell's autobiography, after the first volume, that prompted him to write his own.

The memoir, which ends before his current marriage to Dee Wells, the novelist, contains a candid portrait of his first, to Renee Lees, now the wife of another Oxford philosopher, Stuart Hampshire. (There is a charming vignette of the young lovers setting off together on a continental holiday, the pretty girl riding the motor-bike and the philosopher beside her in the side-car.) Later, many an inference can be drawn that philosophers are also full-blooded *bon viveurs* – a fact brought into some disrepute by Russell. A second volume may follow, depending to some extent on the reception of the first, and to a greater extent on the susceptibilities of those who have known Freddie Ayer sincer 1946. Those he knew, in all senses of the word, before 1946 have been treated with discretion.

If Ayer were to write his own obituary in *The Times*, he says, he would paint himself as a creative and sympathetic teacher rather than as a great philosopher. He places himself in 'the second rank', promoting only his friends Russell, Wittgenstein and perhaps G.E. Moore to the first in this century. He has been much praised in his time and admits that vanity made it easier to quote such remarks in this book: he has also attracted that breed of bitchy obloquy, unique to Oxford's senior common rooms, which regards the 'telly don' as a traitor to Academe. In conversation as in printed self-appraisal, Ayer is properly boastful about individual achievements, and modest about their sum; it will be glory enough, he says, if posterity ranks him Horatio to Russell's Hamlet. I'm not sure, however, that there were more things in Russell's heaven and earth than are dreamt of in Ayer's philosophy.

'Atticus', *Sunday Times*, 12 June 1977

O'Brien's Daughter

A year ago, Edna O'Brien was telling friends she would never write another novel. She had interrupted her long flow of fiction with a passionate book about Mother Ireland – after which she was feeling, and falling, silent. Life in London, besides, doesn't provide much material for a writer like her. People don't open up enough.

Then she met a friend of her son's, a beautiful boy, and asked her son what he was like. He was the kind of chap, said her son, who would share his glass of beer with you if there was no more to be had. The discovery that he was kind as well as beautiful was something of a revelation. As she sat on a park bench one day, thinking about it all, the first lines of a story came to her.

They and a further 50,000 words, written in twenty days, appear this month – Edna O'Brien's first novel for five years, entitled *Johnny, I Hardly Knew You*. The first-person female in the book has an affair with the boy, then kills him. She worries above all else what his friend, her son, will say. The author hopes – optimistically, I ventured – that it is not a gloomy book. She'd like to think she has emerged from all that.

Her two sons, on whom she dotes, have refused to read the book. They think, not without reason, that it sounds too personal. It annoys their mother, nevertheless, to see them sitting around her house reading other contemporary novelists, and she hopes they'll read it when she is dead. She is pretty confident they will.

Her sons are things of beauty, joys for ever. The rest of her conversation is peppered with such stridently anti-male remarks that she is constantly apologizing. But her sons are exempt. The elder is a trainee film director, the younger an architecture student. 'Though God knows', says their mother, 'what British films will there be to direct, what buildings left to be built?'

Somehow, Edna O'Brien always manages to find the pessimistic view. Her own recent past – a holiday in Brittany, a short story written, a hotel with newborn ducks and Chekhovian gardens – is ecstatic enough; but can it ever be recreated? Will she ever again find such peace, such silence, such a place to sleep?

Certainly not on her forthcoming tour of the British provinces to promote her novel. Will she be able to find quiet in her Newcastle hotel? Will the food be edible? And when she is home again, will Chelsea Art College ever stop holding Saturday night discotheques beneath her bedroom window? The omens, for all her warm and wise presence, are not good.

'Atticus', *Sunday Times*, 3 July 1977

Frank and Fearless

Frank Sinatra is wearing a gun on his hip and looking very menacing. He stares at me hard, then turns to play a fruit machine. His third nickel wins him the jackpot – at which, to my surprise, he shakes his head, says 'This goddam machine is fixed', and begins to weep real tears.

There is an awed silence, followed by a cry of 'OK, cut it,' at which Sinatra untenses, dries his tears, and hits someone round the head with a copy of *Playboy*. Then he retires into a corner, where he stands alone, screened by a cordon of personal staff. He appears to be making *sotto voce* wisecracks; his every word provokes as much loyal laughter as the jokes of royalty.

Sinatra is a short man with a huge bulk, which he holds erect in an occasionally convincing attempt to make fat look like muscle. His head of hair, greying fashionably here and there, has had so much major surgery it looks like matted barbed wire. His eyes, like his rich, deep voice, are really scary.

We are in a police station-house in New York's West 30th Street, where I am watching history in the making. Sinatra is once again returning from retirement, this time Thespian retirement, to make a movie about a crusading cop who single-handedly takes on the Mafia. Hence the rod in his waistband. He is 'granting no interviews' right now, but is kind enough to say I can stay and watch.

He then rehearses a scene in which he is forced to give Lieutenant Martin Balsam a wigging, which he does in chilling style.

Sinatra is making the movie, I am told by its producer, for 'no salary' – which, in fact, means the actors' union minimum of £400 a week, plus the rights to the film in Europe, plus a percentage of all profits because he has bought the book on which it is based. He is insistent that the three-hour film is completed in thirty days, and the producer says with some trepidation that this may prove a problem.

I have brought along a photographer, but he is allowed to take no pictures. This, I am firmly told, is because Sinatra allows no photographs except those he can personally approve. He is followed around the room by three personally approved lensmen, constantly shooting. Their films, when finished, are taken from them, and flown to Sinatra's personally approved processing laboratories in Los Angeles. The contact prints are then flown back to New York, where he selects those for personally approved enlargement. The rest are destroyed. After another round trip across the nation, the prints are resubmitted for personal approval. This is why, after a month of filming and photographing, there are still no personally approved photos available.

Pondering all this, I get in the way when the star is making his big entrance. The door he throws open hits me in the back. After another of those looks, I decide it is perhaps time to leave, which I do with as much grace as I can muster, those eyes following me all the way. Last Sunday, he hired three aeroplanes to spell out a happy first anniversary message over Long Island to his latest wife, Barbara; next Sunday, by public demand, he is again coming out of (vocal) retirement to give two concerts in Forest Hills; this Sunday, he is a small-time cop in New York's 23rd Precinct, surrounded by actors who are all taller than he is, and who are more or less walking around on their knees so he doesn't notice.

He's just another guy they've got to work with. He's just another guy I've met on my travels. I decide against offering to ghost his memoirs.

'Atticus', *Sunday Times*, 17 July 1977

In Memoriam Zero

Zero Mostel, who died on Thursday, aged sixty-two, had three helpings of genius: as actor, painter and friend. The first was never in doubt to anyone. The second two were known and appreciated only by a fortunate, and fascinated, few.

To begin to understand him, you had to visit his spiritual home, an attic studio in downtown New York. My fondest memory is of the first time I gained admittance a few years ago, introduced by a mutual friend; Zero was about to appear on BBC-TV as Puccini's Gianni Schicchi, something of a departure, and was wary of a potentially journalistic presence. I survived two giant bear hugs, no joke from such a leviathan, then: 'OK, you've had the full works. Now, whadd'ya want?'

'Just to look at your pictures.'

'No interview?

'No interview.'

'Know anything about pictures?'

'Not much.'

' . . . but you know what you like.'

'I *think* so.'

'You'd better be lying. OK, fix yourself a drink and shut up.'

For the next three hours, Mostel charged around pulling out canvas after canvas – perhaps fifty in all – before he decided enough was enough. Any attempt at comment from me was silenced – 'Let's just look, shall we? That way, we'll stay friends.' But even I could see this was no part-time hick painter. The canvases, like the man, overpowered, infuriated, disarmed. He reckoned he had painted some 10,000 pictures; most were still in his possession, most still officially unfinished.

He had an exhibition once, at the ACA in New York, but he never wanted to sell his pictures.'I give 'em away sometimes, but usually ask for them back. I want them around.' He said: 'When I'm dead, who cares? Someone will find something to do with them.'

Next day, Mostel was going on the road for six months in a

revival of *Fiddler on the Roof.* He created the part of Teyve, and couldn't escape it. A very Jewish man, he loved it for that and other reasons. But he had painted no pictures of the Fiddler. The pictures of his other roles showed which were most important to him: Bloom in Joyce's *Ulysses,* the first and (if you saw it) only Rhinoceros for Ionesco, an undefinable crazy man in Mel Brooks's *The Producers.* 'Mel Brooks's?' I can hear him saying. 'Zero Mostel's, Zero Mostel's.'

Leaving his studio for six months was a sad moment. But in the street, with beret and cane, he was Zee again, shouting to passers-by, gesticulating dangerously. 'This was the original Tin Pan Alley. Over there, where my last studio was, Gershwin wrote all his stuff. Here, where it is now, was the home of a great Vaudeville duo, Weber and Fields. You wouldn't have heard of them, would you? You're hideously British.'

Hailing a cab with Zero was a dangerous business. He had a badly gammy leg after being hit by a truck some years ago, and could only sit in the larger, Chequer variety. The smaller, limo-style taxis answered the wave of his stick, and were not best pleased at being rejected. He pre-empted their anger with a deafening: 'Whadd'ya mean, you don't want my cab? So my cab's not good enough for ya? Look, Buddy, d'ya wanna make something outa this?'

Back in his sumptuous apartment, lined with Picassos, Dubuffets, Rouaults, Matisses and Mostels, I studied a Chagall. 'Hey, you know what happened once? I was in a bar downtown, where the exiled Jewish community used to meet. I went to the men's room, and there was this guy peeing with such beauty, such eloquence.' A demonstration, one hand behind the head, the other in the appropriate place. 'I said to him: Hey, I hope you don't mind my saying this, but you pee just like a Chagall. You know what he said? He turned to me and he said, he really did: "Monsieur, I *am* Chagall."'

As with all Mostel stories, you wondered for a moment. You registered an ambiguous look expressing some scepticism, but primarily enjoyment of the story. He understood. 'Now this one, it *is* true.' You believed him. His most unbelievable stories were always the true ones.

Al Alvarez, the writer, one of Mostel's closest friends, once witnessed another. 'We got out of a cab together, and the driver said to me: 'Wasn't that Zero Mostel? Now that guy, he isn't a New Yorker. He's New York.'

He will be much missed.

'Atticus', *Sunday Times*, 11 September 1977

St Mug Meets his Match

It is Wednesday evening, and we are fortunate enough to be in Madame Tussaud's after closing time. Hush! Before us is the strange yet somehow familiar sight of Malcolm Muggeridge talking to himself. Familiar, because some of us think he never really talks to anyone else. Strange, because he actually *is* talking to himself. Muggeridge is locked in earnest dialogue with his own waxen image – and the conversation, in his own words, is 'really rather interesting'.

Television cameras whirr out of the darkness, as this meeting of great minds is being recorded for Dutch viewers. Why Dutch? Because they asked him, of course. Will British audiences have a chance to sample the repartee? Perhaps; it depends on the attitude of the BBC, these days rather cursory. Muggeridge himself doesn't much care. Nor, I suppose, should we. Unless, as popular rumour had it last week, this is Malcolm Muggeridge's last will and testament. Is this really, positively, his final statement on the human condition he has come so much to deplore?

'Well, it might be. If you're seventy-four, as I am now, anything you say might be the last thing you say. I said just that, in fact, to someone the other day, which is how I think this last testament business sprang up. But you know me well enough to be sure I'll keep on talking as long as I can. My last statement can't be my last statement until it's the one I make before I pack up.'

Not but what Muggeridge's Dutch statement is a sweeping, conclusive summary of his philosophical position to date. That position, grotesquely oversimplified (his own words), is that Twentieth-Century Man has created himself a world of fantasy to live in – through the media. Muggeridge, recognizing this, has tried to locate the reality TCM is missing, and has done so 'in terms of Christian revelation'.

But is there not some irony, nay contradiction, in his passing on this reality through the very medium on which he pins the rap for the fantasy? 'Yes, there is. Of course there is. In a way,

I'm trying to cast out devils in the name of Beelzebub, Prince of Devils, if you see what I mean. And the most serious programmes on television – Clark's *Civilization*, Bronowski's *Ascent of Man*, and so on – are the ultimate in fantasy. The peripheral stuff, the trash – *I Love Lucy*, that sort of thing – doesn't count. Anyway, I don't myself watch television any more. The fantasy can't be pulled into the reality. If the Gospel had been told in television programmes, I don't think it would have got across.'

Yeeees. For a slow, deliberate talker, Muggeridge is remarkably difficult to keep up with. In the middle of our contemporary moral vacuum, meanwhile, the moral vacuum which he sees as the symbol of our collapsing civilization, he is still talking to his own waxwork, which he sees – after some thought – as a symbol of himself. Before Madame Tussaud's closed, he had confused some visitors by sitting near the effigy and meditating upon it. They weren't quite sure which was which. Now, it seems, *he* isn't. He has this idea that he should stand behind the ropes, and the waxwork should go out into the world and be him.

Now he's got me confused. Which one was it I talked to?

'Atticus', *Sunday Times*, 2 October 1977

William Styron and
Sophie's Choice

The lawns of William Styron's holiday home on the island of
Martha's Vineyard, Massachusetts, curve down to meet the
Atlantic Ocean. Sprinklers murmur and swoosh in the baking
summer sun. At the foot of the garden is Styron's private pier, to
which is moored a cluster of bobbing, beckoning boats.

We sit on the verandah, splitting a jug of Bloody Mary, gazing
serenely across the bay to Hyannis and Cape Cod. He sits here,
he says, for hours, just gazing. Occasionally a dot on the horizon
will slowly metamorphose into a large and elegant sloop, which
he knows well. Teddy Kennedy will be sailing over for tea.

'He might look in this afternoon, in fact,' says Styron,
disappearing to recharge the pitcher. 'He called last week to say
he might be over today. So you'll have a chance to ask him
yourself.'

To say that I start is to break new ground in understatement. I
am the prototype guilty-thing-upon-a-summons. I have just
confessed to Styron that my other reason for visiting Martha's
Vineyard, this glorious summer week, is to poke around in the
murky waters of Chappaquiddick. All part of journalistic life's
rich tapestry. Styron in turn has told me that on this very lawn,
a month after the Chappaquiddick tragedy, he was standing
looking out to sea, 'bothered' by what had happened to his
friend, when he felt a tap on his shoulder and turned to find the
man himself had crept up on him from behind. For the rest of our
conversation I kept catching things in the corner of my eye.
Each turn of the sprinkler has me leaping up to greet the good
Senator.

He does not, in the end, materialize. But in six unbroken
hours of conversation, which pass like one, Styron and I have
long since given him the benefit of the doubt, and moved on.
Politics seem remote from this tranquil, other-worldly scene.

We are celebrating the news, telephoned from New York this

morning, that Bill Styron's new novel, *Sophie's Choice*, has today arrived securely at the top of the American fiction bestseller list. For him, it is a doubly rewarding moment. Apart from the obvious fiscal implications, it means that the literary public is squaring up en masse to a book which does not yield its treasures lightly, and which is the product of the last five years of Styron's life. *Sophie's Choice* is the first novel from Styron in twelve years. His last, *The Confessions of Nat Turner*, won him a Pulitzer Prize, but it also earned him the obloquy of a group of angry black intellectuals. They even went to the lengths of publishing their own book in reply.

Styron had chosen to tell the story of America's only black slave revolt through the eyes of its leader, Nat Turner. The book, again, had taken him several years to write, and it was mere coincidence that it reached publication at the height of the civil rights activity around the land.

That a white man could presume to inhabit the mind of a black seemed, in itself, sufficient offence to *Nat Turner*'s detractors. That Styron chose to have his character, for instance, rape a white girl meant that the author, a Southerner, must be the worst kind of bigot.

Throughout the furore, Styron was staunchly defended by his friend James Baldwin, whose conversation had indeed heavily influenced the work-in-progress. But he had one fundamental difficulty. 'I couldn't get it across to these guys that the book was a *novel*. Although it was based on a true story, and a man who did indeed live much the kind of life I described, I felt free to invent things to amplify both character and narrative. The rape was invented. But I felt it was exactly what he might well have done.'

It hasn't happened, but Styron at first had fears that *Sophie's Choice* might provoke another such storm. It is the story of a Catholic Polish girl caught up in the Nazi ravishment of Europe. Sophie survives Auschwitz – her time in the camp is a central, harrowing section of the book – but can never exorcise the experience from her new life in post-war Brooklyn. There is a fatalistic thrust, the brooding presence of a Greek tragedy, behind the long and passionate tale of her decline.

It is central to an understanding of the book to remember that Sophie is not Jewish. Styron seeks to remind us that the Nazis

243

persecuted many people other than the Jews. In the process, he portrays Auschwitz above all as a slave camp, where human beings, reduced to the lowest imaginable level of life, seize any means of survival.

He was immensely gratified, therefore, to receive a 'fan letter' from Norman Podhoretz, the editor of *Commentary*, and one of America's leading Jewish exegesists. 'It meant', says Styron, 'that my point was taken, and that it had caused no offence to Jewish intellectuals. A letter on this subject from Podhoretz is like a letter from the Pope.'

Styron himself grew up in the American South, in Nat Turner country, the scion of Scottish immigrants who had long since taken slavery for granted. His grandmother used to tell him stories of her slave girls, whom she loved, he says, as she did her own children.

The narrator of *Sophie's Choice*, Stingo, also grew up in the South, in Nat Turner country. He too had a grandmother who told him stories about her slaves. He was born in the same year as William Styron, 1925, and like Styron served three years in the US Marine Corps, later being recalled to serve in Korea.

At the novel's opening Stingo is sacked from a job he hates, that of an editor at McGraw-Hill, for refusing to wear a hat to work and for launching balloons from his office window. Those were the very reasons Styron was sacked from his first, humble editing job at McGraw-Hill.

The point need not be laboured. Stingo moves into a seedy Brooklyn bedsitter, starts work on a first novel, dreams one day of writing a book about Nat Turner. Later in the novel he has done so, and it has caused something of a furore. He decides to expand on a similar theme by writing the story of Sophie, who lived in the room above him with her dazzling but disturbed friend, Nathan.

If Styron has chosen to place himself so squarely in his own work of fiction, is he, like Stingo, attempting to exorcise some lurking guilt of his own by writing *Sophie's Choice*? Is this an acute case of the sins-of-the-fathers syndrome?

'It's a good question, but I don't know how to answer it. I don't feel any guilt for the behaviour of previous generations of my own family. But conditions in Virginia when I was growing up were much like they are still in South Africa today. I went to a segregated school. I do, I suppose, feel a need to account for this in a way that others might not.'

The two books, then, are complementary, circling around a central flame, brooding lengthily and deeply on man's inhumanity to man. *Sophie's Choice*, along the way, enjoys moments of high comedy, high drama and high sexual activity. It was denounced in the *Wall Street Journal* – amid paeans of praise on all other fronts – for, in Styron's own phrase, 'onanistic dalliance'. His reply: 'The battle to write explicitly about sex was fought long and hard. We must never begin to surrender that victory.'

Stingo, he thinks, may reappear in his current work-in-progress, a novel about the military mind, which again draws its foundations from his own experiences in the marines. His hero commits an act of unspeakable brutality in the headiness of his military youth, and spends the rest of his life trying to expiate it.

Styron started this novel ten years ago, in the wake of *Nat Turner*, but after five years' work was not very happy with it. He awoke one morning from a night full of dreams, dreams about the girl named Sophie who had lived in the room above his, many years before, in a Brooklyn boarding-house. She was Catholic, and Polish, and on her arm he had noticed an Auschwitz tattoo.

He decided, that morning, to write her story, and it took him five years. Styron writes in longhand, on yellow legal note pads, and reckons 800 or so words a good day's output. He is not a great reviser, but refuses to proceed to the next chapter until the one in hand is in finished form.

I find myself harping on, perhaps a little rudely, about the sheer length of his book. Others have made the point, and Styron is defensive. He's been making comparisons, counting the pages, and the words per page, in his editions of *Bleak House* and *Crime and Punishment*, to reassure himself that each of them is several times as long. 'But it was a story', he concedes, 'that took a lot of telling.'

From the jacket photograph of *Sophie's Choice*, Styron appears a rather menacing figure. 'He looks a tough cookie,' my wife had said as I departed, and I passed her message on. He agreed: 'Rather like Robert Mitchum at his meanest.' The portrait bears little resemblance to the real thing.

He is a big but gentle man, with a particular enthusiasm for sailing and cooking. His wife, Rose, works for Amnesty International, and writes a little poetry. They have four children, from age twelve up, with whom Styron has an understanding. 'I'm what you might call a familial man. I love having my family around me. But I insist that they all leave me alone for equally large chunks of time.'

The Styron family's home is in Roxbury, Connecticut, but the long summers are always spent on Martha's Vineyard. He has his own work-room in each place. The crème-de-la-New-England-crème emigrates en masse, it seems, to Martha's Vineyard each summer, giving the island a flavour of *la vie Bohème*, perhaps of the radical chic at leisure.

The island's newspaper, a paragon of the concerned, helpful and happily self-indulgent local paper, is owned and lovingly overseen by James Reston, the *New York Times* columnist. Around the corner from the Styron home is the Xanadu-like mansion of Kay Graham, proprietor of the *Washington Post* and sundry other influential organs. Styron is due there for lunch next day. He invites me to come along. It's that kind of place.

For a man who works exceeding long hours, and shuns the literary cocktail circuit, Styron enjoys bouts of such gregariousness. He and his wife are prolific entertainers: theirs is the kind of house in which you turn round to be confronted by the famous face you've just been talking about. After most such long afternoons and evenings, your host will suddenly disappear, ostensibly into the garden, in fact to his work-room. He will write late into the night, and sleep late into the next day.

His friends, he says, are the main reason he chooses to live in New England rather than the South, which has such a pervasive and continuing influence on his thinking and writing. His early novels, *Lie Down in Darkness*, *The Long March* and *Set This House on Fire*, were steeped in southern influences: Thomas Wolfe, Robert Penn Warren and, above all, William Faulkner.

But he is not keen to be named as the latest link in a chain, a tradition of southern writing. His first novel read so much like Faulkner that he tore it up and wrote the whole thing again. Now he can securely claim to have found his own voice, while frankly acknowledging a debt to those and other masters. His nearest equivalent on this side of the Atlantic – a writer he much admires, but has never met – is surely John Fowles.

There is a contradiction somewhere in grappling with ideas of the scale of guilt, slavery and unmitigated evil, and rendering into words the unspeakable horrors of Auschwitz, in a setting as idyllic as Martha's Vineyard. He is aware of it, and approvingly quotes George Steiner on the unfathomable 'time-warp': the fact that in New York people were getting drunk and going to parties while at the same time in Auschwitz people were going to the gas chambers. But he dissents from Steiner's conclusion: 'In the presence of certain realities, art is trivial or impertinent.'

Before writing *Sophie's Choice*, Styron steeped himself in the literature of the Holocaust: he even visited Auschwitz, in the true spirit of the documentary novelist. From all that has emerged, more than anything else, a major study of what Coleridge (writing of Iago) called 'motiveless malignity'.

Even speaking of it all in this setting makes one, at length, feel inadequate and guilt-ridden. It is with some relief that we attend to a sprinkler which has stopped revolving. We can even joke about another 'time-warp': the fact that a Polish Pope visited Auschwitz on the same day that, in New York, Random House threw a $15,000 party to celebrate publication of Styron's novel about a Polish Catholic girl's 'visit' to Auschwitz.

'As a publicity stunt,' he says, 'it takes some beating.' There is mockery in his voice, but in his eyes there is guilt at even speaking such a thought.

Observer magazine, 9 September 1979

The Kissinger Industry

Henry Kissinger needs good publicity these days about as much as Jimmy Carter needs bad. No other American, not even Edward Kennedy as he mounts his white charger, enjoys such indiscriminate public awe.

Over the next several weeks, however, we are in for a sudden rush of further reading matter in praise of Dr Kissinger, telling us more than many may need or care to know. Much of it will amount to a well-informed encomium, since much of it has been written by the good doctor himself.

Tomorrow, five weeks ahead of their publication in book form, *Time* begins serialization of the Kissinger memoirs. *The White House Years* is the somewhat saucy name gracing the dust-jacket, though the author's own working-title was, for some time, *Kissinger: a Study in Infallibility*. There would, he told friends, be a brief footnote encompassing his mistakes – if he could find any.

For the last two and a half years, since he left office, the chronicle of Kissinger's eight years in the seats of power has been swelling to mighty proportions. Now it has split into two volumes, this first one alone, which covers the years of the Nixon presidency, running to more than 1,000 pages.

Kissinger's reflections on his role in US foreign policy, 1968-76, will thus be twice as long as those of the two presidents of the period on their entire administrations. Nobody seems either surprised or much bothered. His prominence and influence appear, paradoxically, to have grown greater than ever since he reverted to the status of private citizen.

Kissinger is not merely the most sought-after guest in Washington's highly select social circles. He has managed to give the impression of transcending party politics, and of sharing none of the moral guilt attaching to the Nixon Administration. He has become, in effect, a self-contained honorific branch of the American Government.

He remains a compulsory stop on the schedules of visiting foreign leaders, returning their visits with all the pomp and circumstance of a head of state.

Foreign Governments still canvass his views, which he provides only too readily. His globetrotting dynamism makes a stark contrast with the dull competence of his successor, Cyrus Vance. He is said, moreover, to give the impression that he is still passing on secrets, though the only ones he knows are at least three years old.

At home he feels free, if not obliged, to pronounce on most major issues, secure in the knowledge that his words can shape events. The Carter Administration pays him court, regarding his support for sundry foreign policies, notably the Strategic Arms Limitation Treaty (SALT II), as indispensable.

Witness Kissinger's evidence this summer to the Senate hearings on SALT II, when his demand for a *quid pro quo* increase in arms spending altered the scope and course of the entire debate. Several senators instinctively referred to him as 'Mr Secretary' or 'Secretary Kissinger' – as indeed, on occasion, has President Carter.

There is no name-plate outside his tenth-floor Washington office, any more than there is outside the White House. You are expected to know where you are. Portraits of the occupant with sundry world leaders steer you to his presence. Richard Nixon is conspicuous by his photographic absence.

Kissinger dismisses other recent American political memoirs as 'self-serving' and 'unhistorical'. But his own book, apparently, contains no great surprises. There is, according to aides, some 'good new stuff' on Chile, but 'not a lot else to make waves'. Kissinger's main intent has been to write his own place in history.

He skimmed Richard Nixon's memoirs for references to himself, pronouncing most of them 'okay'. Has he read the tonnage of other Watergate books? He apparently prefers watching late-night horror movies on TV. Kissinger's own verdict on Nixon remains friendly but cautious.

The two remain in frequent and amiable contact, although history alone, perhaps, will pronounce on various disputes between them: the only reason, according to John Ehrlichman, that Nixon didn't burn those tapes was to prove to posterity that he, not Henry Kissinger, was responsible for the worthier foreign policy initiatives of his Administration.

Kissinger, meanwhile, has three full-time attorneys on his staff to fight lawsuits over his wire-tapping of government officials and journalists. He still receives numerous 'hate' and 'nuisance' suits over his part in the expansion of the conflict in South-East Asia.

Kissinger devotes the major portion of his book to defending his own role, as National Security Adviser and as Secretary of State, in the Vietnam and Cambodia wars. Some passages were hurriedly rewritten in the light of recent new evidence from William Shawcross, the English journalist, whose book *Sideshow* denounces Nixon and Kissinger as 'war criminals'.

Kissinger is haunted by those wars, for which America's liberal intelligentsia, guardian of the nation's collective conscience, will never forgive him. Nor will many of those who served, who returned home to a villain's welcome. His critics remain a minority, but an impassioned and vociferous one, who constantly chip away at his prized and otherwise pristine reputation.

Kissinger's apologia, its Teutonic prose perked up by a fleet of editors, has few challengers as the publishing event of the American autumn. Advance deals around the world already guarantee him something in excess of $5 million.

He says he needs it, although his income from directorships, consultancies and after-dinner speeches is already prodigious. Kissinger claims to do more unpaid than paid work. But it has been calculated that just three of his consultancies, occupying a quarter of his time, earn him $1,250,000 a year – more than the annual salary of America's highest-paid corporate executive, Henry Ford.

For Goldman Sachs and Chase Manhattan, giants respectively of investment and commercial banking, he appears at monthly lunches to expatiate on the state of the world. His value to Goldman Sachs, as a rival banker put it, is that 'important clients can go home and say to their wife and friends, "I had lunch with my banker – and Henry Kissinger – today"'.

From the NBC television network he has a five-year contract worth $1 million a year, though the company is now more embarrassed than elated about its distinguished catch. The one 'special' Kissinger made for them, a ninety-minute diatribe about Euro-Communism, came sixty-fifth out of sixty-five in that week's ratings. Since then Kissinger has appeared as a brief interviewee on some fifty news programmes in two years – thus collecting more than $5,000 a minute, out-earning even the legendary Barbara Walters.

Kissinger also holds salaried positions with the Aspen Institute of Humanistic Studies; the University of Southern California; Georgetown University in Washington (where he holds a weekly seminar, travel permitting); and one British company, General Electric. Plans to give him a professorship at Columbia University, New York, were abandoned when 1,200 students and 140 faculty staff protested that 'hiring Henry Kissinger to teach history would be like hiring Charles Manson to teach religion'.

Kissinger frequently spells out his scruples about accepting hire and salary from among the many offers that come his way. 'I'm prepared to advise on foreign policy consequences, the environment in which they operate. I am not prepared to open doors or engage myself in exploiting the contacts I have. I do not intervene with the Government – use my contacts there – on behalf of commercial clients.'

Unpaid positions include a trusteeship of the Rockefeller Brothers Fund (the late Nelson Rockefeller was one of his great patrons and friends), a position on the boards of the Council on Foreign Relations and the Foreign Policy Association, the chairmanship of the President's Alliance to Save Energy, trusteeships with the Metropolitan Museum of Art in New York and the Houston ballet, and honorary membership of the Harlem Globetrotters basketball team.

Demand for him on the lecture circuit is overwhelming, even at a charge of $15,000 for twenty or thirty minutes, plus first-class travel for himself and an entourage of six.

The outgoings, as he is quick to point out, are equally compendious. For a start, there are the five permanent security men he hires to protect him, at a cost of some $200,000 a year, since the Government decided he no longer merited state financed protection. Kissinger's conviction that he is still important enough to be shot at, more or less anywhere in the world, is cited by critics as evidence of a Walter Mitty-style fantasy about his own significance.

There are his homes in Washington and New York, plus his

wife Nancy's current quest for a country house in Connecticut.
There is a staff of eight to run his plush Washington office, plus
those three attorneys, plus other mountainous legal costs fighting publication of 30,000 pages of transcripts of his telephone
calls while in the White House and the State Department.

'He's got it all now,' said a former member of his staff.
'Influence and money are a tough combination to beat.' But why
does Henry Kissinger, at fifty-six, drive himself quite as hard as
he does? Is it purely ego, which he admits to possessing in vast
quantities, constantly in need of sustenance? Or does he still
nourish higher ambitions?

Kissinger certainly experienced withdrawal symptoms on
leaving office. His wife once confessed that he talked diplomacy
in his sleep, adding that he would wake in the morning to say,
'What a relief I haven't still got to worry about all that.' He
himself has said he misses the cables. And he was conspicuously
miffed when Georgetown neighbours insisted on the removal of
the official No Parking sign outside his home.

His German birth prevents him, short of a change in the
Constitution, bashfully stepping forward as a candidate for the
presidency. But the money he is accumulating would certainly
cushion a career in the Senate, where outside income is
necessary to supplement a salary of $57,000 a year.

Kissinger has already indicated his interest in the New York
Senate seat of seventy-five-year-old Jacob Javits, who has not
yet decided whether to run for re-election next year. But in
doing so he made it clear that 'they would have to come to me. I
would make no motion for it myself.'

And if a Republican president is elected in 1980? 'He would
find it very difficult to turn down,' said a senior aide, anticipat-
ing my question. 'Sure he could return to government as
Secretary of State,' says Kissinger-watcher Marvin Kalb of CBS.
'In a Republican Administration he could be God or most
anything else.'

Would a Republican president be content to have God
upstaging him in Cabinet? That may depend, apart from
anything else, on whether Henry Kissinger's divinity survives
the publication of his memoirs.

Observer, 23 September 1979

Milton Friedman:
Free Market Man

A summer's day in New York City, Hollywood of the East, where the air is thick with the clack of clapperboards. On location in Chinatown, Woody Allen is filming yet another of his tortured urban psychodramas, soon to net him a fistful of Oscars.

Just a block away an equally diminutive superstar, this one sixty-seven years old, five-foot-two and even balder, is making his screen debut in a seedy sweatshop, hectoring the camera about the merits of capitalism and the free enterprise system. He may not be in line for an Oscar, but he's already won the Nobel Prize. Yes, it's the Milton Friedman Show.

Down the aisles of the slum factory he goes, singing the praises of an establishment in clear contravention of numerous government regulations. Its workers are paid less than the minimum legal wage. They toil long hours in atrocious conditions. Yet if the laws of the land were observed here, he says, they wouldn't have jobs at all.

He should know. It is how his own mother brought up Friedman and his three sisters after the early death of their father. It is a central part of the economic gospel he has been preaching ever since . . .

Cut (some time later) to San Francisco, where you climb halfway to the stars to reach Friedman's apartment home, one of the ritziest in town, commanding a stunning view across the bay to Alcatraz. 'It *is* rather nice, isn't it?' says your host, producing a photograph of the even more stunning view from his ski lodge in Vermont. 'The free market has worked pretty well for me.'

The man is American entrepreneurism made flesh, one of the millions who bear living witness to the opportunities presented by this brave, if presently troubled, new world. The

253

son of Austro-Hungarian immigrants, born in Brooklyn and raised in New Jersey, Friedman has weathered poverty, anti-semitism, academic isolation and plain abuse en route to an extremely comfortable retirement, punctuated by the odd lect-ure at some $8,000 a throw.

The Nobel Prize for economics, awarded in 1976, conferred international respectability on a reputation torn by dissent. There were, and are, people all over the world trying to prove Milton Friedman wrong. But even the staunchest of his opponents now concede that Friedman seems destined to prove the most influential economic philosopher since Keynes.

It comes as something of a surprise, therefore, when the high priest of monetarism shudders at the very mention of the word. The label, it is quickly apparent, is an albatross around his neck, giving him credit where it is due, but obliterating the rest of his life's work. Friedman sees himself as a broader social philosopher, in the tradition of Edmund Burke, Adam Smith and John Stuart Mill, of Thomas Jefferson, Jeremy Bentham, even George Bernard Shaw.

'The Mighty Mite' his colleagues call him, and you quickly see why. This tiny man has been responsible for something approaching a revolution of thought, free in his view (though not that of others) from political affiliation.

The hellos have scarcely been exchanged before even the small talk comes under his sway. The lot of a foreign corres-pondent, for instance, has been ameliorated by the lifting of foreign exchange controls. (A good thing.) The fact that I may smoke in his home proves he's giving freedom of choice. (Not everyone would.) My wife's inability to acquire a work permit in this country is evidence of government strangulation of economic, social and cultural life. (A bad thing.)

There, down the road, out the window, are the sleazy emporia of Fisherman's Wharf, all red lights and cheap admis-sions (somewhat akin to our own 'new' Piccadilly and Leicester Square). The greed of free enterprise may vulgarize, okay, but consumers are happily consuming and thus providing a living to those who might otherwise die.

He yanks you onto the balcony to point in their direction. He bets they don't pay any income taxes. They are part of what is now called the 'underground economy', that section forced by government interference to make their own rules, to cheat to survive. However much you try to contain it, free enterprise will out.

He's the champion of the individual. He's the defender of liberties. He has the solutions to the problems of the world. The trouble is that no one would ever listen – or, even if they would, they wouldn't understand and take action. Now, given scientific blessings not enjoyed by Smith, Burke, Bentham and Co., Friedman has an opportunity to get his message across. He has seized it with a vengeance.

The *Observer* last week invaded Friedman's living-room because for the next several weeks, in the televisual tradition of Clark, Bronowski, Galbraith and others, he will be invading yours. Friedman and his wife of forty-two years, Rose, a fellow economist and associate producer of the TV series, could not have been more accommodating. They are particularly partial to Britain now that a Friedmanite Government is in charge.

'She's moving in the right direction,' he says of Margaret Thatcher, with whom he dined in London shortly before the Tories took office. 'She's cutting government spending and dealing with the tax rates. But she shouldn't have raised Value Added Tax, and she hasn't yet taken proper control of the money supply. That will require some rearrangement of your banks' reserve system. Given that,' he says, 'she can turn the economy round in five years, oh yes.'

Any doubters will be pleased to know that all this will be hammered out on BBC2 over the next five weeks, as Milton Friedman sets forth his ideas and then defends them in half-hour discussions, chaired by a TV star-cum-economist with some recent knowledge of the United States, Peter Jay. Friedman will be only too happy if you choose to tune in and let the wonders of modern science ease your approach to his ideas. But he'd much rather you spent the time reading his new book, also entitled *Free to Choose*.

'Television', he says, 'is hard to turn down, given the chance to address such an enormous audience. But it is not a medium of serious thought or reflection. Since the series began here in the United States, I've had several hundred letters a week, mostly pro, some hysterically anti. I've never had a response like that to any of my books.'

He leaps to his desk and begins to read examples, one correspondent saying, 'I cried, because your solution is so simple, yet those dumb jerks in Washington can't grasp it.' Another accuses him of 'animalistic sadism'. Yet the sheer volume of letters, he says, proves what's wrong with television, not what's right with it. 'I regard the TV series as a giant advert for the book.'

The book, already riding high (thanks to television) on the American bestseller list, is a summation of the Friedman economic philosophy, translated into terms accessible to the layman. It is no lightweight bedside volume, but nor is it the kind of coffee-table tome now associated with such series. 'I wasn't going to do something I'd be ashamed of. It was a chance to get people to *understand*.'

Friedman's metamorphosis into TV star began in the small Pennsylvania town of Erie, where the head of the local TV station spluttered with rage some years back as he watched the (to him) incoherent liberal ramblings of John Kenneth Galbraith. Something had to be done. Money was raised and Friedman launched on a longish lecture tour, all videotaped and now available from his New York publishers. His effectiveness as a popularizer of his ideas was tested and proven. The lectures formed the basis of the TV series.

Friedman, too, had been watching Galbraith. *The Age of Uncertainty*, he says, baffled him. 'I looked in vain for any central idea. All I could see was a man sneering at conventional solutions, without offering any of his own.'

'That's because he hasn't got any,' interjects Rose, co-author of the Friedmans' reply. 'No wonder it was called *The Age of Uncertainty*. Ken was far from certain what he was talking about.'

The two purport to be friends off screen, but there is clearly no love lost in that corner of the economic pantheon shared by Friedman and Galbraith. 'I've often called him a Tory radical,' says Friedman. 'He's in the direct tradition of those early nineteenth-century British Liberals, Lord Shaftesbury and his fellow aristocrats, who thought they knew what was best for lesser mortals.'

What, I inquire, would Galbraith call Friedman?

'Oh, the darling of the business community,' suggests Rose.

'No, the front-man for the rich,' says her husband, with some grandeur.

The argument should continue elsewhere. But it is striking that in an era when economics dominate government, when figures like Galbraith have been central to the lives and times of Democratic presidents, Milton Friedman has never held a government post. He's turned down many offers, he says, 'Because it just wouldn't be worth it. You'd be bound, sooner or later, to be forced into compromise.'

Instead he has been 'a gadfly, I hope, a thorn in the side of all recent administrations', influencing them much more in his writings than he could ever have done in their counsels. He was Barry Goldwater's economic adviser in his 1964 campaign against Lyndon Johnson, though a veil should perhaps be decently drawn over that. Some of the Nixon Administration's early economic policies were, however, pure Friedman. Everything went well until August 1971. The dollar had been detached from gold and allowed to float, tax rates were being reduced, government spending was being reduced, government regulations were being reduced – all the gospel according to Friedman. Then Nixon introduced wage and price controls.

'That was the end of the line. I wrote and told him so. He didn't reply.'

Travel around with any Republican candidate on the 1980 campaign trail, however, and all you hear is undiluted Friedman. 'Abolish the minimum wage,' says Ronald Reagan (of the Chinatown sweatshop). 'No more wage and price controls. They haven't worked since the days of the Emperor Diocletian.' (Friedman cited this rhetorically useful example in a lengthy *Playboy* interview in 1973.) 'A superb book,' writes Reagan on the dust jacket of the American edition of *Free to Choose*. 'Must reading for every American, from the president to the private citizen.'

'Yes,' concedes Friedman, 'I'd endorse Reagan. I would like to see him elected. He's very receptive to ideas.' (A slight smirk.) 'He would be the president most likely to implement my philosophy.'

Another reason Friedman has never been in government, however, is that he was for years an intellectual pariah. To some extent, he still remains one. His wife is writing a book about it, a biography of her husband which relates the world's recent economic crises quite simply to the rejection of his ideas. 'It's the one area', she says, 'in which Milton and I disagree. He is much more generous than I am in explaining why his views took so long to win acceptance. Do you know, before he won the Nobel Prize the *New York Times* didn't review a single one of his books? Now, with this new one, they're writing news stories about it and reviewing it twice.'

For all his academic reservations about television, Friedman for years took part in radio discussions out of Chicago. They were in part responsible for the growing renown of 'The Chicago School'. His ideas attracted hate mail, seeming (as, to many, they still do) to discriminate against the poor, the minorities, the underprivileged.

'That's what I like about the TV series,' says Rose Friedman, smiling at her husband. 'To listen to him, you think he might be a monster. To look at him, you just know he isn't.' Friedman smiles beatifically. Reluctantly, he concedes her point. At last, through television, the poor and underprivileged might realize that the abolition of the welfare state would work in their favour. That they would spend less money assisting the lives of others and have more money to assist their own.

Will they listen? 'I don't know,' says she. 'I rather doubt it.' 'Well,' says he, 'look at our own lives.'

They met in Chicago, where both were postgraduate economic students in the early 1930s. Rose had been born in Russia, a part of Russia which later became part of Poland but is now Russia again: when she was eighteen months old, her parents came to Portland, Oregon, and set up a retail shop. His parents were from Austro-Hungary, a part which briefly became part of Czechoslovakia before also being swallowed by Russia. Neither has ever been back.

His parents, too, set up shop: 'A familiar saga', he says of both their origins, 'of Jewish immigrants coming from Eastern Europe to the land of opportunity ... to find the streets weren't paved with gold.' Friedman's father died when he was fifteen. His mother worked twice as hard, but young Milton won a state scholarship to Rutgers University, New Jersey, whence he graduated to Chicago. (The older Milton, of course, disapproves of such state subsidies to education. 'There is no other government programme which so clearly imposes taxes on low-income people to assist high-income people.')

Milton courted Rose during the Depression, which more than anything else influenced their subsequent economic thinking. The Great Crash of 1929 and the years of depression which followed it were assumed to be the death-knell of 'one hundred per cent pure capitalism', the system Friedman is proud to defend. The received wisdom was and is that market forces had collapsed, proving their inability to survive independent of government. Not so, say the Friedmans. The crash was caused by too much government interference, and the subsequent depression accentuated by same. The market has never since been properly free.

Economists who come up against Friedman have trouble with such ideas, so apparently complex yet expressed with such breathtaking simplicity and confidence. 'Part of the trouble', says Peter Jay, a convert to the monetarist cause, 'is that Friedman's thought is always confused with political ideology. It need not be, and it should not be. For instance, the fundamental tenet of monetarism – that it is the money supply alone which should determine the amount of spending in the economy – is a purely technical argument, not a matter of partisan political dispute. Yet it is always interpreted that way. Denis Healey, when Chancellor, largely abided by Friedman's teachings, though loudly disclaiming any such notion.'

With unabashed monetarists in Downing Street, however, Milton Friedman now has a chance to see if a government acknowledging his influence can put principle into practice. Given those few aforementioned minor adjustments, the British economy will be pure Chicago. But will those adjustments be made? It has never happened before. One of Friedman's most respectful critics, the American economist Walter Heller, once said that his ideas could work 'only in heaven'. Friedman, not surprisingly, says the criticism is unfair. 'It's unfair, because my ideas have never been properly applied.'

When the Chilean junta of General Pinochet ousted President Allende, Friedman happened to be lecturing in Santiago, as part of an exchange scheme with the University of Chicago. Many of the newly installed government ministers happened to be economics graduates of Chicago University, thanks to the same exchange scheme. Friedman's name and notions were suddenly all over the Chilean newspapers.

He has borne heavy criticism ever since, for having any truck with a regime which so openly flouted human rights. 'I was only there six days,' he protests. 'I was not an official consultant or anything like that. Yet,' he concedes, in a satisfied afterthought, 'the Chilean economy has recovered amazingly well.'

When Menachem Begin came to power in Israel, Friedman happened to be lecturing in Jerusalem, and found himself 'suddenly sucked into long talks with members of the new Government'. Again they started out on the right track, again they deviated from pure Friedmanism. 'But it went well for a while.'

Well, where have his principles worked in practice?

'Take Japan. In 1973, it had inflation of 25 to 30 per cent. Monetarist policies were adopted, and by 1978 inflation was between 4 and 5 per cent. Look at Korea, Taiwan, Singapore, Malaysia – all countries with the fastest growing economies in the world, all countries whose economies place a far greater reliance on market forces than on any government controls.'

Monetarism, says Friedman, is susceptible to scientific proof, like gravity. It's either right or wrong. He is open to contradiction, but no one has yet adduced, he says, any contradictory evidence.

He hopes he might see Mrs Thatcher while he is in Britain for the TV series, to sort her out on a few technical niceties. Might he then stick around to watch Friedmanism finally bear fruit in a great contemporary democracy? 'No, no. I don't think so. I'm afraid British politics will have to try and survive without me.'

Would they survive *with* him? 'You bet. Properly applied, the system works. The tide is turning. You wait and see.'

Observer, 7 February 1980

Rosalynn Carter:
The Steel Magnolia

The annual dinner of the White House Correspondents Association is a very grand affair, held in Washington each May in honour of the President of the United States and his First Lady. Twelve months of jibes, wounds and mutual recrimination are exorcised in a haze of cigar smoke, alcohol fumes, after-dinner wisecracking and general over-indulgence.

This year, the President decided to stay away – a calculated insult, doubly bold in an election year, to a group of people he holds in mixed regard. In his place his hapless Press Secretary, Jody Powell, struggled to his feet before a distinctly hostile audience.

'Ladies and gentlemen,' he began apologetically, 'you've no idea of the efforts I made to persuade the President to be here tonight. I strode right into the Oval Office, looked the leader of the free world squarely in those steely blue eyes, and I said: "Rosalynn, please make Jimmy do it".'

Mrs Carter, also absent, would have enjoyed the joke. She revels in her reputation as America's most political First Lady since Eleanor Roosevelt – even as, in *Time* magazine's judgement, 'the second most powerful person in the United States'. She herself has said: 'I am in the eye of history. I know I have influence, and I enjoy it.'

The extent of that influence has become a matter of some controversy in the last year. As with the President's Chief of Staff, Hamilton Jordan, there has been concern that someone unelected to public office should hold such sway over the leader of the world's most powerful democracy.

Mrs Carter attends most Cabinet meetings, not hesitating to speak her mind. She has a business lunch with the President every Tuesday, for which she draws up an agenda of non-family topics. She is known to have influenced many appointments, and indeed some dismissals. Hers was the dominant role at last summer's 'Camp David domestic summit', when the Carter presidency was taken back to square one to be reborn.

Last autumn, after Camp David, the President made his wife stay home for a few months because she was getting too much publicity. It had been Rosalynn, America discovered, who was responsible for the rise of Pat Caddell, the President's youthful pollster, a latter-day soothsayer and reader of entrails whose statistics-based theories are the nearest Carter gets to a political philosophy.

It had been Rosalynn who insisted on the firing of Joe Califano, the popular Secretary of Health, Education and Welfare, partly because he had not been supportive enough of her work for mental health. It was Rosalynn's idea that her husband, while he was at it, might get rid of a few more. Michael Blumenthal, the Treasury Secretary, was next on her list of those insufficiently loyal. Then there was Brock Adams, Secretary of Transportation.

All, and more, were gone within the week. Jordan and Caddell were given more power, again at Rosalynn's bidding. Visitors to the 'summit', Americans from all walks of public life, reported back that the President had sat quiet while his wife ran the meetings, taking notes, slipping him messages. All had felt a need to ingratiate themselves with her quite as much as with the President.

'If Rosalynn's on your side,' said one White House insider, 'you're all right. We often take things to her first, and ask her to put in a good word. And she's a great second line of defence, to get him to change his mind about something.'

So after cover stories in *Time* and *Newsweek* (where she was dubbed 'a second vice-president'), after even undoing the top three buttons of her blouse for *Cosmopolitan*, Rosalynn lay low for a while. It had all gone a bit too far. People were beginning to say they'd rather have her as president than her 'Jimmeh'.

Come January, however, and the start of the primary campaign, Mrs Carter was once again to the fore. The President having decided to campaign from the White House, she led a team of surrogates who worked the hustings for him. Every week for five months she travelled the length and breadth of the country, telling the faithful that 'Jimmeh sends his love. He's just so sad he can't be here today, but he's kept mighty

busy, what with Iran and Afghanistan and the economy an'
all.'

It seemed to do the trick. Carter's renomination at the
Democratic convention in New York next week will be as much
Rosalynn's triumph as his. People who know them well say the
First Lady is even more intent than her husband on hanging
on to the White House – and that's sure saying something.

It was thirty-four years ago last month that eighteen-year-
old Rosalynn Smith, the belle of Plains, Georgia, married the
boy-next-door, a smart and ambitious young man who had
already won a place at the US Naval College in Annapolis,
Maryland. Rosalynn was the best friend of his favourite sister,
Ruth. To his formidable mother Lillian, however, she was 'just
a child, a poor slip of a thing'. Even during the White House
years, Rosalynn and Miz Lillian have not managed to conceal
their somewhat strained relations.

As the eldest of four children in a fatherless home, Rosalynn
recalls an impoverished struggle of a childhood. Other folks
around Plains don't remember it quite that way; the family,
they say, never went short of much. Either way, she soon
escaped all that, travelling the world as a navy wife whose
husband was away four or five nights a week.

They had three sons in quick succession, and after eleven
years in the service moved back to Plains to take over the
family peanut firm, on the death of Carter's father. Rosalynn,
who always insisted on being involved in the decision-making,
kept the books. They prospered, and began to nurture political
ambitions.

When Carter lost his first race for the governorship of
Georgia in 1966, Rosalynn – like her husband – converted to
the Baptist faith. When, at the second attempt four years later,
he won, she had a face-lift and swapped her specs for contact
lenses. She gradually began to conquer her fear of public
speaking. Her prime motivation in life was to further her
husband's career.

During Carter's improbable run for the presidency in 1976,
Rosalynn campaigned as hard as he did, on her own separate
schedule. When they equally improbably came to Washington
that autumn, she shared her husband's loathing of northern
sophisticates. As President and First Lady, they have incurred

the wrath of Washington hostesses by refusing all social invitations.

Now she occupies the White House more confidently than the President, a hard, calculating and rather frosty First Lady who has earned herself the sobriquet of 'the steel magnolia'. While obsessively protective of her husband and his political interests, she has worked just as hard to carve her own niche in history.

'First Ladies', said President John F. Kennedy, 'are not public officials.' His wife Jacqueline used her position to beautify the White House and promote the arts. Lady Bird Johnson beautified Washington and campaigned for the environment. Pat Nixon was a stay-at-home; Betty Ford became a symbol of contemporary American motherhood – right down to a drink problem, which she overcame.

Rosalynn Carter has worked energetically and effectively in the cause of mental health, but she has also become an overtly political figure. It was Franklin Roosevelt's infirmity which propelled his wife Eleanor, on his behalf, into the public domain, where she championed civil rights and the notion of a United Nations. Mrs Carter has consciously gone even further.

She is the first First Lady since Eleanor to have addressed the National Press Club, the first in forty years to have testified before a Senate committee. She is the first in history to have represented the President at dinners for visiting heads of state, to stand in for him at political occasions in Washington, to have travelled without him to Rome for talks with the Pope, and to have invited groups of congressional leaders to the White House for their very own First Lady-like tongue-lashing.

From her own suite of offices in the White House's east wing, she has become almost a surrogate president, dealing with the kind of pleas for help which would in previous times have been addressed to the chief executive. She has a staff of twenty headed by Kit Dobelle, wife of the first (now moved sideways) chairman of the Carter-Mondale Re-election Committee. Mrs Dobelle has a salary of $56,000 a year, the same as the President's Chief of Staff, Hamilton Jordan. She sits in on the daily meetings of senior White House staff, to ensure that the First Lady's interests are represented.

Mrs Carter has travelled extensively as her husband's

ambassador-at-large. In 1978 she whistle-stopped around Mexico and seven Latin American countries, conducting negotiations with heads of state on such hefty matters as nuclear arms control, foreign aid and the curbing of drug traffic. As Air Force One carried her home in triumph, a radio message arrived from the White House: 'The President of the United States requests you to dine with him this evening at Aspen Lodge, Camp David.'

'The First Lady of the United States', she radioed back, 'accepts your kind invitation with pleasure.' Like children playing with grown-up toys, perhaps, but the Carters are also a couple seemingly preserved in an aspic of teenage love. Politicians always make a fuss of their wives in public – it wins votes – but when the Carters kiss, cuddle and hold hands, to the cringing embarrassment of public officials and visiting dignitaries, they really mean it. 'She thinks Jimmy hung the moon and stars,' says one of their staff.

'She is a perfect extension of myself,' the President has often said – increasingly to his wife's annoyance, as she has worked hard to become the very model of a modern liberationist.

The highlight of her day, she says, comes at 4.30 each afternoon, when the President saves an hour to be alone with her. 'He'll call and say "Let's go jog" or "Let's go play tennis". Or we'll watch a movie together in the White House cinema.' Or they'll do some homework with their twelve-year-old daughter Amy, the publicly paraded apple of their eye.

Rosalynn Carter occasionally expresses feelings of guilt about Amy, with whom she would like to spend more time. They share violin lessons in nearby Arlington, Virginia, and the twenty-minute car ride together each week is an unassailably fixed point on her calendar. But the President and his wife frequently exploit Amy's saccharine public appeal – pushing her towards the microphone at public meetings, making her play her violin (excruciatingly) at state banquets – to an extent that must have helped fashion the profoundly miserable look usually upon the child's face.

But then Amy's parents have become consummately political animals, who will seize any prop to help them occupy the centre-stage for another four years. It is significant that Mrs Carter, amid all her furious public activity, has soft-pedalled

265

her initial crusading for the Equal Rights Amendment. Even Betty Ford did more. It is the one issue for which a First Lady is ideally placed to campaign; but it is a politically sensitive issue, and this is an election year.

The Carters have their rows too, of course, and even these are occasionally leaked – for strictly cosmetic reasons. They have to appear human. It is now public knowledge, therefore, that Rosalynn thinks Jimmy has shed too much weight – 13lbs – with all that jogging. And she gets upset when he plays his favourite bluegrass singer, Willy Nelson, too loud on the White House stereo. She will turn the volume down, and he, without a word, will turn it up again. That's how the family rows tend to be conducted: Rosalynn gets worked up and does the shouting, while Jimmy goes tensely quiet. But he always gets his way.

Rosalynn Carter's influence over her husband is as strong as it is because they have very few such differences. Neither is a political ideologue; both are single-minded in their pursuit of electoral goals.

Rosalynn's belief in her husband, meanwhile, is unshakeable and palpably sincere. For the next three months, America will be incessantly presented with two alternative styles of uxoriousness. Nancy Reagan will sit on platform after platform, watching her husband's performance with a look of drop-jawed idolatry, as she has done eight or ten times a day, seven days a week, for the past six months. (The actor, it should be remembered, married an actress.)

Rosalynn Carter, by contrast, will be on her feet paying her husband (usually *in absentia*) compliments so fulsome as to transcend the realms of mere embarrassment. During the primary campaign, moreover, having been briefed on the anti-Kennedy innuendo tactic, she would sing his praises as husband, father, human being *and* president.

'She really believes it all,' said a party worker at my table in Pittsburgh, Pennsylvania, during one such Rosalynn after-dinner litany. 'I wish my wife talked about me like that.'

If other people's opinions paid the rent, and the landlord was turning ugly, maybe she would.

Observer magazine, 3 August 1980

Walter Cronkite:
That's the Way It Was

At the 1976 Democratic convention in New York City, Walter Cronkite of CBS News was asking Edward Kennedy about his decision not to run for the presidency. Surely it would mean, suggested Cronkite, that Kennedy would make 'less of a difference' to American society?

'You don't have to be a president of the United States to make a difference,' said Kennedy. 'You don't even have to be a congressman.' He paused, and fixed television's original anchorman earnestly, almost enviously, in the eye. '*You* make a difference, Mr Cronkite.'

Millions of Americans have spent the past week wondering whether there can be such a thing as life after Cronkite. After twenty years hosting America's most watched evening news broadcast, everyone's 'Uncle Walter' has finally hung up his headphones, leaving the nation asking itself if the news – which is to say the world – will ever be the same again.

I do not exaggerate. Walter did not merely read the news; he decided what the news was, and had a way of implying how you should feel about it. If it was bad – if America was losing a war, or someone had shot the president – Walter was somehow reassuring. If it was good, or dramatic, or funny, he helped you enjoy it.

'Go, Baby Go,' enthused Walter as Apollo 11 lifted off for the moon, willing it on its way on the nation's behalf. As in the old *New Yorker* cartoon – 'Daddy, was there news before television?' – events didn't seem to be news unless Walter was there to explain them. He came, in effect, to articulate his fellow countrymen's emotions. With Walter gone, many of them won't know what to think any more.

Since inventing the job in 1961 – in Holland, the land of his fathers, the word for anchorman is 'Cronkiter' – Walter has always been a dominant public figure, transcending politics,

267

representing the aspirations of the little guy, making events take place by his very presence. But it took his retirement last week to demonstrate the full and extraordinary extent to which a television newscaster can establish a hold over a nation's psyche.

It was not just a question of his immense celebrity, though it was always entertaining to see the cameras turn away from presidents and prime ministers to record Walter's arrival on the scene. When he travelled on the Kennedy campaign plane last year, his own CBS jet flying escort, the Senator was left to talk to himself as everyone rushed off to interview Walter. And at the Democratic convention in New York, after Carter's acceptance speech, the whole of Madison Square Garden turned towards the CBS 'anchor booth', waving signs screaming 'We want Walter.'

It was, and is, much more a question of the ultimate anchorman's unparalleled, almost Orwellian, influence on events. He is credited, for instance, with swinging American public opinion towards withdrawal from Vietnam. In 1968, after a trip to the war zone, Cronkite concluded an evening special by urging the Government to negotiate 'not as victors but as an honourable people'. It was as if, said *Newsweek*, 'Lincoln himself had ambled down from his memorial and joined an anti-war demonstration'. Watching in the White House, President Johnson turned to his Press Secretary and said: 'If I've lost Cronkite, I've lost Middle America.'

Walter's boyish excitement about the moonshots – more down-to-earth than Patrick Moore's, less patronizing than James Burke's – did more to raise public enthusiasm, and thus the space budget, than NASA and all its works. At the turbulent 1968 Democratic convention, Walter spoke for Everyman (apart, perhaps, from Mayor Daley) when he called the Chicago police 'a bunch of thugs'.

Highly aware of his unsought power, and not altogether comfortable with it, Cronkite presented himself not as a pundit but as a reporter. He rarely loaded his newscasting deliberately. It just came out that way, the way he and so many other Americans felt about things. He became a kind of incarnate national conscience, keeping a mixed bunch of politicians in line, much as *Webster's Dictionary*'s subsidiary definition of an anchor: 'a source of reassurance'.

When it suited the Carter campaign to play down the Tehran hostage crisis last summer, Cronkite refused to let them get away with it, adding 'on the x-hundredth day of captivity for fifty-two Americans in Iran' each evening to his famous payoff line '. . . and that's the way it is'. He was accused, of course, of everything from political bias to abuse of power, but somehow, with Walter, such charges could never be made to stick.

That was his greatest asset. Whatever nuance he chose to give an item of news, it never came across as an intrusive personal opinion. It was what everybody thought – or would be once he'd said it. It wasn't arguable; it was just plain right.

Cronkite's farewell broadcast was in itself such a major news story that his last '. . . and that's the way it is' was carried live by the two other major networks, NBC and ABC, whom he had humbled in the ratings all these years. Now they are paying sundry other anchor-persons – as are CBS with the hectoring young Dan Rather – millions of dollars a year to try to fill the vacuum left by Walter in the national consciousness.

He had become such a national institution that his power was, as LBJ once conceded, greater than that of the president. Opinion polls over the past two decades have consistently shown him to be 'the most trusted man in America', outpointing politicians of all shapes and sizes. Few care to speculate what would have happened last year if Walter had accepted John Anderson's invitation to join him on the Independent presidential ticket.

Both major parties have also, over the years, made overtures to Cronkite. But he has always remained so scrupulously above party politics that even 'Independent' would have seemed too specific a tag. President Kennedy thought him a closet Republican, Nixon a closet Democrat. Nobody ever knew how Walter voted, though we did know – he gave us a little lecture last November – that he took a dim view of those who didn't bother to vote at all.

People like to touch Cronkite. He exudes power and responsibility. On the island of Martha's Vineyard last summer, I took part in the bidding for an afternoon's sailing with the great man, who was auctioning himself for an island charity. I had to drop out when the price tag reached four figures.

But the winners, Mr and Mrs Berge M. Heede of Greenwich,

Connecticut, weren't merely intent on a brush with fame, like Mrs John Bull gasping to cuddle Reggie Bosanquet (or Mr Bull Anna Ford). They wanted, they said, the benefit of Walter's wisdom. They wanted to know how he saw the future of the world. They wanted him to tell them how to vote.

It's a relief that such mesmeric powers were held by so middle-of-the-road a man. A son of the Midwest, born and raised in Missouri, Walter always spoke for the heartland, which is of course why it in turn came to look on him as Mr America, representing its interests in the capitals, palaces and war zones of the world. One hopes that a more eccentric figure could never, by definition, become the focus of so many aspirations.

In Britain, as yet, it is the institutions rather than the anchor-persons who command respect. People believe Angela Rippon because she is the voice of the BBC, not because she personally influences our beliefs with the flicker of an eyebrow. What weight will she carry with us at breakfast time, sandwiched between cereal ads and jogging tips?

If the late Richard Dimbleby had presented the news every night for two decades, he could perhaps have acquired influence on a par with Cronkite's. But even after twenty years, will folks in Birmingham come to regard Alastair Burnet as the fount of all worldly wisdom? Will Dundee look for moral and political leadership to Sir Robin Day?

In the United States, with Uncle Walter, that's the way it was.

Observer, 15 March 1981

Jerry 'the Zip' Zipkin:
Nancy Reagan's 'Walker'

Jerry Zipkin is short, fat, bald, sixty-six years old and a multi-millionaire. He's been called 'the flamboyant prince of New York society' and he holds equally celestial court in California. Now he's the man every Washington hostess wants at her dinner table. Jerry the Zip, Baby Zip to his friends, is Nancy Reagan's walker.

A 'walker' is that essential thing in the lives of rich, elegant women married to dashing, dynamic men: someone to squire them to their hairdresser and clothes designer, to accompany them to the opera and escort them to smart parties. Hubby's far too busy making money or running the world, so he's only too happy to pick up all the tabs.

The walker must have certain obvious characteristics. For starters, he must be unmarried – no scandal, please, we're famous – and have plenty of time on his hands. He too must therefore be rich. He must be witty, discreet, loyal and blessed with endless patience and impeccable taste.

Jerry Zipkin is all these things and more. He owns most of Park Avenue, reeks of sandalwood perfume and never leaves home without eighty-six pairs of cufflinks in his suitcase. His shirts and suits are hand-made, with buttons specially flown in from London. He is, as he himself once put it, 'a New Yorker, born, bred and buttered', and, as Nancy Reagan once put it, 'a sort of modern-day Oscar Wilde'.

For fifteen years now, Nancy has relied on Jerry the Zip to see her through those long, arduous hours waiting for the White House. While Ron was off making speeches, Nancy and Jerry would share a limo first to her hairdresser – in New York, Monsieur Marc – where Jerry would make enchanting conversation to beguile the boredom of the blow-drier.

Then on to the salon, where Jerry's flawless judgement about colour schemes and hemlines would ease the agony of those multi-thousand-dollar decisions. No migraines for Nancy in the shoe department: Jerry would know exactly what was for her.

A quiet lunch *à deux* at La Grenouille, perhaps, or Quo Vadis, or the Palm, spiced with a little gossip about friends, some guarded advice about skin care, more charmingly turned compliments. After an afternoon's rest from all these exertions, on by dark to a first night, a gala or a little white-tie dinner party with friends.

Without Jerry the Zip, Nancy doesn't know how she would have managed. Nor do Betsy Bloomingdale or Pat Buckley, Nan Kempner or Diane von Furstenberg, Mary Lazar or Estée Lauder, Diana Vreeland or Lee Radziwill. Jerry, in his time, has walked them all.

The son of a real-estate magnate, Jerry's never exactly had to sweat to survive. Born into a Park Avenue apartment block owned by Daddy, he went off to Princeton but failed to secure a degree. The 1936 *Princeton Year Book* lists the intentions of Jerome Robert Zipkin as 'to attend Harvard Business School and engage in banking'.

Jerry never managed either. He was always too busy travelling and socializing. He has been ever since. After conquering New York he moved to Hollywood, where he quickly became an intimate of George Cukor, Louis B. Mayer, Claudette Colbert, Paulette Goddard, Old Uncle Ron Reagan and all. In the mid 1940s, wandering around Europe, he also met Somerset Maugham.

Gravitating, like a homing pigeon, to the Riviera, Zipkin spent the summer of 1949 staying at Maugham's home. The writer later told his secretary, Alan Searle, that Jerry had gone on a 'completely mad' spending spree. 'We had the greatest difficulty in preventing him from buying up the entire contents of every shop he went into,' said Maugham. 'As it was, he went back laden with antiques, shirts and pullovers, most of which he could have got in New York at half the price, but as he owns not apartment houses on Park Avenue but *rows* of apartments, I don't suppose it mattered.'

Maugham's biographer, Ted Morgan, says that a 'warm and enduring friendship' grew between them. The Zip became old Somerset's 'favourite bridge partner'. And Jerry may, thinks Morgan, be the original of Elliot Templeton, the raving snob in

The Razor's Edge, who makes his way in the world by conscious cultivation of the right people at the right time.

Well, you can't say fairer than that about Jerry the Zip, who has finally made it to White House walker and is fast becoming a household name in the US. He spent election night with the Reagans in Los Angeles, rode in the victory motorcade to Ronnie's jubilant press conference, and shared a quiet dinner with the new leaders of the free world the following evening.

When the Californian limos took over Washington in January, seizing up the nation's capital as they cruised from party to gala to banquet to ball, Jerry was in most of them. His name cropped up as often as Frank Sinatra's in the published lists of those escorting the Reagans around town. He might have had an ambassadorship, they say, had Nancy been able to survive without him. But the Presidential Medal of Freedom is clearly a mere heartbeat away.

'Jerry has more depth than a lot of people in our lives,' the First Lady says of her walker. 'He is constructive, has an ability to amuse everyone, from our chauffeur to the sternest secret service agent.' Nancy relies on him, says her friend Betsy Bloomingdale, for 'his marvellous ideas and suggestions about clothes . . . whatever. We think he's terrific. When he says something to Nancy or me – you know, your skirt's too long, something like that – you say stop! stop! Then you think about it, and you say, well, maybe he's right. Jerry's got that eye for the perfect detail. He always tells the truth; he doesn't care. He's never phoney-baloney.' Diana Vreeland says she has adored him for twenty years: 'He's a naturally affectionate person, and his friends *rely* on him.'

With friends like that, can Jerry have made enemies? Well, Truman Capote once told him his face looked like a bidet, but then that's our Truman all over, eh? It's been suggested that they hate each other because there is a certain physical resemblance between them. When Capote ratted on chic Manhattan society in his megabitch, *Answered Prayers*, the Zip spluttered: 'Disgusting! It's disgusting! Truman is ruined. He will no longer be received socially anywhere.'

But the Zip is himself capable of stinging abuse. 'He can have a very sharp tongue,' says Betsy Bloomingdale. 'Once we were at a barbecue in California, and he looked down at one of the men's shoes and said: "Ugh! *Who* wears Gucci buckles anymore?" The man went into a swoon!'

Whew. Betsy remembers another occasion, when the Zip entered a friend's house to find it adorned with artificial flowers. 'Ugh!' he said (it seems to be one of Jerry's favourite words). 'What are you *doing* with artificial flowers?' The hostess, reports Betsy, 'was devastated'. No one ever saw artificial flowers in *her* house again.

All these years Jerry has stayed in the same Park Avenue apartment – when he's at home, that is – which he shared with his mother until she died recently. The few who have been privileged enough to enter report that it is stuffed with priceless antiques and objects, overflowing with Clyfford Stills and Henry Moores. *Women's Wear Daily*, once allowed in to take some pix, said the place was 'perfumed with the cypress scent of Rigaud candle'.

When he's touring, however, Jerry likes to take his creature comforts with him. Once upon a time, at the Colony Hotel in Palm Beach, the Zip found that the cupboards in his room were too narrow for his large clothes, and that they were 'hurting' the shoulders of his jackets. He complained to the manager, who obligingly sent up the carpenters to enlarge the cupboards overnight. Next day, by way of thanks, Jerry checked out, never to return.

Jennifer Allen, writing about the Zip in the *New York Daily News*, came up with someone who called him 'an awful sucker-up to the rich' and another who described him as 'nebulous, bitchy, very, very pretentious and affected. . . . Interested only in sophisticated girl-talk.' Poor Jerry. That seems a bit harsh on a man also said to be 'essentially lonely' and who has never, according to friends, had much of a love-life. Perhaps we should settle for the description of New York columnist Liz Smith, who says Jerry's got a very big heart. 'Underneath that chi-chi veneer, he's just a sentimental slob.'

Even Truman Capote would settle for half of that.

Tatler, April 1981

Jean Harris:
The Homicidal Headmistress

'When I read about *crimes passionels* in the papers,' says one of Anthony Powell's characters,'I am struck not by the richness of their emotions, but by their desperate poverty. On the surface, the people concerned may seem to live with intensity. Underneath it is an abject egotism and lack of imagination.' George Orwell took a similar line, with due irony, when reviewing an account of the wartime Cleft Chin Murder for *Tribune*; the case was 'pitiful and sordid . . . interesting only from a sociological and perhaps a legal point of view'. Lamenting the passing of such stylists as Joseph Smith, who played 'Nearer, My God, to Thee' on the harmonium while his wife was drowning in the next room, he complained 'You never seem to get a good murder nowadays.'

Orwell was protesting on behalf of the piped and slippered Englishman at leisure, who liked to digest his Sunday lunch with a dash of *News of the World* gore. The demise of the death penalty seems to have somewhat diminished his appetite, reducing even such spectaculars as the Yorkshire Ripper trial to their properly sordid dimensions. Americans, however, suffer no such dearth of material. The reintroduction of execution in some states has provided cannon-fodder for such authors in search of a character as Norman Mailer; the murderous small-town psychopath was celebrated at lucrative length by Truman Capote long before he became a movie cliché. Earlier this year the trial of Claus von Bulow, convicted of injecting his wife with insulin, held high East Coast society in thrall. Nothing in recent years, however, can compare with the astonishing appeal to Everyman (and, more particularly, Everywoman) of the case of Mrs Jean Harris, headmistress of a chic Virginia ladies' college, convicted last year of the second degree murder of her lover, Dr Herman Tarnower, a fashionable New York physician also celebrated as the author of the best selling *Scarsdale Medical Diet Book*. Just as Britain's own Moors Murder trial in 1966 drew such writers as Pamela Hansford Johnson and Emlyn Williams to authorial seats on the press benches (and the Ripper trial Piers Paul Read), so we are now promised a glut of literary rumination on the mind and motivation of Mrs Harris. The first comes from Diana Trilling, who has hitherto distinguished herself in altogether different fields.*

Mrs Trilling, to her credit, is herself not unsurprised by the mysterious forces which drew her to Westchester for the trial; she spends much of her prologue and epilogue – the bulk of the book is a day-by-day courtroom diary – engaged in agonized self-justification. On slow days in court, she tells us, her new-found friends in the press box would turn to her for interviews about her interest: 'I'd been asked, not too unkindly, whether it wasn't ghoulish, an exploitation, to make a book out of so terrible a personal tragedy. I don't recall how I replied . . .' Yet 200 pages earlier, she has already told us at some length that in response to just such inquiries she would express fascination in 'the kind of world that Dr Tarnower and Mrs Harris inhabited together and what happened between them for their relationship to ensue in such tragedy'. She launches, indeed, into a protracted wail about the state of contemporary fiction and its inadequacy in the face of the complexities of our contemporary lives.

> It had once been the high function of literature to deal with just such material, to acquaint us with our social various-ness and our human complexity, provide us with the surro-gates of our known and unknown strengths, terrors, perils . . . But literature no longer gave us this instruction. It had become abstract, remote from the objects of our immediate personal and social curiosity.

The world of the Harris-Tarnower drama, she argues,

> was by and large the same as that of readers of books: it was the world of the educated middle class. If its two chief characters were more ambitious or successful than the rest of us, this merely gave an advantage that had always been

Mrs Harris: The Death of the Scarsdale Diet Doctor

given to the protagonists of drama; the traditional hero or heroine always had more to lose in defeat than commonplace people had. Their emotional histories nevertheless fed our natural curiosity about ourselves.

So why, were we to accept her thesis, aren't people writing novels about all this any more?

Love and sexual passion, honour, money, envy, jealousy, greed, death, greatness and meanness of spirit, the anguishing anatomy of class differences: all these, which were once the major themes of the novel, were disappearing from literature to find their home in television, whose falsifications steadily weakened our understanding of life even while we boasted our superiority to its influence.

So *Dallas* has superseded Dickens, and a contemporary Dostoevsky must now seek his Raskolnikov down at the Old Bailey. It's a thin self-defence against the charge Mrs Trilling levels at herself later in the same paragraph: 'To write a book about someone's murder was to make capital out of another person's tragedy.' But the die is cast, the thesis persists, and by the time of Mrs Trilling's coda Mrs Harris 'belongs to the novel in the way that Emma Bovary does, or Anna Karenina'. The harsh truth, apart from the fact that Mrs Trilling is neither Flaubert nor Tolstoy, is that Anthony Powell was right all along: the Harris-Tarnower saga is one of 'abject egotism and lack of imagination'.

The facts, insofar as they can be summarized, are these. On the night of 10 March 1980, the fifty-six-year-old headmistress of the Madeira School in MacLean, Virginia, just outside Washington, drove the 500 or so miles north to the home of her lover, apparently intent on suicide. The sixty-seven-year-old doctor had transferred his affections, after fourteen years of world travel and proxy domestic bliss, to his thirty-five-year-old secretary. She was going to have a final chat with him, then shoot herself.

Mrs Harris did not prove too welcome when she entered the doctor's bedroom. He was asleep, and asked her to leave so that he might remain so. The pistol was drawn and there was a struggle, during which Tarnower suffered four fatal gunshot wounds. Mrs Harris was driving away as the police arrived, summoned by a servant; she led them back inside to the spectacle of the doctor dying on the floor between his bed and the 'guest bed' he kept beside it. The headmistress argued that his death was accidental; neither the investigating authorities nor, in the end, the jury believed her.

I was living in Washington at the time, and can testify to the popular obsession with the case in that already scandal-ridden town. Its universal appeal, and its capacity to provoke fierce domestic and social arguments, lie in the suggestion that Mrs Harris was some kind of avenging angel acting for womankind, settling centuries of scores by at last cutting down Polygynic Man – and, moreover, at the scene of his crimes, in his bedroom. 'She was not thought to be a criminal', Mrs Trilling observes, 'since she had acted rightly and on behalf of all women.' The same society had recently been shaken by the murders of John Lennon and a fashionable Washington doctor, Michael Halberstam (brother of the writer, David) on their front doorsteps. But the Harris case became a veritable archetype, its protagonist a martyr to some perverted subcurrent of Feminism.

It is clear, whatever else she may say, that this was Mrs Trilling's driving force. Her opening words confess that she approached the project 'in a spirit of partisanship ... my initial response was one of unqualified sympathy for the headmistress'. As the trial proceeded that sympathy waned, but more in the face of Mrs Harris's Lady Macbeth-like lack of remorse than for any sense that a man had been unjustly deprived of life. A self-conscious, forced female sensibility dominates the book. When random examples are required of middle-class respectability unbuttoning itself, they turn out to be Edith Wharton and Vita Sackville-West; the most instructive suicide case is that of Marilyn Monroe; a Stendhal heroine, Mina de Vengel, is called in evidence that women don't use guns: 'Her ardour was too strong for her sex, and hers was a masculine heroism.' The only man cited as any kind of social parallel, in a passage mumbling about people killing the things they love, is Oscar Wilde. 'Was Mrs Harris a female victim, as she thinks?' asked Mrs Trilling. 'Yes, I guess she was, in the limited sense of having yielded her own standards in return for advantages that could be given her by a sex more privileged than her own.' And a final drubbing for mindless masculinity: 'People aren't solved. Even women aren't to be solved . . .'

There is no denying, and it is amply chronicled here, that Dr Tarnowner appears to have been a highly unpleasant man, whose behaviour none of his gender would particularly care to condone. But the lady doth protest too much. She is nearer the mark with an earlier, more considered judgement: 'In killing Dr Tarnower, Mrs Harris was killing something other than just the cruel lover who had rejected her. She was killing the poor object of her social gratitude.' Mrs Trilling is at her best in shrewd analysis of American class structure, social snobbery and the eternal quest for upward mobility. To have a Gentile on his arm, for instance, bought the Jewish diet doctor access to certain clubs and dining tables; for Mrs Harris, his company took her to loftier social levels than she would have reached in this otherwise Jewish-dominated suburban society. He was a man who thought money conferred class as much as bought it; she was a woman of unimpeachable integrity and social standing in her own Virginia fastness, anxious to shine outside her natural habitat amid the upstate New York fat cats. Mrs Trilling: 'Mrs Harris was in the wrong company. She should never have been in this society; it didn't fit her personal style or her moral style. Or rather, it shouldn't have fitted her style as well as it turned out to . . .'

At the last William Hazlitt, writing of the 1750s case of Eugene Aram, offers the most succinct judgement on Mrs Harris's culpability: 'The very coolness, subtlety and circumspection of his defence . . . prove that he was unconscious of the *crime*.' She certainly, it seems, managed to convince her defence lawyer of her innocence, for all the wrong reasons, and he nearly managed to convince the jury. Joel Aurnou, an embattled, slightly out-of-his-depth Westchester attorney, well drawn by Mrs Trilling, so well drawn as often to be more the protagonist of her account than either Harris or Tarnower, fell for the class argument. 'Aurnou's worst mistake was to assume that Mrs Harris was so indisputably a "lady" that in itself this was virtually enough to win her case for her. Aurnou appeared to be convinced that no one could convict anyone as "classy" as

Mrs Harris of murder, and he was almost right.'

I cannot think of a less likely analogue than Dr Tarnower for Jay Gatsby, but Daisy Buchanan is invoked by Mrs Trilling to make a telling indictment: 'Along with the ability and permission to make social distinctions we lose our ability to make moral distinctions.' That this should be true of a bluestocking headmistress, symbol of chaste community propriety, gave the case its especial élan.

Mrs Trilling closes, again on behalf of the Daughters of the American Revolution, by disagreeing with the verdict: 'Had I been on Mrs Harris's jury, I could not have voted as it did.' Anguished by the prospect of so evidently worthy a woman languishing in jail, her closing sentence offers the ultimate in anti-climactic redemption: 'Her gifts of mind may now be put to use as they never were before. There is work to be done in the sphere of prison education, serious work of a kind for which she has the training, energy and intelligence. She may now be splendid in a way that she never knew how to be or dared to be.'

From one institution of learning to another, this time not as headmistress but as head girl. As she goes cheerfully about her duties let us hope, with Mrs Trilling, that Mrs Harris 'may also find much emotional comfort in being punished for her hidden anger at her lover'. It is a solace pretty conclusively denied Dr Tarnower.

Times Literary Supplement, 17 May 1982

Personal File

Home Town

Anyone born in Southport is called a 'Sandgrounder'. I never understood why, let alone what the word meant. But the label always gave me a proprietorial feeling about the place, especially as neither of my parents was born there. And it used to come in handy during boarding-school arguments, giving one's fibs about home an ethnic backdrop which somehow made them ring true. I was always immensely proud of it; and I suppose, in a maudlin sort of way, ten years after leaving home I still am.

Southport is no Rochdale, no Burnley, certainly no Wigan; it is not the kind of place sharp-suited novelists revisit to make TV films about their formative years in the zinc bath by the kitchen fire. It is even a cut above Blackpool. Southport is a town people retire to. Its air is healthy, its habits genteel, its pace slow. In its heart of hearts, it has always really wanted to be a spa. Southport folk don't walk, they promenade; they feed ducks in parks more than slot-machines on piers; they prefer flower shows to pantos, play golf well and football extremely badly, don't visit the cinemas but are cross when they become bingo halls. A few vote Liberal when no one is looking, but the rest still – and probably always will – re-elect a Tory MP. It is a place to grow old in; anyone who grows up there does so in a state of sleepy, well-behaved content.

We lived up the posh end of town, Birkdale (locally pronounced 'Bahkdale'), where football in the street was discouraged and life revolved around the golf club. Cavalry-twilled and sports-jacketed, droves of us giggled at the etiquette but would never dare breach it. To be accepted as an adult, you had to be able to beat your parents' friends at golf, and so graduate from sports jacket to blazer. Failing that, you had to find a pal who didn't mind whether or not your bike was smarter than his.

My mate was Kiffy (his bike was smarter), and the choice of rides confronting us daily was daunting. There were the sandhills, the beach, the boating-lake, the swimming baths (two) and the fairground to choose from, not to mention the seedy downtown coffee bar where there just might be some nymph prepared to hold hands. It rarely came to more than that. Southport girls are very well brought up.

The beach, and especially the fairground, were more attractive out of season. Kiffy and I would wander through their silent gaudiness, reflecting gravely on the innate sadness of clowns – an off-peak *Hamlet* with two princes. Unconsummated loves were inscribed poetically in the sand, to be washed safely away by the tide. At night we would shiver through inefficient sandhill barbecues, envying the lovers we tormented through their steamed-up car windows.

There's many a Lancashire music-hall joke about the breadth of Southport beach, the invisibility of the sea. To me, that was the glory of the place; you could get lost, be out of sight of anyone, even when summer heat-waves filled the foreshore with cars and ice-cream vans, buckets and spades, braces and knotted handkerchiefs. We Sandgrounders knew the sea was too filthy to bathe in, thanks to the sewage of the industrial coastline to north and south; it was a great game to watch the trippers discover this for themselves.

The big day for indigenous superiority came each July with the Orange invasion. Hordes of Liverpool Irish would swarm off trains and open buses into what would have otherwise been a ghost town, as Southport mothers sensibly locked up both sons and daughters. Lord Street, Southport's elegant main artery, was deserted, whilst the little streets leading from it to the prom and the pier were jolted into unwonted life.

The rest of the year, Blackpool Tower was visible across the bay, a reminder to residents of what Southport might have been. To us kids, it was a symbol of our annual excursion to The Lights (Blackpool Illuminations) and Al Read at the Opera House. I was sent away to school at the age of eight, so all such memories are filtered through the rose-tinted mind's eye of one perpetual holiday. It was the Beatle era, and there was an unforgettable week when the entire Epstein stable packed us all in every night at the Southport Odeon. We all knew then, I guess, that we would later boast we'd grown up in Liverpool during those heady days.

Like everybody else, we even tried to form our own pop group; after a one-night stand at St James's Church Hall, with Kiffy on bass being mobbed by toddlers, we broke up because we couldn't agree on a name. On reflection, it was rather because it was no use Southport kids trying to be anything other than they were. We drank our gins-and-tonics, we went to the points-to-points, but we weren't playing golf so much, we were coming home from university rather than school, and our thoughts were already turning south.

Luckily, my childhood had had a cocoon: the stockroom of my father's toyshop, most of whose contents my childish guile and his soft heart conspired to transfer home. It was an antidote to growing up too quickly.

At Christmas, when my friends and their parents were beating on the doors, I would serve them from behind the counter – and mine was unquestionably the superior role.

The toyshop, and my softhearted father, are both still in Southport, and it remains a wonderworld to me. It will be a magic moment when my son is old enough to explore his granddad's stockroom.

Sunday Times Magazine, 14 November 1976

Chic to Chic

It is hot in the big city, hot and humid. The air sticks in your throat, unsure whether it's trying to get out or in; your clothes don't know whether to stick to your seat or your skin. The visiting Briton, ill-equipped without the crumpled canvas *everyone* is wearing this year, longs for the Wimbledon winter back home. The New Yorker thanks God for air-conditioning, and echoes the words of Liza Minnelli in her late, unlamented musical, *The Act*: 'Ah don't wanna breathe anything ah can't see.'

Outside 254 West 54th Street, in the steam-heat of midnight, a large and exotic crowd jostles on the sidewalk. Limousines and battered yellow taxicabs add to it by the minute, disgorging all manner of human creature in all manner of apparent apparel. For a moment the newcomers stand on tippy-toe, crying 'Steve, Steve' over the heads of the mob; they tug excitedly at their clothing, which appears to be the object of Steve's attention. A few receive his nod, and the sea parts with some reluctance for them to disappear off the street. The rest, by now the majority, join the dispirited, bewildered gaggle of rejects.

We are outside Studio 54, the world's best-known, most chic and most lavish discotheque – and the word discotheque, these days, means not so much dance-floor as life-capsule, alternative realm, ultimate experience. Inside this ultimate of ultimate experiences, the dance-floor of our alternative dreams bears the weight of Andy Warhol and Bianca Jagger, of Warren Beatty and the said Liza, of Mick Jagger (not with Bianca) and Farrah Fawcett-Majors, of Truman Capote and Margaret Trudeau. We may hope to gyrate alongside these people, for all the world as if they were mortal. At present, however, we are still stuck out on the sidewalk.

Steve is looking us over. His surname is Rubell, and he is Studio 54's joint owner. We know that he delights in his pavement power, that he has turned away such notables as Arab oil sheiks, kings even, and that he's not going to like the look of us. Trouble is, alas, we are not in crumpled canvas; we are in the T-shirt, jeans and sneakers most comfortable in such weather, but which Bianca and the gang would not be seen high in. Fortunately, we have taken the precaution of arriving with a canvas-clad party, on whose crumpled coat-tails we are admitted. As we reach Cerberus, the seething resentment of the rejects is redoubled; dressed like that, we can't possibly even be gay.

Ethereal sounds beckon. Impatient to see the technological spheres from which such music issues, we part with a mere $20 and advance to behold a scene worthy of all our expectations: beyond a dimly lit, circular bar, a vast arena of elegantly swaying, shoulder-strutting grotesques, seething, bobbing and weaving amid kaleidoscopic hues, against panoramic backdrops, a vision of gently perpetual motion. Strobe-lights flash; things rise and fall from the ceiling; paper rose-petals are wafted softly through the lower air; the ears, and soon the mind, are lost in a womb of dazzling sound, as if the head were being beaten by a sledgehammer of cotton wool. This, we reflect, is life as it must be lived aboard that giant spaceship at the end of *Close Encounters*.

We are drawn, ineluctably, wishing another adverb were available but knowing better, knowing such things just don't matter any more, to the floor. We are alone, but we are dancing in the Temple of Narcissus, where all that matters is to move to one's own satisfaction, and to convince ourselves that we are moving as stylishly as the huge bare-chested negro at our side. We admire our style. We're all John Travoltas now.

The spell is cracked by the collapse of our shoe, an elderly one which had hitherto displayed considerable grace under pressure. We retire, amid some distaste at our incompetence, to the gallery, whence we meditate upon the giant man-in-the-moon who occasionally descends from the ceiling. Somewhere down there, amid the pungent throng, are under-cover federal narcotics agents. Somewhere behind those metallic walls, according to some of the more investigative journalists who have visited Studio 54, people are not having such fun. As if on cue, a fistfight breaks out in the corner, and heavies descend to ensure its continuance out of sight. We watch idly – but at least, unlike the dancers, we are watching.

There has also been a lot of trouble with the liquor licence. Rubell, who seems about as nice a guy as any twenty-eight-year-old millionaire entrepreneur, which is not very, is rather vague about such matters. At present, he is planning to open a London Studio 54, in the New Victoria Cinema, but may encounter unforeseen problems. My inquiry to his New York office about the doubts of various London councils met with giggles. 'What are they so scared of?' Well, the club might not be able to open without various bureaucratic permissions. 'Hey, really? Oh yeah?'

Not but what he is big on egalitarianism. Answering the complaints of his founder-members, who paid their $150 fee only to find it didn't necessarily qualify them for admission, Rubell says: 'Membership is no guarantee of getting in the door. Cardholders only get reduced rates and mailing shots.' His street selection process is based not on who you are, not even just on what you look like, he says, but 'where you're headed'.

Well, we're headed for the john, through the smoking room, the focal point of many an aromatic vapour. Even the loungers here are alone, not conversing much, staring into space, enjoying – literally – themselves. By now we are feeling sufficiently heady to consider all this a paradigm of contemporary American life. 'After the anarchic hugger-mugger of the Sixties,' says *Esquire*'s music critic, Albert Goldman, 'Americans are really into segregation: a trend that was launched, incidentally, by blacks, not whites. Everybody sees himself as a star. The only thing they all lack – talent – is precisely what is most lacking in those other, nearly identical, young people whom the world has acclaimed as stars.'

And Rubell is going to bring all this to London? Are there enough stars, we wonder, worldly or off-the-street, to fill the New Victoria Cinema, even if it is made to look like a special effect from *Star Wars*? Are there enough exotics, even in the demi-monde of Chelsea, to evoke Manhattan bezzazz? As we watch a gold-painted, all but naked sylph swing through the air, wrapped around a giant illuminated guitar, we rather doubt it. We limp into the street, our one shoe evoking wide eyes of admiration.

On the sidewalk they still arrive, they still wait, whining and moaning, being fingered only by the dawn.

'Atticus', *Sunday Times*, 9 July 1978

The Rev. Tony Holden

In response to countless inquiries to this office – well, a few – I wish to make it absolutely clear, on the record, for quotation, that I have not taken holy orders. Friends and readers have been taken short by the sight of an advertisement suggesting there might be another, hitherto unrevealed string to the decidedly singular Holden bow.

Not so. There is, however, another Holden *in* Bow. Intrigued by this valiant churchman, his cap set so boldly against the National Front, and having never in my life come across another Anthony Holden, I decided to track him down. The path started (as did mine) in Lancashire, and proceeded via Accrington and Wolverhampton to the Methodist Mission in Bow, just a substantial stone's throw away in London's Mile End Road.

Tony Holden – I have always wanted to write this sentence – is an extremely pleasant, intelligent and dedicated fellow. Not bad-looking, either. He is thirty-eight years old, married with two children and reads Atticus (who is thirty-one years old, married with two children and reads Atticus). All very commendable.

But he, unlike Atticus, is a Methodist minister working in one of the country's toughest parishes. His church is in Stratford East, where he has a highly cosmopolitan congregation. His mission work takes in a larger area of the East End, where the National Front have considerable strength. The notorious Brick Lane is in his patch. It therefore took some *chutzpah* to publish an anti-NF tract.

At this point, I had contemplated a passage of sustained irony, comparing the Rev. Tony's life with the dangers of working in the combustible world of gossip. But that, even by my standards, would be in the direst taste. I could only admire the man, and told him so.

He told me a bit more about his work: projects with the homeless, the unemployed, the alcoholic, teenagers, pensioners, children, students, West Indians, Asians – all, he said, tinged in their way by the presence of the Front in Bow. Street incidents, he says, are increasing both in number and in ugliness. This was why he decided to publish his pamphlet.

There has been a strong response, several believers in such democratic rights as free speech now accepting arguments for the Front's being denied them. He has not yet, however, suffered the fate of a neighbouring Anglican clergyman, who last week received excrement through his letter-box, with a note saying: 'The next call you receive will be from your maker.' Holden has so far had one somewhat unpleasant phone call.

So Tony Holden felt a touch abashed by his meeting with Tony Holden, and caught himself reflecting mistily on life's priorities. The two parted friends, intrigued by their encounter, and returned to their very different worlds just a few miles apart.

All other Tony Holdens reading this piece, and thinking they're good for a bit of free publicity if they play their cards right – look to your credentials.

'Atticus', *Sunday Times,* 16 July 1978

On Being a Diarist

I write this in the middle of a delightful North Portuguese vineyard, in the middle of an equally delightful journalistic perk: The Free Trip. My fellow-travellers – just as well they can't hear me call them that – are out for their third day amid the *quintas*, watching grapes being squashed, churned and massaged into wine. Mostly wine-and-food or travel writers, they are busy taking notes and writing pieces before breakfast. (Ask any journalist about The Free Trip and he'll huff and puff a bit before admitting he accepted it, being ostentatiously candid about his source of patronage, but *these* people really earn their money.)

Me, I'm unashamedly here for the beer – in this case, the drowsy port and table wines of the upper Douro valley. The thing is, you see, that the weekly column I write (Atticus in the *Sunday Times*) was marinated for several years in wines of every hue (by a predecessor whose name I was not surprised to find, among others equally unastonishing, in the visitors' book here), and I have made it a rule never to mention the word. Whatever identity I have hard-won for the column over the past year would go straight out the window. Being a down-to-earth sort of a chap, I made all this quite clear to my hosts – whose name, Sandeman, I won't mention for fear of reprisals – before departure, but they were still quite happy to have me along. I look forward to further such long weekends (the most I allow myself, being, alas, a journalist of some appearance of principle). The extraordinary thing is that, even having laid my cards on the *Punch* table like this, I will still be offered them.

Being a diary writer is thus a privileged calling. Public relations people are there, of course, to be exploited or abused at will. More important, one moves hither and thither, also at will, among the rich and the lucky, the distinguished and the merely famous, with enough freedom of literary movement to make them appear one's closest friends. (A whiff of boredom when dropping a particularly heavy name is most effective here.) I spend the majority of my week, as it happens, behind my office desk, preferring to charm people off their guard over that greatest of all euphemisms, The Working Lunch. And I spend most of my weekends at home, in the ample bosom of my family, entertaining a lot of not very famous friends at a modest table. It is quite possible, meanwhile, to make this appear the most hectic of social rounds, which is what diary writers are supposed to have.

I tried an HSR, in fact, in a fit of initial enthusiasm, and found it not very productive. The best definition of my kind of story (as of a news story) being something that someone, somewhere, doesn't want you to print, the best way of finding it is not by going in search of that someone, somewhere. It is by incessantly talking to (i.e. buying drinks for) the same, always increasing round of companionable, gossipy people, who will tell you all the things they themselves cannot print or get printed – which they do primarily for the fun of daring *you* to print them. In a pukka column, however, it is necessary to check the veracity of such information, an arduous and usually embarrassing process which often proves a disappointment to your source, thus proving the source a disappointment to you.

A fact, anyway, is much more exciting when it has been checked. (NB all journalists: This is a truism. No correspondence, please.)

Having graced myself with the name of diarist – in case you think I'm going on a bit, I have actually been *asked* to write about all this – I should say it is a real pleasure to be called, as I sometimes am, a gossip columnist. A diarist is not really a journalist; he is a writer given space in a newspaper to write about himself and how he spends his time. (This, before anyone else says it, is a diary.) A gossip columnist, by contrast, is someone who actually reveals things about other people: 'ALAN COREN TO EDIT PUNCH', scoops like that. He may well reveal things about himself in the process, but that is only because gossip and diary writing are activities that go straight to the head.

But, given the story, how to write it? Let us take ALAN COREN TO EDIT PUNCH – surely, I must repeat, a Pulitzer Prize winner – as our example. It perfectly illustrates two important rules, which we may dub The Pub Principle and The Exercise of Rat-Like Cunning. The first is simple; it is a fact that any journalist, telling you in the pub about the assignment from which he has just returned, will be immeasurably more entertaining even over a single Scotch than he will be on the same subject in the columns of his newspaper. Always, therefore, look for these kind of details. If, for instance, Alan Coren is washing his car, on a *Saturday morning*, when you ring him up to check the veracity of your information, you should reveal this fact. It is not something satirists are supposed to do.

But wait a minute. What of The Exercise of Rat-Like Cunning? If you make a monkey out of Mr Coren, will he continue to commission you to write articles for *Punch*? This is a real dilemma. It can be solved only by using as much rat-like cunning as Nick Tomalin used when he pinched the phrase 'rat-like cunning' from his and my colleague Murray Sayle, and then went on to *admit* he had pinched it. You've got it. You *don't* insult Mr Coren.

Finally, the vexed question of invasion of privacy. This is something my editor does not believe in; *ergo* nor do I. But what exactly is it? Let us take further examples. If Nigel Dempster reveals that I am having an affair with Margaret Thatcher, that would be a clear invasion of both our privacies, (a) because we wouldn't want anyone to know about it, and (b) because we would both argue – or I hope we would – that it was not interfering with our ability to perform our respective functions, both putative public services. It would, however, be a matter of some public interest, and would not require Auberon Waugh to add to his already Everestic defence of Dempster.

If, however, Dempster were having an affair with Margaret Thatcher, I would not reveal this fact. There would be no problem about checking its veracity – Dempster would admit to anything – but it would be a clear invasion of both their privacies, and it would anyway be a matter of no public interest. Even Bron Waugh would yawn.

No, I shall stick to the colour of Mrs Thatcher's mascara, and the fact that she'll drink the odd nip of somebody's Scotch – the kind of privacy invasions worthy of my sophisticated readership. At which point it occurs to me that this entire piece is an invasion of somebody's privacy – not to put too fine a point on it, yours – so I'll go away. See you on Sunday?

Punch, 26 October 1977

Fear and Loathing at the Cambridge Union

Friday: to Cambridge, for the Union's end-of-term presidential debate. The motion is that 'Journalism is an honourable profession', and I am opposing it. (Memo to editor: please note, this is supposed to be a humorous debate.)

I arrive to the delightful alfresco scene of sherry with Lord Butler on the Union lawn, my humorous speech tucked safely in my pocket, only to discover this is *not* supposed to be a funny debate. 'No, no, no,' a Union official chides me, 'We had the funny one *last* week.' My confidence is completely undermined. We have our formal group photograph taken, and the photographer further undermines me. 'Keep your feet together,' he shouts. 'Do your jacket button up. *Please*.' It wasn't like this in my varsity days.

The proceedings are preceded by the splendid presidential dinner (cream of asparagus, smoked mackerel, sirloin steak marchand de vin, etc.), at which Greville Janner MP looks on with pride as his son, the incoming president, proposes our host's health. A presentation is then made to Lord Butler, to mark his retirement as Master of Trinity.

First guest speaker on his feet is Derek Jameson, editor of the *Daily Express*, who rather surprisingly admits he was wrong to put round-the-world Mormon Joyce McKinney on the front page on the same day as the Kolwezi massacre. He quotes an Old Lady of Fleet Street – known, he says, to *Private Eye* as Sid Yobbo's mother – as telling him: 'Of course journalism is an honourable profession, son. Otherwise, why would that toff Union place in Cambridge ask you to get up and talk to them in your monkey suit?' Mr Jameson, I should add discreetly, was much more entertaining over dinner beforehand.

Me next. Modesty requires that a veil be drawn over my remarks.

Just as well, for I suddenly realize that the entire evening is to consist of an attack on gossip columnists. As the only speaker in any way approaching that breed of journalist, I am taking all the stick for Hickey and Dempster. Listen to Desmond Wilcox, next up: 'Their rotting lies and malicious half-truths . . . . The world of Hickey and Dempster is a world where facts are seldom checked, the lie is to be believed, and innocent, decent people traduced . . . . They are outcasts and lepers . . . . The weak and whining ravings of illicit and twisted men . . . . scabby and disreputable.'

And he is *proposing* the motion that journalism is an honourable profession? (He tells me afterwards that he and his wife, Esther Rantzen, were the subject of some comment in such columns before their marriage.)

Simon Jenkins, editor of the London *Evening Standard*, complains that Lord Janner asked him over dinner: 'And which Union office are you standing for, young man?' Opposing away, he rightly declares that journalism surrounds itself with more cant than does any other profession, and calls his Express group stablemate Derek Jameson 'the Archie Rice of journalism'. William Deedes, editor of the *Daily Telegraph*, suggests that Willie Johnston should become sports editor of the *Daily Mirror*. He goes on to confess that people accuse even him of belonging to the gutter press – to which he usually replies: 'Try living without gutters. They're rather useful things, you know.'

Star of the evening, however, is Ms Maureen Colquhoun MP, who is scarcely on her feet before she declares that she is Proud To Be Lesbian. The august chamber walls creak slightly. Why, she asks, does every story about her have to be headlined Self-Confessed Lesbian MP says blah? Why aren't stories about Margaret Thatcher headlined Heterosexual MP says blah? And why, if comment about her private life is justified as being of public interest, does it not appear in the political rather than the gossip columns? There's no answer to that. She makes a triumphant exit, her friend Barby on her arm.

The motion against all historical precedent, is lost by acclamation.

'Atticus', *Sunday Times*, 11 June 1978

To Tea with Her Majesty

Thursday: to Buckingham Palace, for the third and penulti-mate of Her Majesty's 1978 garden parties. Strolling across Green Park, congratulating myself on not attempting to arrive by car, I am worried by the storm clouds stacking overhead. Should I have brought my umbrella?

The grey toppers and floral hats stretch to the crack of doom (which is how I have always thought of Hyde Park Corner). But it is the fastest moving queue in Britain. Within five minutes, I have passed through the gates, across the central courtyard, and into the Grand Entrance. The invitation stipu-lated morning dress or lounge suit; having opted for the latter, I notice that I am in a distinct minority. Memo to self: take out shares in Moss Bros.

Through the Bow Room, onto the terrace and there is the sight we are all waiting for. A mere 7,000 of us are Her Majesty's guests today, and we fill only a corner of her magnificent garden. Tea tents beckon: those for toffs to the right, those for the likes of me (6,900 of us) to the left. Beneath two elegant canopies, the bands of the Coldstream Guards and the Royal Marines bash out hits from *Oklahoma* and *South Pacific*. Mayoral chains abound.

We all tuck in. The iced coffee – I have been briefed – is more tasty than the tea; the swiss rolls, rather disappointingly, taste just like they do at Joe Lyons (which is where they come from). Suddenly it is four o'clock, and all munching jaws are stilled. The royal party is emerging from the Belgian Suite. We stand for the National Anthem. They begin to pass among us.

The Queen, Prince Philip and the Queen Mother each have their own 'lane' – down which they pass, through solid blocks of guests flanked by beefeaters, pausing to chat to a fortunate few. Many of these have been pre-selected and are standing, waiting, a few paces in front of the rank-and-file.

I nod to the Chancellor and Mrs Healey, who distinctly fail to nod back. I pass Mr Jeremy Thorpe, the cares of the world seemingly upon his shoulders, and decide not to intrude on his reveries. Sir Harold and Lady Wilson are here. So is their friend Edward Heath. The Archbishop of Canterbury and his lady glide by. By gum, I think to myself.

I then ruin the effect by waving to my friend Heath – the *other* one – who is up on the roof recording the occasion (having entered, as per his instructions, via the tradesman's entrance).

I am handed a piece of paper saying that the Queen is wearing a loose white woollen coat over a navy blue and white silk dress; her hat is large, white, felt, and trimmed with navy flowers. The outfit has been seen before, I am told, during her recent state visit to Germany. She is accompanied by some gentlemen called White Staves, led today by the Rt Hon. Walter Harrison, Deputy Chief Whip and Treasurer of Her Majesty's Household. They are called White Staves, apparently, because on the death of a sovereign one of their functions is to break their white staves and place them in the coffin.

I am disappointed that they don't actually appear to be carrying anything white or stavish. Their attendants, however, mostly military men, make up for this by spending much of the afternoon walking backwards. They are forced to do this, it seems, to clear a path through the guests for their royal charges. Sir Eric Penn, the Comptroller of the Lord Chamberlain's Office, and Sir Peter Ashmore, Master of Her Majesty's Household, supervise the proceedings with appropriate aplomb.

I cannot, alas, reveal the contents of my conversation with the Queen. Two reasons; it is strictly against the rules, and in fact I don't have one. To tell the truth, I can barely get within fifty yards of her. Her husband and her mother are even further away. I do, however, manage a brief exchange with the Prince of Wales, for whom people are queuing twelve deep. He is looking bronzed and very dashing, a red carnation setting off his striped red shirt.

I retire back among the throng, and allow an eager few to touch my coat-tails. After inspecting the ablutions – green-striped tents, complete with Georgian dressing-tables, discreetly hidden behind the lake – I set off on the Grand Tour. The garden is vast and very beautiful. Along the edge of the lake, past the tennis courts, round the herbaceous border, back past the bridge, I stop and contemplate the flamingos. I also sympathize strongly with the Royal Family's mixed feelings about the Hilton Hotel. There are very few points from which one cannot be observed.

It is an hour or so later, and the Queen has reached her pavilion. Her companions today are high commissioners from I to N (India to Nigeria) and ambassadors from H to U (Honduras to Upper Volta). My feet are beginning to ache, and I notice that she too occasionally lifts one foot from the ground, to ease it. I see no more, for an armada of large-hatted women proceed to stand on their chairs for a better view. The behaviour of one or two lady mayoresses leaves something to be desired.

Rain has threatened all afternoon, but mercifully given us the benefit of the doubt. Already, in the distance, I can hear tannoys calling the chauffeur-driven cars from the Mall. Bishops are returning to the tea tent for a last sausage roll. The decent thing to do is leave gracefully, before you're asked to, so I climb the steps to the terrace, and take a last, lingering look. As I pass back through the Grand Entrance, I overhear a pair of evident regulars. 'Funny, you know,' says wife to husband. 'I didn't see anybody we knew this year. Apart, of course, from Philip.'

'Atticus', *Sunday Times, 23 July 1978*

The Kid

Las Vegas, Nevada

From Binion's Horseshoe Casino in Las Vegas, Nevada, I bring glad tidings of great joy to those aged twenty-five and under, tidings of great gloom to those of us ageing fast enough to think that senior citizens, let alone policemen, look younger every day.

The 1980 world professional poker championship, known hereabouts as the World Series of Poker, has been won by Stuart 'The Kid' Ungar, a twenty-six-year-old who looks sixteen, and who is today some $900,000 richer than he was last week, when still in nappies.

The Kid, a professional poker player for precisely one year (having become so adept at gin rummy that no one in the world – and I mean *the world* – would give him a game), stands four-feet-six in the saddle. He strained to reach the microphone on CBS Network News, his voice breaking with emotion rather than age, as he paid gracious tribute to such poker greats as Doyle 'Texas Dolly' Brunson, Amarillo 'Slim' Preston, Walter 'Pug' Pearson and Johnny 'The Man' Moss, over whose collective poker wisdom his tiny feet had trampled to devastating effect during four days and nights of unremitting card-sharpery.

That Monday, seventy-three of the world's greatest poker players had sat down for the championships, each placing $10,000 on the table in front of him (or her; four women were taking part). By Thursday afternoon, The Kid had won the lot, thus earning the right to keep half – a cool $365,000 – as his first prize.

Across the street in The Golden Nugget, where your correspondent was celebrating his birthday in a brash game of five-and-ten-dollar stud, the news from the Horseshoe fell like lava from nearby Mount St Helens on a table of hitherto expressionless faces. Winners joined losers in an exchange of glances which might plausibly have signalled cardiac arrest. Their faces then sagged into drop-jawed aspects of ineffable gloom.

The game had just got going again, all arms feeling just that much more geriatric as they stretched for their chips, when a runner arrived from the Horseshoe with the kidney-punch. The Kid had placed a $10,000 bet on himself to win – at 50-1. Another half million stacked away.

Things at my table turned ugly. 'Silent Harry', across from me, a man from whom I had not heard one word in three days and nights of play, sought out the youngest face at the table with his meanest look. Though no chicken, and indeed a year older than he had been twenty-four hours before, the youngest face at the table belonged – disown it as he might – to your correspondent.

'You kids,' said Silent Harry witheringly, shooting a morose glance at my (then) satisfying pile of chips. 'You kids oughta go find a job, not sit here all day playing poker. It's no life for a youngster. Get a lifetime's work behind you before you sit down here again.'

I got what seemed like a lifetime's sleep that night (day? in Las Vegas, it's hard to tell) before gingerly returning to the table. Silent Harry, summoning all the eloquence at his command, grunted disapprovingly. His companions, known to him man and (hard-working) boy these fifty years, nodded their endorsement of his remarks. I had them psyched.

It was due to no skill of mine, but to their own simmering rage, that I proceeded to mop up, quitting (uncharacteristically) while ahead. Blinking into the sudden sunlight, a reminder that there was a world outside, where people walk up and down pavements unaided, putting coins into newspaper stands in the belief that they are slot machines, I decided to seek out The Kid.

The Kid was holding court jauntily in the back room of the Horseshoe, oblivious to the popping of flashlights and the whirr of TV cameras. Someone thrust a box of brand-name cigars into his hand, asked him to smile and popped another flashlight. A few more grand, I supposed morosely.

The Kid, according to him, was running a fever. It had dampened his concentration a bit, or the whole thing might have been over a bit quicker. Was he married? No. Make that yes. Make that no. He had a girl-friend? Er, yes. In fact, come to think of it, where the hell was she?

The next bit did for me. The Kid had told his girl that morning to get to the Horseshoe at three sharp. He thought he'd have the thing wrapped up by then. I looked at my watch. It was five past three.

I was aching for a bossy nanny to come and scoop him away, tuck him up and mop his fevered brow, tut-tutting that he'd run off downstairs like that. But I couldn't hang around. There was unfinished business across the road.

Attempting to emulate The Kid's sashay, I strode back to Silent Harry's side thinking myself into whatever role Clint Eastwood played in *The Good, the Bad and the Ugly*. Throwing back my chair, I cast a contemptuous glance at my swollen pile of chips, designed to indicate that I assumed someone would have pinched some in my absence, but there were plenty more where they came from. No one seemed to notice.

Silent Harry, with all the excitement of Sheik Yamani finding his premium bond had come good, was raking in the biggest pot of the night. He played two more desultory hands, losing nothing, before getting up to leave. From the window of 'the cage', as he cashed in his chips, he shot me a significant glance.

I knew what he meant, but it was no use. I had one more day in Las Vegas before returning to an American election I assumed was still going on somewhere, and these guys had 365 more hard-working days at the poker table before I could join them again next birthday. (It's become my annual treat.)

I lost remorselessly for a few hours before it happened, that uncertain turn of events which starts you winning again. It was Silent Harry, slipping back into his seat across the table, his dollar bills turned fecklessly back into hunks of plastic. I looked at him inquiringly, with what was supposed to be Jimmy Cagney's expression at the end of *Angels with Dirty Faces*.

'OK, Kid,' he said, 'so I couldn't sleep. So I'm back. Well, we're all kids under the skin.'

He called me 'Kid', I thought, entranced, and went on winning till my plane left without me.

Punch, 25 June 1980

Tales from the Washington Embassy: Peter Jay

Zbigniew Brzezinski – the Henry Kissinger *de nos jours* (apart from Henry Kissinger) – is a lovely mover.

I am dancing with him right now, in fact, in so far as people who disco in close proximity, their every move rendered Chaplinesque by strobe lights, occasionally look up from self-obsessed reverie to find themselves opposite a total stranger.

Urgent questions flood the front of my mind. What are the prospects for Senate ratification of SALT II? Has Anwar been on the line lately? How was Leonid looking in Vienna? Will Zbig succeed Cyrus Vance as Secretary of State next year?

But the National Security Adviser is lost in a little world of his own. A world untroubled by the slings and arrows of foreign policy. His movements are Chaplinesque even without the strobe lights: he dances with what might politely be called abandon. It's well after midnight, what's more, and he's due for breakfast with the President at 7.30.

So is Jody Powell, currently pinned to the bar by a press gang of Washington correspondents. Elliott Richardson, these days a man of past distinctions, has nothing so pressing on his mind. The White House charabanc purrs not for him. He's jitterbugging on the other side of me, with what must be his twelfth partner of the evening. He is what may politely be called somewhat the worse for wear.

Where, I hear you clamouring, is the scene of this exotic assemblage? Where is it possible, where in the world, to cross-examine Senator Howard Baker on his prospects for the presidency to the strains of Charlie Drake singing 'Splish, Splash, I was taking a bath'? Rub your eyes, British taxpayer, and eat your heart out. The whole shindig is at your expense.

We are foregathered in the Palladian splendour of the British Embassy residence in Washington DC , to honour the birthday of Her Majesty The Queen – and to bid farewell to our much lamented outgoing Ambassador, Mr Peter Jay. As has been customary during Mr Jay's tenure of office, the occasion is informal (which means you're spared black tie, but should look pretty damn chic). The scene is one of sumptuous elegance.

Mr Jay, towered over only by John Kenneth Galbraith, his sole rival for the title of the world's tallest economist, moves from group to group with consummate diplomatic aplomb.

Mrs Jay is dancing alternately with Bob Woodward and Carl Bernstein. Miss Jay, until a brief month ago a prime minister's granddaughter, is charmingly handing round drinks. The champagne has strawberries in it.

We drift onto the elegant terrace, for a waft of the balmy night air. Alas, it is raining, precluding the immortal alfresco scenes of last year, when David Frost and a nymphet led the guests headlong into the pool. Some of tonight's guests blame the meteorological conditions on a piece in one of the British Sunday newspapers, which predicted a 'presumably cloudless summer sky'. The culprit lurks somewhere in the shadows. But few spirits are to be dampened.

Everyone save the President is on hand – apart from Senator Edward Kennedy, but that amounts to the same thing these days. (It is not done, I am told, to invite the President to social occasions. Which seems a bit tough on him, but then he doesn't drink or smoke or anything, and it's too wet for jogging.) Vice-President Mondale, it is whispered, has been spotted in an ante-chamber, but in vain do I search for an exclusive tête-à-tête.

Heavy-duty conversations abound. No-one in Washington talks about anything but politics anyway, but tonight one has the feeling that the future of the world is being sorted out to the sound of Golden Oldies. The Ambassador has hired a Washington discotheque, which goes by the name of Mac's Music, for the evening; Sir Edwin Lutyens, architect of this noble pile, would be astonished by the goings-on in what appears to be the ante-room to the sub-dining chamber of the east, or perhaps it's the blue, wing.

Ambassadors are in huddles with what are known as 'key White House staffers'. Behind the Corinthian pillars senators plot, like bit-players in *Julius Caesar*. Tall, distinguished, grey-haired gentlemen, each as powerful as God and as rich as

Croesus, steer editors gently by the arm to corners spared Mac's decibels. Bishop Muzorewa's fate is settled over an Everly Brothers medley.

The scene brings a lump to the throat. It has been fun having a fellow scribbler installed in such other-worldly magnificence. Popping in to chat about the state of the world has been like visiting the editor of *Punch* in Buckingham Palace.

The last conversation I had had with Peter Jay was in the Blue Lion, one of the less salubrious hostelries of the Gray's Inn Road. The first here was in an office presumably unparalleled in the Western world – large enough, indeed, to have the Western world mapped out to scale on one wall, another – entirely glass – affording a view on what I at first took to be Kew Gardens: on recovering my composure, I realized it was the Ambassador's back lawn.

The next was in his study in the residence, which – I have to say it – upstages some of those in Buckingham Palace. The third was in one of the sitting-rooms, which I took in error for the ballroom. No wonder Mrs Jay feels some relief at the prospect of moving. 'It will be nice', she says, 'to live in a house where I can shout at my children and they'll hear me.'

(One of those children, seven-year-old Patrick, has been in the habit of standing at the foot of the imposing Lutyens double-staircase, waiting for his father's approach, and crying: 'Here he comes. Yes, folks, here's Peter. Let's hear it for PETER JAY .')

Alas, no more. Peter Jay is, as you read this, in mid-Atlantic, sailing home in a three-week yacht race. His wife has preceded him to their holiday home in Ireland. At the end of the summer, they will be returning to live in Washington – he as an economic philosopher, she as a radio and TV producer.

3100 Massachusetts Avenue, meanwhile, will have been restored to the hands of an orthodox career diplomat. No longer will one have the feeling that it's all a game, a journalist's dream-come-true, that somebody's had a whip-round and rented this terrific pad for the evening.

If Peter Jay ever does wake in the fastness of the Washington night, and wonder if it all *really* was a dream, there will be reassurance to hand. In the lobby of the Chancery building there is a marble plaque, on which his name – one of the very few without a handle to it – will now be inscribed among the mighty who have preceded him.

Back at the party, there is a feeling that the fairy tale is ended, but that our host has even greater heights to scale. The wicked witch of Downing Street has had her way, but Peter Jay will live happily ever after.

We are at the door. *Washington Post* editor Ben Bradlee (by kind permission of Jason Robards) wipes his eye and growls: 'Say goodbye to the only Socialistic ambassador this goddam place will ever see.'

Goodbye, Peter, we hardly knew ya.

Punch , 11 July 1979

Tales from the Washington Embassy: 'Nico' Henderson

Can it already be a twelvemonth since last I chronicled the events of this magic annual night, the night of Her Majesty's birthday, when we expatriates at last get our (and your) taxpayers' money's worth at Embassy bashes the world over?

Eheu fugaces! Can Phoebus's cart full once have circumscribed Neptune's salt etc. since Peter Jay departed the majestic pile bestriding Massachusetts Avenue, to be replaced by a career diplomat symbolizing the acceptable face of Thatcherism?

Tempus fugit, plus ça change, and all the other things career diplomats are wont to burble in their cups. The times, hereabouts, they certainly have a-changed.

Loyal readers will recall that this time last year, in the interests of the special relationship, your correspondent was jitterbugging with Zbigniew Brzezinski, whom he then described (somewhat crudely) as 'a lovely mover', but who has since proved him right by managing to budge Cyrus Vance out of the State Department.

They will recall that the heavens opened on the stately scene, precluding action replays of such vignettes from the Jay Years as the night David Frost led a pack of nymphets modesty first into the ambassadorial pool. Peter set his farewell to Elvis and the Everly Brothers, and we gave him a good send-off. *Erant lacrimae rerum.*

Imagine, therefore, the impatience with which your correspondent panted to get back on the *Punch* hot-line as he returned to the same scene the other evening, wondering if the balmy, caressing night air, the absence of the merest cloud above old Lutyens's Palladian terrace, were ultimate proof that the Almighty votes Tory. It was like climbing aboard a time-machine.

Last year's invitations prescribed informal dress – which, in

Washington parlance, means pretty damned formal. No need
for a monkey suit, but designer jeans not good enough. None of
that trendy Socialist stuff as the present Government drags us
into the 1980s. Black tie, it said, or national dress.

Our current house guest – known in your circles, I understand, as the Horizontal Man – shared my meditations on the
most appropriate form of national dress. As a sometime public
schoolboy from Lancashire, a brusher with royalty fiercely
proud of his Albert Finney credentials, I suggested an Eton
boater with built-in miner's lamp. Horizontal preferred the
Queen Mother's racing colours over a jockstrap specially flown
in from Wigan. I settled for my Union Jack underpants.

Svelte Anton figures (a reference which requires no further
explanation to more mature *Punch* devotees) crowded the
terrace as the wife and I desperately tried to silhouette
ourselves against the Glenn Miller moonlight. Tender tram-
beams truckled at the eye as the *Washington Post* popped its
flashlights, and for the first time I saw what F.R. Leavis had
been on about.

But there was a problem. My most gracious hostess, Lady
Henderson, had herself handed me an engraven card assign-
ing me to Table Thirteen – an inauspicious omen, to be sure –
while the wife was smugly settled amid the White House
honchos at Sixteen. Search as I might, past the creaking buffet
table, I could locate no Table Thirteen.

A hesitant word with a flunkey. Ah, Thirteen has – for
obvious reasons – been dispensed with. Instructions are to find
a seat at Twelve or Fourteen. I pile high my plate with goodies,
while discussing the European initiative on the Middle East
with the man who tried to scupper it, only to find that Twelve
and Fourteen are already deep in Reagan's choice of running-
mate.

No room at the Inn.

Miffed, I waylay a familiar Embassy face. 'Well, the man
that went to Mrs T's White House banquet in a green corduroy
suit'* – ahah, so they read *Punch* – 'can't expect the royal red
carpet here you know. It's the kitchens for you, me lad.'

I go straight to the top. Table Twenty-one, the top tells me,
has been assigned to those assigned Table Thirteen. I locate

* *See p.314*

Table Twenty-one, utterly bereft of pre-, during- or post-prandial conversationalists. In a word, empty. I return to the top. ' OK,' I say in my best working-class, Mogadishu-via-Belfast In-sight tones, 'either I get a seat or I expose you in *Punch*. I'm quite happy to be seen sitting all alone at Twenty-one, discussing the President's oil import tariff with myself, but I suspect I'd be preaching to the converted. Could I borrow a newspaper? Haven't finished *The Times* crossword in Cutty Sark time since this time last year.'

As if by magic, a seat materializes at what has to be the chic *Table du moment,* stuffed with White House, State Department, special advisers, *crème de la Carter crème. Pas de problème.* The food – which, we Socialists have to confess, has improved under the Tories – melts on the talkative tongue. But hush, the Ambassador has risen to propose the loyal toast.

He has a message from Lord Carrington, flown in by Ariel, fleetfoot as Concorde, for our distinguished Commonwealth guests. It pays tribute to the free, democratic standards now applying to all Commonwealth countries, which draws a few *sotto voce* comments from our distinguished State Dept brethren. The Ambassador, Sir Nicholas Henderson, lists the names of the mighty in our midst – most prominently Mr Cecil Andrus, Secretary of the Interior. (So that's what he looks like.)

As if by magic, at a snap of His Excellency's fingers, the Moog Synthesizer behind him Moogs out the British national anthem. All rise, and drink to Her Majesty. There follows a Mooging of the 'Stars and Stripes', alas faded out just when it gets to the good bit. The distinguished guests, notably Mr Cecil Andrus, look faintly disappointed, even disgruntled.

Viennese waltzes are then Mooged upon the air, and once again we are reminded of life's little niceties, so hastily abandoned by the short-lived Socialists. Dizzy at the sight of the revolving couples, a too brutal reminder of all those BBC 2 soap operas, I repair to the bar, where I fall into conversation with Mr Donald McHenry, Andrew Young's successor as US Ambassador to the UN. Mr McHenry is this evening a man of few words, as are all those anxious to promote the President's (and thus their own) re-election.

Back on the terrace, above which every star is a sequin sewn by Miss Universe, I seek to remind a clutch of inebriated and irreverent Britons of what it is we are really celebrating. The elevation of Mr Victor Matthews to the peerage. The knighthood so long denied the editor of the *Sun*. We mere Washington correspondents, our fingers perilously near the cosmic button, are as an unread Page One to their dog-eared Page Three.

I am, on my way out, once again accosted by the very top. 'You won't be writing about all this in *Punch*, will you?'

Punch, 9 July 1980

Divided by a
Common Language

As another American presidential year opens, Punch Consumer Concepts Inc. is proud to unveil a new reader service explaining something of the complex foreign tongue in which these quadrennial rites will be conducted. 'We are', as George Bernard Shaw so aptly said (not, as you may be told, Oscar Wilde or General Patton), 'two nations divided by a common language.'

Over the next few months, we will be providing coverage of these momentous events in parallel text form, explaining such obscure transatlantic concepts as 'elevator' by translating them in parentheses (lift, I mean brackets).

First, however, number one in a series of handy tips for those who may actually venture across the pond (sea) to the United States (Stateside) to witness the events in person. If you fall sick (ill) and have to go to the doctor's office (surgery), remember that a first-floor office is actually on the ground floor, a second-floor office is on the first floor, and so on. Above all, if asked to remove your vest and pants, do not strip. Vest (waistcoat); pants (trousers). Geddit?

Right. To begin with, we will put phrases and sayings on the back burner (in cold storage) and concentrate on simple substantives. If you're sitting comfortably, our narrative opens in the private presidential apartment (flat) in the White House (Ten Downing Street – or Buckingham Palace, depending on your view of the imperial presidency).

'Good morning, America (former British colony),' said President Jimmy Carter as he jogged (untranslatable) from his bed to his 6 am tub (bath). 'Adjust the antenna (aerial), Rosalynn, and let's see what's on TV. Could I borrow a bobbie pin (kirby grip) to hold my quiff straight under the douche (shower)?'

'Good morning, America (America),' intoned Walter Cronkite (Robin Day). 'This morning brings more bad tidings for

President Carter. The latest poll shows that only 19 per cent of Americans approve his performance as president, and that Senator Kennedy would defeat him in a presidential race (contest) by two to one.'

'Goldarn (drat) that Kennedy,' said Carter, leaping from the tub. 'If he runs I'll whip his – (defeat him). Rosalynn, where are my suspenders (braces)? No, no, woman, that's my garter belt (suspender belt). Look, I've got some thinking to do. I'll meet Hamilton Jordan (Deputy Prime Minister, Secretary to the Cabinet, Head of the Civil Service, Second-in-Command of the Armed Forces) downstairs for some grits (a disgusting Southern breakfast food beloved of the President, resembling nothing so much as cold semolina).'

'Hi Yo' All (Good Morning, Sir),' said Jordan as he entered the Oval Office. 'Seen the mail (post)? Seems them truck (lorry) drivers want a pay hike (rise). I done told them where they can put it (I have responded in the negative). So what's new?'

'Ham,' said the President (addressing his Chief of Staff, not ordering more breakfast), 'Ham, ah'm bugged (bothered) by that Kennedy. I feel like switching (swatting) him with my paddle (ping-pong bat). Feisty (cocky) little pollywog (tadpole) reckons on how (thinks) he can whup (defeat) me next year. How're we gonna settle his number? (What course of action do you suggest?)'

'Jimmy, sure as hell seems to me (I think) ain't no sense gettin' riled (we should keep calm). Deep six (dispose of) that junk (this morning's newspapers) in the trash can (wastepaper basket). Gimme some more lox 'n' bagels (smoked salmon and buns) and let's play tic tac toe (noughts and crosses). I'm ten bucks (dollars) up, mind (remember).'

'Ham, stop joshing (kidding) around. Don't rile (annoy) me. And it's time you started wearing a business (lounge) suit around here instead of them jeans (blue denim trousers) and sneakers (gymshoes). I know I'm still in my bathrobe (dressing-gown), but Rosalynn's pressing my papal necktie (tie) in preparation for today's visit from His Holiness. Fetch the Kennedy file from the hutch (Welsh dresser) and let's talk turkey (get down to business).'

'Back up (go into reverse) there, Jimmy. A stand-off (confrontation) with Kennedy's no problem. Pass the eggplant (aubergine), please. No, he can take a raincheck (postponement) on the White House. He's far too liberal (conservative) to carry (win a majority of votes in) the South, whereas your moderate centre (extreme right) position will make him seem like a lefty (Trotskyite) and Reagan (Genghis Khan) look like Genghis Khan.'

'Ham, you're a dingaling (person of limited intelligence). Anyone who figures (suspects) I can zonk (defeat) Kennedy on policies (figurative political positions) is a schmuck (person of even less intelligence). This thing is about politics (public relations), not about positions (political philosophies). I gotta hit him where it hurts (Chappaquiddick).'

'No problem. You make a lot of speeches saying you don't muss your pants (panic) in a crisis, then send him a private (public) letter telling him you weren't fixing to (intending to) make any inferences (implications) about him. Maybe a wire (telegram) would be more sexy (politically significant). Keep freshening up (refilling) that Chappaquiddick cocktail, and you'll push him so far toward (towards) the edge that he'll soon fall (autumn) out of sight.'

'Ham, that's just the frosting (icing) on the cake. I'll make him stand in line (queue) to meet the Pope, and put Joan on that love-seat (sofa) near the liquor (booze) during the White House reception. I'll make liverwurst (liver sausage) of that guy before I'm through.'

Enter the maître d' (headwaiter). 'Mr President, Senator Kennedy's calling (telephoning) you on the hot line (the red one in the middle of the desk). Says he's got the Holy Father (Pope) in his office, and would you like to make your number (greet His Holiness) now before they go into closed session about the problems of Boston (the Catholic Church) and Massachusetts (World Catholicism)?'

Next week: The chips (french fries) are down.

Punch, 17 October 1979

Gatecrashing the White House

Washington

Of the many advantages of becoming an expatriate Briton, seeking shelter at least temporarily in the United States, pretty damn high on the list comes the headlong flight from Margaret Thatcher.

When the lady, therefore, flies at short notice in this direction, as she did on her Christmas goodwill visit, it feels very much as if an irate and finger-wagging mama has finally caught up with a distinctly prodigal son.

We in America have taken an unwonted theological interest in Islam of late, for reasons with which I won't detain you. It was thus in a spirit of self-flagellation – possibly (though you said it, not me) in a quest for martyrdom – that I dogged La Thatcher's footsteps around this neck of the Eastern seaboard.

I was not disappointed. I returned duly flagellated, and duly intent on avoiding a Thatcherized, but otherwise beloved, Britain for the indefinite future. There is clearly no hope for us middle-classers. No matter how assiduously we try to make our modest way in the world, she'll see us bankrupt. (And cackle all the way to the polls.)

Anyway: that's your problem, not mine. The thing I thought you'd like to hear about this week was my lowering of the tone (wilful, I know, but on all your behalves, and indeed on that of Punch Consumer Concepts Inc.) at Jimmy Carter's White House state dinner for Madame. It all happened – I wish I could pretend otherwise – rather by accident.

The long and the short of it is I Was The Man Who Crashed The President's Party In A Scruffy Green Corduroy Suit.

I'd been down to the White House lawn for the welcoming ceremony that morning, and had waved my miniature Union Jack (distributed in liberal quantities, special relationship by television, for the use of) until I was beyond hope of putting her off her speech. The day was a familiar litany of Oval Office, Pentagon, British Embassy, Capitol Hill. I began to get worried about *Punch*.

Then came the evening. Nipping dahn the White House, to pick up the official guest list, I found my hard-earned accreditation entitled me to listen to the toasts – as long as I pretended to be the unacceptable face of television crewery, given that I hadn't slipped into a monkey suit.

Thus disguised, Your Correspondent found himself elevated on a podium in the centre of the ornate East Room as the guests arrived. Friends from the British Embassy, tackling their finest hour with wonderfully diplomatic nonchalance, were thrown off-stride slightly to see this Frankenstein leering at them from a modest height. One kindly attempted to steer some champagne in my direction, but was told by the White House 'downstairsers' that the media did not qualify.

Amid suitable fanfare, the President of the United States of America entered with Mrs T. There followed toasts spiced with transatlantic jokes (viz, don't forget your ancestors tried to burn this house down – Don't forget George Washington was born a Brit, etc., etc.) until the monkey suit mob retired for the pheasant, and Your Correspondent was, not to put too fine a point on it, ejected. (Via, it should be said in self-defence, the front door.)

Nothing daunted, he retired across the block to a Washington hostelry called the Class Reunion, where he knew the action would be. There, indeed, was Jody Powell, scornful of the presence of this woman prime minister from a former colony (isn't that the way it was?) tossing back many a 'light' beer. There was Patrick Caddell, the President's pollster (soothsayer, seer, entrail-reader), runner-up only to Rosalynn Carter and Hamilton Jordan as the second most powerful person-figure in the United States – also ignoring the cream of the father/mother/parent-land.

A quick natter, and I had to be back for the post-prandials. The Nigel Dempsters of Washington, all female and approximately eighty to eighty-five, were assembled in the Press Room for the 'pick-up'. Mrs Carter's Press Secretary arrived to, as it were, pick us up. The Dempsteresses were in their White House best – stylishly antique Victorian evening gowns; had they not been purchased at the time and reeked of mothballs ever since? The *Punch* correspondent, they assured him, eyeing his ever tattier green cords with right Victorian disdain, would never be admitted.

The *Punch* correspondent, as you, gentlish reader, will have discerned, was by this stage (pretty late) bloody determined he was going to be admitted. Though not a genuine eccentric at heart, as much as he would like to be thought one, he posed as the eccentric Brit prepared to brave the wrath of Washington's brightest and best – and he made it.

Through the West Hall, down the LBJ Corridor to the Red Room, where – according to Mrs Carter's Press Secretary, the media were not, repeat not, to 'mix and mingle'. But there were the Brits. There was good copy in mixing and mingling. Sure enough, the strange eccentric in the green corduroy was either a wino of the street or ' . . . must be a journalist, French or German, I should think'.

One friendly British diplomat, it has to be said, offered to take me through the receiving line as his gay guest. (By this time, I was so totally in the wrong place that not merely was I mixing and mingling, I was about to shake hands with the President of the United States and the Prime Minister of Great Britain and Northern Ireland in a green corduroy suit.) For my friend's sake, and for his sake only, I declined the offer.

I nipped through the non-mixing-and-mingling bit only to find that Jimmy and Rosalynn were having a brief discussion about who should make what speech when, and had thus briefly abandoned Mrs T to her own fate, and that she had thus discreetly turned away – to be confronted by this apparition in a green corduroy sort-of-suit amid the finery, whom she had last seen two years ago attempting to keep up with her as she Gordon Piried her way up the Great Wall of China.

To give her her due – and I hate to do it, but journalistic impartiality takes its toll – she didn't bat an eyelid. 'Ah, Mr Holden, we're having breakfast tomorrow, aren't we?' (True, should I wear a monkey suit?) 'Early. Very early? Yes, Mr President. Quite ready, thank you.'

What a fine woman. You Brits are in good hands. I take back everything I said – so please consider this piece so far, in the immortal word of Nixon's hapless Jody Powell, Ron Ziegler, 'inoperative'. She didn't even bat any further eyelids when, jet-lagged, Tip O'Neill-lagged, hack-lagged, she watched (like the rest of us) with wild surmise as Cyrus Vance, Kirk Douglas, the President's daughter-in-law and assorted dignitaries from states hosting important early primaries, sang songs as part of the after-dinner entertainment.

Mrs T, I'll watch from a safe distance, but by me you can from now on do no wrong.

Punch, 9 January 1980

The Diarist Bows Out –
In Heroic Couplets

The diarist bows out today. He has expressed his feelings on this nostalgic occasion in verse : the sonnet with apologies to J. Keats, the remainder with apologies to everyone else.

Much have I travell'd in Bodoni bold,
And many guilty men and doorsteps seen;
Round many sweaty newsdesks have I been
Which hacks in fealty to Lord Copper hold.
Oft of one wide expanse had I been told
That deep-brow'd Hickey ruled as his demesne;
Yet did I never breathe its foul serene
Till I heard Dempster speak out loud and cold:
Then felt I like some thro'er of custard pies
When a new Bianca swims into his ken;
Or like swart Rumour, when with narrow'd eyes
He stared at Marie-Astrid – and his pen
Hung o'er his notebook with a wild surmise –
Silent, until he enter'd Gossip's den.

1 : Our Hero's Day Off
THE DIARIST wakes at dawn. Or is it noon?
These summer evenings draw in all too soon.
The phone rings. 'Atticus . . . I mean, Hello?'
(Got my home number. Bloody PRO.)
'A lunch? Alas, old boy, it's my day off:
Hobnobbing here at home with some poor toff.
Forgive me, but I can't reveal his name;
Well, since you ask, it's Lord Extremely Fam-
Ous Person. Got a thing or two on him.
Come Sunday, he'll be pushed to sink or swim.
Know what I mean? Well, mustn't keep you now.
Let's meet sometime – but this week's hectic. Ciao!'
The Diarist opes his eyes. What has he done?
Lunch with that starlet might have been quite fun.
Why tell that lie? Perhaps a quick call back?

No: why appear a low-down, wheedling hack?
(For that, my boy, is what you really are,
Though no one else has rumbled it – thus far.)
Stick to routine. Yes, snatch a solid brunch,
Then join the boys for an *El Vino*'s 'lunch'.

By four that afternoon, our hero's knell
Is drinking out of hours *chez Muriel*.
By six, he's gossiped out. He's told his all.
Filled with remorse, he heeds his nature's call
To head downtown, through *Soho*'s grim delights
To *Mayfair*, where he's spent his favourite nights,
Recouping gossip old with gossip new,
Some fair, some foul, some dank, some even true.
On through the night, poor souls to buy and sell,
Till he winds up – where else – *chez Annabel*.
He never gambles, save of course with *Fame;*
His blackjack's chip's the price of *Someone*'s name.
By dawn, where we came in, he can but stutter.
He falls asleep. At home? Or in a gutter?

2 : The Inner Man
Such, gentle reader, so I'm always told,
Is life as lived by *Gossip*'s Fleet Street fold.
I wouldn't know. I've spent a mere two years
Attempting thus to emulate my peers,
But always falling short. Can't take the booze;
Can't fib; don't like Some Win, Some Lose
As life's philosophy; get fond of those
Whose candour lends enchantment to my prose.
Can't dance (that disco story from *New York*
Was all pretend). Prefer some nice Roast Pork
To *Tournedos Rossini*. And, of course,
I never gamble, never back a horse.
I can't play poker (though please do come round
If you're prepared to risk the odd half-pound).
And I'm discreet. Your secret's safe with me:
Let's wash it down with cups of *Mum*'s best tea.
I'm never rude. If I had rank to pull,
I'd hurt about as much as cotton-wool.

I don't stay up late, need my full eight hours.
I'm happiest kissing kids and planting flowers.

So you can see my eyes were wide indeed
When fickle *Fortune* offered me this steed
To ride around old *London*. 'No,' I said,
'Give me a *Sunday Times* white horse instead!
Let me expose, reveal, seek truth, jet set!'
'Precisely so,' said *Fortune*. 'On you get.'
From that day forth I've flatter'd, oil'd and fawn'd
My way around a trendy demi-monde
In which I've been a worried refugee
From all that's decent and – well – odour-free.
The things I've seen. The tales that I could tell.
The names I could besmirch. The famous . . . well,
That's quite enough of that. It's over now.
I'm free to prune my roses, milk my cow.
It's all a ghastly memory, soon suppress'd:
I'm through, thank God, with women half undress'd,
With punch-ups, insults, *Gossip*'s view-halloo.
Get thee behind me, *Dempster*. I've won through.

When *Vino*'s boys read all this guff, I'll rue it.
But that's my story and I'm sticking to it.

3 : Ten Commandments
When I consider how my nights were spent
– I'm sorry, *Milton*. You're a proper gent –
Burning *Sheik Midnight*'s oil, Being Seen Around,
Observing *Joyce McKinney* run to ground,
Powd'ring *Felicity Fark*'s delightful nose,
And tickling *Emma Jane Crampton's** tiny toes . . .
Was it all worth it? What else could I do,
Poor little me, a plucky young father-of-two,
An innocent abroad, cast quite adrift,
In a world where people seem so easily miffed?
I played the part. I tried to cut a caper.

---

*She claims, in *Penthouse* mag, to know my flat.
  A *Lawyer* writes: 'We'll soon see about that'.

The Diarist Bows Out – In Heroic Couplets

I bore in mind that I work for a family paper.
I learnt the ropes. The boys taught me the code.
At last, I thought, my show is on the road.

But now it's off, I think I'm going to blow it.
The gaff, that is. It's not like me to go it
All alone like this, but then, you see,
I'm off on hols for the next week or three:
To *John o'Groats, Land's End,* to *Ulster, Beachy
Head, Southport* . . . some place they'll never reach me.
So look both ways and light up a High Tar.
The gossip writer's Ten Commandments are:

Write first about thyself; none can gainsay
The rest will follow as the night the day.
Ne'er write about unknowns, however grand,
When famous names are readily to hand.
Take every name in vain, as far as poss,
And you will reap good copy out of dross.
Labour all seven days : endless the quest.
Let no man ever say you're not the best.
Honour thy father and mother, on the whole,
But never spare another mortal soul.
Adultery is out. Thou hast thy name
To think of: others' sins are all fair game.
Thou shalt steal only stories from thy riv-
Al columns. Bear false witness, and thou'lt thrive.
This above all: There's no one does it worse,
So let it go to thy head. Think big. Write verse!

4 : Lady Luck Hits Out
These precepts lodg'd at heart, I gave up gin
For *Pimm's,* wore velvet and a safety pin,
But things did not go well. I shunned the perks
Of my new trade, thought *Chelsea* stiff with jerks.
My sense of history would get in the way:
To me, *Muhammad Ali* was still *Cassius Clay.*
The problem grew. I wanted to succeed;
In vain, howe'er, I feigned campness and greed.
Each cause at which I threw my feather weight

321

My alter ego would invalidate.
Try as I might, I couldn't get the goods
On *Godfathers, Train Robbers, Mafia* hoods.
E'en small-time crooks would wriggle out my grasp,
E'en debutantes evade my am'rous clasp.
I was a flop. There wasn't anybody
Else, just *Atticus,* whom even *Roddy*
Failed to recognize at *Harrington*'s.
My love of cricket missed *Ken Barrington*'s
Keen eye. Just once, I met *Bianca J*
(When grooving to *George Davis Rules OK?*)
And failed to recognize her. No amends
Could e'er be made for that. I lost my friends.
My memberships were cancelled. All alone,
I sought the company of my own clone –
But even he avoided me. My fate,
It seemed, came down at last to one blind date
With *Lady Luck.* But even that I blew.
'I'm not consorting with the likes of you,'
Quoth she. 'You're too big for those fancy boots.
You think the crowd at *Tramp* aren't worth two hoots.
Say *Kennedy,* and you think of *Ludo.*
You've never even heard of *Meg Trudeau.*
You don't like punk. You're at the *Albert Hall*
Instead of *Chelsea Arts Club*'s New Year Ball.
You'd give *Antonia Fraser*'s do a miss
To talk of *Washington* with *Alger Hiss.*
I fix you that free trip to *Monte Carlo*;
Oh no: you're interviewing *Kenneth Barlow.*
Warhol, you say, is boring, *Caine* a creep,
Vidal – *Sassoon* or *Gore* – sends you to sleep.
I go up-market, fly in *M.Soares*
And find you snigg'ring with *Al Alvarez.*
You won't invade the privacy of Royals –
Too busy literary lunching down at *Foyle*'s.
You won't give plugs. You'd run a minute mile
To miss a soirée chez *Margaret Argyll.*
You're writing limericks with *Kingsley Amis*
When *Larry Adler*'s ego's in extremis.
I fix a fur protest with *La Bardot*

And you dine at the House with *John Pardoe.*
You like that *Melvyn Bragg.* You'd rather sup
With *Eamonn* than with *Mick.* Well, I give up.
I'll bet you'd rather meet *Sir Toby Belch*
Than spend a night alone with *Raquel Welch.*

That did it. *Lady Luck* had finally hit
Beneath the belt, as 't were. I took the bit
Between my teeth, and rang up *Esther Rantzen.*
The line went dead. Had I called up *Charles Manson*
I would have got more joy. That *PRO,*
From out the shadows, whispered, 'Well, you know,
I shouldn't tell, but just the other day
I overheard the *Duke of Bedford* say:
'Ah, *Atticus.* So sad. Top of his tree,
But just about as liked as *Richard Three.*'
Thus crack'd my heart. I'd failed as a back-scratcher,
So I flew East with cuddly *Margaret Thatcher.*
From out *Air China*'s window I saw years,
Stretching ahead, of thoughts too deep for tears.

5 : Down Memory Lane
The memory grieves me still. I was a mess.
My new-won laurels drooped . . . . But I digress.
Where was I now? Ah yes, time to recall
Those moments that have held me most in thrall
During my heady sojourn on this page.
When I began, *'Peanuts'* was all the rage,
To office new elected, not so silly
As all the world thinks now. His brother *Billy*
Sank more canned beers than diarists ate hot dinners.
But *Atticus* could scarcely call them sinners.
So off he went to lunch, at great expense,
With *Spiro Agnew*, desperate for a mench
For his first novel. Charming man. True blue.
'Integrity?' he said. 'See *Lee Kuan Yew.*'
I saw *George Brown* instead. In pin-striped trews,
He'd lost a lot of weight, forsaken booze,
Could do no wrong in my eyes. Off I went
To *Paris* – lots more waning budget spent –

To see *O. Mosley* and his wife *Diana*.
I'll knock 'em dead, I thought. Another spanner
In the *Atticus* works. Delightful pair!
Then *Jimmy Goldsmith* got into my hair.
I washed him out, but still I needed dirt:
I mocked that *André Previn* roll-neck shirt.
No 'sources close to . . .' lost. But a near miss.
And so it was when I exchanged a kiss
With *Ms Diana Dors* – by phone, that is,
And got *Encounter*'s editors in a tizz.
Ah, halcyon days! I rivalled *Private Eye*
At games of 'It is whispered . . .' and I-Spy.
In those days, paedophilia was strange
And *Caroline* unmarried. How times change!
Sir Harold, as he now is, scored a hit
When he did me his Great Historian bit.
And so did *Enoch Powell*. Much better. Well,
I'm giving up this job. Now I can tell
The truth behind those stories. Did you know,
For instance, that when *Jackie O* . . .
But no, I mustn't. Ethics. Then *Ted Heath*
(Who rivals the said *Rantzen* for fine teeth)
Had me aboard his train. I draw eight veils
O'er that, er, literary day. *The Prince of Wales*
– Against whom I won't hear a syllable said –
I chased to *Canada*. I did see red,
I must say, when a bolshy *Kremlin* cog
Prevented me accompanying *JY* 's prog
To *Moscow*. Then I thought my luck had changed
When meetings with *Sinatra* were arranged
In *New York City*. Via the *Alfred Beits*
In *Wexford* I went out, but then the lights
All o'er *Manhattan* did the same. *Lord Grade*
Lit my cigar: I glimpsed *Virginia Wade*.
An age of gold! Alack for woe now lost!
Apart from the odd breakfast with *Dave Frost*,
Asking *A. Wesker* if his *Sunday Times*
Still gives due satisfaction . . .
                              'All these rhymes,'
Chips in *Pam Ayres*. 'You want to be Poetry Prof

At Oxford, don't you. Eh?' *'Evita* off,'
I say. 'Here comes my final requiem':
No more will I catch mumps from the *PM*.

6 : His Just Deserts
The diarist's day is done. As he lays down
His batter'd pen, the shadow of a frown
Comes o'er his features. Can this be regret?
Does he perceive he owes the world a debt?
Quite so. All he's achieved, free with one bound,
Is privacy for others to confound.

'Atticus', *Sunday Times*, 30 July 1978

Anthony Holden, who graduated from Oxford University, was a reporter for the London *Sunday Times* and then wrote their "Atticus" column, for which he was named Columnist of the Year in 1977. He left the paper to write *Prince Charles*, and then spent three years in Washington, D.C., as Chief U.S. Correspondent for the *Observer*. Holden returned to England in 1981 as features editor of *The Times*, and resigned a year later in protest over Rupert Murdoch's dismissal of Harold Evans. He has since become a regular contributor to leading journals on both sides of the Atlantic, has hosted his own radio talk show in England, and presented a major BBC TV documentary. Now a free-lance writer, Holden lives in London with his wife, Amanda, a pianist, and their three young sons.